High-Perform
Jeep WRANGLER TJ
Builder's Guide
1997 – 2006

CHRISTIAN LEE

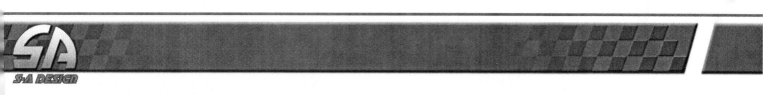

S·A DESIGN

CarTech®

Edited by: Travis Thompson
Designed by: Christopher Fayers

ISBN 978-1-61325-027-3
Item No. SA120P

Printed in USA

Cover:
Author Christian Lee spent quite a bit of time building up his project TJ. They all start out stock, but some end up looking—and performing—just like this.

Back Cover:

Top:
What's the difference between that cheaper lift kit and the one that costs twice as much? The difference is in the details, and you'll need to cover them all if you want to lift your TJ the right way.

Right
Your stock TJ NP231J transfer case is great for off-roading, but there's always something better. Learn to upgrade your case with lower gears and stronger parts, or swap it out for something better.

Bottom:
Whether you're into rocks, sand, mud, or snow, High-Performance Jeep Wrangler TJ Builder's Guide will help you modify your TJ to get there and back. When modifying a Jeep for trail use, many of the parts (tires, gears, suspension lift, axles) need to be selected with the others in mind, so it's important to educate yourself before you start buying parts.

Title Page:
Imagine jumping your Wrangler without destroying it. The Poly Performance TJ coil-over system makes stuff like that possible.

CarTech®
39966 Grand Avenue
North Branch, MN 55056
Telephone (651) 277-1200 • (800) 551-4754 • Fax: (651) 277-1203
www.cartechbooks.com

TABLE OF CONTENTS

CONTENTS

I wish I had a grand reason why I drive a Jeep, but after great thought (or at least some), the best reason I can think of is that it makes me feel like me. It messes up my hair and puts dirt and grease under my fingernails. It rattles my head around and jumbles my stomach like a roller coaster. It makes my teeth chatter, my cheeks rosy, and gets dirt in my ears, and I like it. Maybe I'm weird, but that's what driving a Jeep means to me.

As for who I am and where I come from: I was born and raised in Long Beach, California. I grew up riding dirt bikes with my dad in the California desert and Baja California, and I found myself in a 4x4 as soon as the DMV would let me drive. I graduated from CSULB (California State University Long Beach) in 1997 with a Bachelors degree in English and Creative Writing. At school people always asked what the hell I planned to do with a degree in English. I'd tell them, "I like Jeeps. Maybe I'll write about Jeeps." I kind of fell into the automotive magazine industry after that and never really dragged myself away. The first gig I landed was with *Petersen's 4 Wheel & Off-Road Magazine* as a features editor. I also helped out at a Petersen Publishing start-up called *4x4 Power*. I have also free-lanced for *Off-Road Magazine*, *Dirt Rider*, *Dual Sport Rider*, and *Off-Road Adventures Magazine*. In 2001, I began my current position as Technical Editor of *4 Wheel Drive & Sport Utility Magazine*.

What qualifies me to write this book? Well, aside from my fore-mentioned employment, I think the fact that I'm damn fond of Jeeps qualifies me pretty well. I don't have any Jeep tattoos but I do wear Jeep T-shirts from time to time. I happen to know a thing or two about Jeeps, too—the TJ in particular. I've had the pleasure of operating a 2001 TJ Sport as my daily driver since it rolled off the showroom floor. After driving a '69 CJ-5 for a few years in the same capacity, the TJ felt like a passenger car and handled like one, too. I was immediately sold and had a build plan set before I even got it home. It turned out 2001 was a good year for the TJ, as the first-available aftermarket long-arm suspension kit had recently hit the market, and the aftermarket in general was hot with parts for TJs. Before I knew it, my once-girlish-looking Solar Yellow TJ was leaping boulders in a single bound. Well, it was built big and strong, anyway. I could hardly drive it without being stopped and asked about its construction. I'd suddenly spout off the details, offering finer points on the design, which I'd probably learned from a Jeep engineer I met in Moab or the head fabricator from a suspension company that I ran into on some desert trail. The inquisitors listened intently to what I had to say. Somewhere along the line, after many hours building my TJ and surviving every pitfall along the way, I realized that I actually knew what I was talking about. Does this make me an expert on all things Jeep? Not a chance. An expert on all things Jeep Wrangler TJ? Well, I wrote the book, didn't I?

– Christian Lee

Acknowledgments

Though my name is on the cover, there are many, many people that helped me with this book. Jason Bunch, Mike Montana, and the entire crew at Tri County Gear in Pomona, California, were especially helpful, sharing their many experiences with these vehicles and revealing the kind of details that only come from working in a 4x4 shop on a daily basis. Jason was kind enough to open his shop to me for multiple photo shoots as I continually gathered material, never once shooing me out.

Jeff Sladick at Don-A-Vee Jeep in Placentia, California, was another great source of information. Jeff was my go-to guy for all the oddball questions; he never failed to produce an answer. Kevin McNulty, the Editor of *4 Wheel Drive & Sport Utility Magazine* and my boss man du jour, also aided my plight by going easy on the assignments when I'd remember to ask him to, and excusing my late morning arrivals at the office after pulling yet another all-nighter in front of the screen. Travis Thompson, my editor at CarTech, never gave up on me, even when it was looking impossible. My parents, Olaf and Nancy Lee, were also immensely helpful and always eager to lend a hand, whether it was some form of monotonous data entry or making a jillion phone calls to obtain photos or check my facts. But mostly, thanks to my new wife, Tina, for sacrificing many evenings of being together so I could sit in front of the computer and get this thing done.

P.S. Thank you, Toledo.

There is quite a bit of Jeep Wrangler TJ info in this book. It includes the most up-to-date information, including a good overview of the factory-installed components and how each can be upgraded to improve overall vehicle performance on the road and on the trail. It will be helpful whether you're looking to begin your Wrangler buildup or are still shopping for that perfect used rig and want to narrow down which TJ best suits your needs.

Chapter 7 should help you determine exactly what type of suspension and what size lift will suit your needs.

For power-up ideas, Chapter 3 has you well covered, whether you're looking for a bolt-on upgrade or a complete engine swap. Chapter 10 discusses the vast amount of interior and exterior accessories available for Wranglers, including clues on the available aftermarket roll cages and tips on how to cover up body damage using steel panels. You'll also be pleased to know I included every bit of tech advice I could muster on the Wrangler axles and transfer case (Chapters 6 and 5, respectively).

After you've learned how to properly outfit your TJ for the trail, you can look to the massive Source Guide, filled with contact info for the various parts manufacturers and retailers mentioned throughout the book. If you have more time than money, you'll certainly enjoy Chapter 11, which offers suggestions on making the most out of your Wrangler on a budget. You'll also gain a few ideas on how to operate your TJ safely, so both you and your rig get home in one piece. Also check out the section on packing for the trail, which includes advice on what tools and spare parts to bring, just in case the trail takes its toll on your TJ.

This is your Wrangler before reading **High-Performance Jeep Wrangler TJ** *Builder's Guide. (Photo courtsey Daimler Chrysler)*

And this is your Wrangler after reading **High-Performance Jeep Wrangler TJ Builders Guide.** *Are you prepared for the trail? Learn what to bring for any adventure, including spare parts and all the tools you'll need, as well as recovery items to get you home in one piece.*

THE BIRTH OF THE WRANGLER TJ

The Jeep Wrangler TJ is one of the most awesome production 4x4s. It is fun to drive, but it's also capable of handling virtually any terrain you may encounter. On the road, it offers car-like handling characteristics, at least when compared to earlier Jeeps. The Jeep Wrangler TJ is most at home, however, when navigating off-road trails and living up to its "Trail Rated" badge.

The Jeep Wrangler TJ was introduced in 1997; one year after the Wrangler YJ was discontinued. The TJ experienced a 10-year production run that included three different engines and eight transmission offerings. The most refined TJs came in the later years, so owners of earlier models may find their TJs to be a bit deficient in engine power and transmission strength. However, the chassis and suspension components remained largely unchanged. The same goes for the interior and exterior, which received minor changes and improvements through the years.

Despite the Wrangler's off-road prowess right out of the box, it does have its limitations when it comes to conquering more extreme trails. Those of you who have traveled off the pavement in your Wrangler have likely experienced these limitations. A stock Wrangler per-

With ample power and ever-capable off-road ability, the Jeep Wrangler TJ has become a modern-day legend for the brand. (Photo courtesy DaimlerChrysler)

forms well through a variety of terrain, but if you take on obstacles that are taller than the suspension can flex, you'll probably be looking at some damage. Tire size is typically the first improvement TJ owners make, and upsizing is one of the most common upgrades. Larger tires are often paired with a suspension or body lift for the correct fit, and engine performance and axle gearing usually follow shortly thereafter. The best part? All of these components and more are abundantly available from a variety of aftermarket parts manufacturers, giving you the choice to build up your Wrangler TJ just about any way you like.

Jeep History

The first Jeeps were produced in 1941 when the U.S. military recruited automakers to build a "light reconnaissance vehicle" to assist in the war effort. Three companies stepped up to the plate to design and build prototype vehicles to meet the Army's desired specifications. Requirements included a fold-down windshield, a two-speed transfer case with 4WD, a wheelbase less than 75 inches, and a 600-lb load capacity. Willys-Overland produced what it called the Willys Quad, while Ford Motor Company offered its Pygmy, and the American Bantam Car Manufacturing Company submitted its Model 40 BRC. After extensive testing and a second round of contracts for 1,500 vehicles each, the Army selected the Willys Quad as its choice. It went into production as the Willys MA, and eventually as the Willys MB. Ford also produced a great number of these vehicles, then called the GPW, under license by Willys-Overland. Other military models followed, including the M38 and M38-A1, the latter of

The release of the Wrangler TJ in 1997 fueled the aftermarket into a parts manufacturing frenzy. Upgrade parts from bumper-to-bumper are available for this model Wrangler.

The Jeep Wrangler TJ Unlimited was introduced in 2004. It features a longer wheelbase and more cargo space. A Rubicon Unlimited model was released in 2005. (Photo courtesy DaimlerChrysler)

Jeep introduced its most capable vehicle ever with the release of the Wrangler Rubicon in 2003. The rig came equipped with 31-inch Goodyear MT/R tires, 4.11:1 axle gear ratio, a transfer case with a lower 4:1 low-range gear ratio, and front and rear Dana 44 axles outfitted with air-actuated lockers.

which eventually served as the basis for the design of the CJ-5.

After World War II, Willys-Overland turned its attention back to the U.S. auto market. In 1945, Willys-Overland developed its first civilian-model Jeep, the CJ-2A. It was followed by other civilian Jeeps through the years, including the CJ-3A, CJ-3B, CJ-5, CJ-6, CJ-7, and the CJ-8 Scrambler. The CJ-5 was discontinued in 1983 after a 30-year production run. The CJ-7 lasted until 1986, marking the end of the CJ-era and making way for a completely redesigned CJ-type utility vehicle called the Wrangler YJ.

Over the years, the Jeep design changed hands a number of times. The manufacturing rights started out with Willys-Overland, which was sold to the Kaiser Company in 1953, which was then purchased by American Motors Company (AMC) in 1970, and then purchased again by the Chrysler Corporation in 1987. Jeep survived a buyout by Daimler-Benz in 1998 and is now trademarked and built by DaimlerChrysler, the fifth-largest auto manufacturer in the world.

Evolution of the Wrangler

The 1987 Wrangler YJ threw a lot of people off because it had rectangular or "square" headlights, which meant to most Jeep aficionados that it was not a true Jeep. Shortly after its release, however, the initial shock wore off and many of those same Jeep connoisseurs came to relish in the Wranglers finer interior amenities, such as air conditioning and premium comfort. This first Wrangler continued in production until 1995, with each model year receiving upgrades. However, Wrangler YJs still utilized a leaf spring suspension and sat lower to the ground than many of the CJ models. This presented issues for going off-road in a stock YJ, but aftermarket manufacturers already produced leaf spring lift kits for Jeep CJs and other

The 1941 Willys MB was the start of a 65-year span of ever-capable utility vehicles, including the Jeep Wrangler TJ. The TJ is a bit more user-friendly than the MB on the inside and around town. (Photo courtesy DaimlerChrysler)

The Jeep CJ-5 enjoyed a 30-year production run that began in 1953. The TJ's round headlights and smooth bodylines are reminiscent of these popular vehicles.

A precursor to the Wrangler Unlimited, the Jeep CJ-8 Scrambler was roughly 24 inches longer than the CJ-7. Its 103-inch wheelbase was only 10 inches longer than the CJ-7's, leaving a lengthy rear overhang that functioned well as a truck bed. The Scrambler was only produced from 1981 to '86, and fewer than 200 units left the assembly line in 1986. (Photo courtesy DaimlerChrysler)

This "El Jefe" CJ was one of the vehicles used to cross the Darien Gap in a 20,000-mile, 120-day trek from the tip of South America to the top of North America. The 1978–'79 "Expedicion de las Americas" was led by Mark A. Smith, who went on to found Jeep Jamboree USA in 1982.

Square headlights are the telltale sign of a Wrangler YJ, which was introduced in 1987 and produced through 1995. Unlike the TJ, the YJ features a leaf-spring suspension front and rear.

vehicles, so lifting a YJ to fit larger tires and improve its capability wasn't too hard. The YJ was a hit with buyers and enjoyed a relatively long nine-year production run. The YJ is still one of the best used Jeep values available today as CJs become increasingly more expensive due to their "classic" nature.

In 1997, Jeep changed the design of this historically styled vehicle to create the finest rendition to date. The Wrangler took a few cues from its brother Grand Cherokee and received a four-link coil spring suspension. It also received a host of interior upgrades, including a completely redesigned dash with driver- and passenger-side air bags. With a nod to the CJ, the TJ went back to round headlights and shared a similar body appearance. The '97 Wrangler also benefited from a good degree of performance upgrades. In all, the Wrangler TJ received nearly 80-percent newly designed parts in its recreation from the previous model of this vehicle.

Though the 4.0L I-6 remained relatively unchanged, it boasted increased horsepower and torque output. It was also mated to the same transmission and transfer case selections that were offered with the Wrangler YJ. The TJ was upgraded with a standard-cut Dana 30 front axle with unit-bearing hubs, rather than the troublesome vacuum-actuated axle disconnect that plagued the Wrangler YJ. The Dana 35C was the standard TJ rear axle, but in 1998, a Dana 44 rear was an option on some TJ models.

Wrangler Rubicon

The biggest change for the TJ came in 2003 with the introduction of the most capable Jeep ever produced. The Jeep Wrangler Rubicon was the end-all beat-all 4x4 pre-packaged with everything you'd need to conquer the well-known Rubicon Trail. The Rubicon model featured front and rear Dana 44 axles equipped with 4.11:1 gears and air-actuated selectable lockers, a heavy-duty NVG241OR Rock-Trac transfer case with a 4:1 low gear ratio, increased skid plate protection and rocker panel guards, and 31-inch Goodyear MT/R tires. Rubicons are awesome rigs for any one looking for a 4x4 that's ready to rock without turning a wrench.

Wrangler Unlimited

In 2004 Jeep upped the ante once again with the release of the Wrangler Unlimited. Continuing the legacy of the CJ-8 Scrambler, the Wrangler Unlimited features a 103.4-inch wheelbase, up from just 93.4 inches for the regular Wrangler. The Unlimited is 15 inches longer overall, with 13 additional interior cargo-space inches. The longer wheelbase gives it a better highway ride and increased off-road capability. The Unlimited is designated an LJ and shares the majority of its components with the TJ.

What's a TJ?

You're going to be hearing the term "TJ" quite a bit in this book so I think it prudent to fill you in on exactly what it means. If you've been Jeepin' long, you've probably already heard the 1997–2006 Jeep Wrangler called a TJ. This two-letter code name is simply the first two letters of the body style designation assigned by the manufacturer. In Canada, the Jeep Wrangler is designated simply as the Jeep TJ.

It was more than just round headlights that made the Wrangler TJ a hit with consumers. The coil suspension and upgraded interior were also great selling features. Though Jeep began production of the Wrangler TJ before its 1997 introduction, it was never sold as a '96 model.

The Jeep Wrangler TJ and Unlimited are assembled at the Toledo South Assembly Plant in Toledo, Ohio. Here, various models receive a host of optional equipment as they're readied for shipment. (Photo courtesy DaimlerChrysler)

A metal body code plate is attached to the floorpan beneath the driver seat in every Jeep Wrangler TJ produced. The body type, TJ, is listed on the third line on the plate as "TJJ". The second "J" indicates that the vehicle is left-hand drive. A "U" after the TJ would indicate that the vehicle is a right-hand-drive Wrangler.

Right around the time the TJ was introduced, the sport of competitive rock crawling was also gaining popularity. Many Wrangler TJs served as the basis for competition vehicles as the sport took shape.

Jeep Life

Owning a Jeep isn't something that you keep to yourself. If you drive your Wrangler daily you'll inevitably be inundated with hand waves from fellow Jeepers, conversations in the supermarket parking lot about what trails you've run, and debates about how you like whatever suspension system you may have installed. That's all part of the program, and has been since 1941. Along with these traditions, you'll enjoy a host of other annual Jeep activities, including trail rides with your local Jeep club or one of the many traveling outdoor Jeep galas hosted by Jeep itself or private companies such as Jeep Jamboree USA. One thing is for certain: When you own a Jeep Wrangler TJ, you'll never run out of ways to use it. From hitting the trail with friends, reaching a remote camping or fishing spot with your family, or just exploring

There are many ways to experience the Jeep lifestyle. Hitting the trails with like-minded souls is just one method. The Mark A. Smith Rubicon Trail Adventure is just one of the Jeep Jamboree USA guided trail rides. (Photo courtesy Jeep Jamboree USA)

the great unknown, your Jeep Wrangler TJ will get you there and back again.

Jeep Jamboree

Jeep Jamboree USA hosted 32 events in 2006, including a number of its classic adventures and a few new ones introduced that year. The three-day excursions typically include all meals and offer guided trail rides across terrain that varies in difficulty to suit many levels of driving. The organization was established in 1953 with a trek across the Rubicon Trail in California, and now makes stops at many popular 4x4 destinations throughout the United States, including Moab, Utah; Slade, Kentucky; and Hot Springs, Arkansas. These events offer a great introduction to using your Wrangler off-road, with experienced crewmembers on hand to "spot" your vehicle through difficult obstacles and assist you in making repairs if necessary.

Camp Jeep

Another taste of Jeep life can be explored at Camp Jeep. These are events put on by Jeep to encourage a celebration of its brand. They offer trail rides, but most of the activity seems to take place on the event grounds, including new-vehicle demonstrations and test drives, the Off-Road 101 driving course, where an onboard driving instructor helps you navigate difficult terrain, a multitude of activities for the whole family, and plenty of live music. Also, these events usually provide an opportunity to meet with Jeep engineers and pick their brains about issues you may have with your vehicle or regarding what's on tap for new Jeep models. One of my favorite aspects of these events is seeing all of the cool display vehicles. This often includes unique concept Jeeps that may never see production. After you've seen everything on display, check out the parking lot to see all the classic and modified Jeeps owned by all the other attendees.

Catching sight of all the classic Jeep vehicles is a great aspect of Camp Jeep. Shown here are a Golden Eagle Edition Jeep CJ-7, a Jeep Scrambler, and a Wrangler YJ.

A few movie star Jeeps sometimes make the Camp Jeep scene, including this Wrangler Unlimited used in the movie Sahara.

The '07 Wrangler takes this classic 4x4 to a new plateau, offering the finest in interior amenities, heavier-duty drivetrain components, and increased off-road capability. The '07 Wrangler JK is longer and wider than the TJ, lending more on- and off-road stability and vehicle control. (Photo courtesy DaimlerChrysler)

With room for five, the '07 Jeep Wrangler Unlimited 4-door is designed to bring the whole family to the trail. The unique top and four full hard doors set it apart from earlier models. (Photo courtesy DaimlerChrysler)

Looking to the Future: The 2007 Jeep Wrangler

It had to happen; it always does. CJ owners dealt with it, as did Cherokee XJ owners. Jeep ended production of these popular vehicles to make way for supposedly bigger and better vehicles. Wrangler TJ production lasted 10 years. There's no argument that it went out at the top of its game, but it was sad to see production of this fine vehicle come to end. However, it looks like the '07 Wrangler JK learned plenty from its predecessor.

Jeep went with the "more, more, more" philosophy with the design of the '07 Wrangler JK. Convenience, safety, interior space, and comfort were some of the largest issues addressed, but off-road capability and on-road performance and handling were also tended to, resulting in a longer wheelbase, wider track width, and increased horsepower and torque output. Though I had yet to drive an '07 Wrangler at the time of this book's publication, I must say that it looks promising. Of course, my heart will always be with the TJ, as it was with the CJ-5 before that—but there's always room for another Jeep 4x4 in the stable.

MODELS, SPECIAL EDITIONS AND OPTIONS

The Jeep Wrangler comes in many shapes and forms, with plenty of models and special editions. It's important to know what you're starting with, whether you plan on modifying your TJ or wheeling it stock.

One of the great things about the Jeep Wrangler is that one model, trim level, or special edition was just never enough. It seemed that something new would pop up a few times every year, and each new attribute or special edition created another unique vehicle to choose from. This chapter gives you a better idea of what models came equipped with what options and equipment, and in what years each particular special edition was produced.

As with most vehicles, the price of each Wrangler is determined by its options and trim level. Jeep marketed several models in order to appeal to a broad buyer base, so the big-buck guys could get all the bells and whistles and the lighter-wallet crowd could still have fun. Even in 2006, the final year of TJ production, Jeep offered four Wrangler TJ models and two Unlimited LJ models. The most expensive Wrangler cost over 30K, but you could still get into the base model TJ for less than 20K.

Wrangler SE

The SE is your base-model Wrangler. Pretty much every TJ you find for sale "cheap" is a Wrangler SE. All model years were equipped with the available four-cylinder engine, a manual transmission, NP231J transfer case, and Dana 30 front and Dana 35 rear axles. Gear ratios varied by year and ranged from 4.11:1 to 3.73:1. This model is also typically equipped with a 124-amp alternator, power front disc brakes with rear drum brakes, and tires in the 27- to 28-inch range mounted on 15 x 7-inch full-lace steel wheels. Half-hard doors with zip-out upper windows were included, as were black fender flares, vinyl seats, a mini center console with two cup-holders, and a four-speaker stereo system.

Options were limited on the SE and most were dealer installed. An engine block heater was offered, as was air conditioning, cloth seats (later models with tip-and-slide capability), and carpet floor mats. A locking gas-cap, a dash-mounted ashtray alongside a 12-volt cigarette lighter, and front and rear tow hooks were also available as options. Full hard doors were another option and could be combined with a hard top, though the Sunrider soft-top option retained the hard half doors. A rear seat was also an available option in early SE model TJs, but became standard equipment in 2005, as did the 4.0L engine when the auto transmission option was selected.

If you miss the utility Jeep days, then the SE will suit you well. It lacks the niceties of some of the over-optioned models, but it's still a true 4x4 with plenty of grunt for the trail. In fact, SE models are usually the Wranglers you see sporting LS1 and HEMI swaps and macho axles, since they come cheaper from the dealer and have less bullshit to

TJs not equipped with air conditioning use a factory-installed A/C bypass. The absence of the A/C system frees up quite a bit of extra space under the hood.

All Wranglers feature a raised "Jeep" stamp on the cowl sides with a decal on top of that. Each TJ model features a designation decal on the cowl sides, except the SE, which offers a bare minimum of options and a 4-cylinder engine.

deal with under the hood and under the dash. Besides the "Jeep" and "Trail Rated" badges that appear on all TJs, the SE bears no additional decals calling attention to its designation. Instead, it relies on lower-cowl-side "Jeep" decals that rest upon "Jeep"-shaped patterns stamped into the steel.

Wrangler X

The X model was introduced in 2002 as a means of appealing to younger buyers, falling between the Sport and SE models in terms of features and price. It came with many of the typical Wrangler features, such as a 4.0L engine, a manual

SE Model Specifications

2.5L Power Tech I-4 engine ('97–'02)
2.4L Power Tech DOHC I-4 engine ('03–'06)
4.0L Power Tech I-6 engine ('05–'06)
AX-5 5-speed manual transmission ('97–'02)
NV1500 5-speed manual transmission ('03–'04)
NSG370 6-speed manual transmission ('05–'06)
30RH 3-speed automatic transmission ('97–'02)
42RLE 4-speed automatic transmission ('03–'06)
Dana 30 front axle*
Dana 35c rear axle*
Command-Trac 4WD System (NP231J transfer case)
*refer to Chapter 6 for available ring-and-pinion gear ratios

1997 MSRP: $13,470
2006 MSRP: $19,050

Jeep aimed the X model Wrangler at younger buyers. It was first offered in 2002 and was available through the end of TJ production in 2006. It also served as the basis for most special edition TJs. Notice the "X" in front of the door. (Photo courtesy DaimlerChrysler)

With most models, you could choose an option package that included four-wheel disc brakes, 30-inch tires, and a Dana 44 rear axle with a Trac-Lok limited-slip differential.

X Model Specifications

4.0L Power Tech I-6 engine
NV3550 5-speed manual
   transmission ('02–'04)
NSG370 6-speed manual
   transmission ('05–'06)
32RH 3-speed automatic
   transmission ('97–'02)
42RLE 4-speed automatic
   transmission ('03–'06)
Dana 30 front axle*
Dana 35c rear axle*
Dana 44 HD Rear Axle (special
   edition models only)
Command-Trac 4WD System
   (NP231J transfer case)
*refer to Chapter 6 for available ring-and-pinion gear ratios

2002 MSRP: $18,485
2006 MSRP: $21,310

packaged with a leather-wrapped steering wheel. Full interior carpet and a folding rear seat were standard equipment on these models.

You probably see more X model Wranglers on the road than you realize, since the majority of the special-edition Wranglers are based on this model. Most special editions were equipped with the Dana 44 rear axle, while standard X models never were. Even so, the standard-equipped Wrangler Xs are still up to hitting trails in stock form. Like the SE, these models often become the most modified Wranglers since their initial cost is lower, leaving a few extra dollars for aftermarket goodies.

Wrangler Sport

You get a lot more standard equipment and quite a few more available options with the Wrangler TJ Sport. Though the Dana 35c was still the standard rear axle, the Dana 44 was available with a Trac-Lok limited-slip differential

transmission, cloth seats, and other standard equipment that came with the SE model. As with all Wranglers, a variety of options were also available.

Four-wheel disc brakes were an available option for the X-model Wrangler as part of a brake and traction group, which also included a Trac-Lok limited-slip rear differential, 30-inch tires, and 15 x 7-inch aluminum wheels. Cast aluminum wheels with premium tires were another alternative, but 15 x 7-inch full-face steel wheels and 215/75R15 Goodyear A/T tires were standard. The dual-top option became available in 1998, meaning original buyers received a folding soft top along with a hard top of the same color. Full doors were included with this package. A premium stereo system with an in-dash six-CD changer was another available option for later models. The upgraded stereo included seven speakers, including a subwoofer mounted in the full-length center console. Sirius Satellite Radio became an option in later model Wranglers and used a sport-bar mounted

antenna on the driver's side of the vehicle. Electronic, steering-wheel-mounted speed control was also an option and was

You get a lot more with the Sport model Wrangler, including a Dana 44 rear axle as part of the Brake and Traction Group, which also came with a Trac-Lok limited-slip differential. In earlier midels, a script "Sport logo" appears on the cowl sides above the Wrangler designation. (Photo courtesy DaimlerChrysler)

Sport Model Specifications

4.0L Power Tech I-6 engine

AX-15 5-speed manual transmission ('97–'99)

NV3550 5-speed manual transmission ('00–'04)

NSG370 6-speed manual transmission ('05–'06)

32RH 3-speed automatic transmission ('97–'02)

42RLE 4-speed automatic transmission ('03–'06)

Dana 30 front axle*

Dana 35c rear axle*

Dana 44 HD rear axle (optional)*

Command-Trac 4WD System (NP231J transfer case)

*refer to Chapter 6 for available ring-and-pinion gear ratios

1997 MSRP: $17,140
2006 MSRP: $24,170

and four-wheel disc brakes. Full hard doors with roll-up windows were standard equipment for later Sport models, as were fog lamps, air conditioning, tip-and-slide reclining cloth seats, and a seven-speaker premium sound system with an in-radio six-disc CD changer. The standard tire and wheel package was also a step up from that offered on lesser models, using a P225/75R15 Goodyear Wrangler A/T tread.

Though the base-model Sport is merely a step above the fully-equipped X, it can still be outfitted with nearly every available Wrangler option from the factory or dealer, whereas the others had limited options. Some of these items include the Sentry Key theft-deterrent system, an auto-dimming rearview mirror with reading lights and compass and temperature readout, high-pressure gas-charged shock absorbers, 30x9.50R15 Goodyear Wrangler A/T tires mounted on 15 x 8-inch cast-aluminum wheels, the dual-top option, a matching full-size spare, and four-wheel anti-lock (ABS) brakes.

The Wrangler Sport is extremely versatile at being a 4x4 on the weekends and a daily driver all week long. It features all the interior comfort items that make it easy to tote passengers who might object to vinyl seating and a lack of air conditioning, while at the same time appealing to the rough and tough crowd that doesn't mind having the top down with dirt blowing in their ears.

Wrangler Sahara

A continuation of a model first introduced as a Wrangler YJ, the Sahara has traditionally represented the flagship model of the Wrangler fleet. Distinctive exterior styling included unique body coloring, Sahara badging, wider painted fender flares and extended flares with entry steps, and unique seating upholstery with the "Sahara" logo used throughout. Available options gave the Sahara a different look from vehicle to vehicle since both hard and soft tops were available, as well as half and full

doors. Paint choice also varied and included colors that were only available on a Sahara. Through the years, available colors included black, Stone White, a shade of khaki or tan (Light Khaki, Desert Sand), and a shade of green (Moss Green, Shale Green, Forrest Green). Sienna Pearlcoat also appeared in 2001 and was available for the remainder of Sahara production, which ended in 2004. Interior colors also varied and included a shade of khaki, tan, or camel mixed with a green or dark green.

Sahara owners weren't left wanting for standard features, but many were merely for comfort and cosmetics. Think of the Sahara as a top-of-the-line Sport model. The standard rear axle was the Dana 35c but the Dana 44 HD rear was an available option and most Sahara models I've spotted around town and on the trail (yes, I check every time) are equipped with the 44. The 4.0L, of course, was the only Sahara engine and was mated to both manual and automatic

The Wrangler Sahara had a consistent theme through the duration of its production and was offered in limited colors, which added to its uniqueness. (Photo courtesy DaimlerChrysler)

This early Sahara interior shows the tan and green colors used throughout. Steering-wheel-mounted cruise controls were an optional on the X, Sport, Sahara, and Rubicon. (Photo courtesy DaimlerChrysler)

transmissions. The NP231J transfer case was also utilized. Four-wheel disc brakes and 30x9.5R15 Goodyear Wrangler OWL A/T tires on 15 x 8-inch Canyon aluminum wheels were standard. Most Sahara TJs were also available with heavy-duty front and rear shocks, a full-size alloy spare wheel and tire with cover, tow hooks, skid plates, fog lamps, a premium seven-speaker sound system with in-radio CD changer, full interior carpet, Sentry Key theft-deterrent system, and steering-wheel-mounted speed controls.

Though the Sahara was largely popular, production ceased after the '04 model year. After that, Jeep applied the Sahara title once more as a special-edition Unlimited that was available in 2005. This is a great model to pick up used since you'll almost always get a bunch of optional equipment.

Wrangler Unlimited

The 2004 Wrangler Unlimited was a dream come true for fans of the earlier Jeep Scrambler. Like the Scrambler, the Unlimited offered a longer wheelbase than standard Wranglers. For the Unlimited, Jeep added 15 inches in overall length, including 10 inches to the wheelbase and 5 inches behind the rear wheels. This produced an overall length of 170.4 inches and a wheelbase of 103.4 inches.

Sahara Model Specifications

4.0L Power Tech I-6 engine
AX-15 5-speed transmission ('97–'99)
NV3550 5-speed transmission ('00–'04)
NSG370 6-speed transmission ('05)
32RH 3-speed automatic transmission ('97–'02)
42RLE 4-speed automatic transmission ('03–'05)
Dana 30 front axle*
Dana 35c rear axle*
Dana 44 HD rear axle (optional)*
Command-Trac 4WD System (NP231J transfer case)
*refer to Chapter 6 for available ring-and-pinion gear ratios

1997 MSRP: $19,210
2004 MSRP: $25,275

The Wrangler Unlimited was introduced in 2004. It featured a 103.4-inch wheelbase and a good deal more rear passenger and cargo space. Its longer wheelbase created greater vehicle handling on the road and increased its capability on the trail. (Photo courtesy DaimlerChrysler)

A Dana 44 rear axle was standard on the Wrangler Unlimited, as was the 4.0L I-6. A 4-speed auto trans and a 6-speed manual were also offered.

Wrangler Rubicon and Unlimited Rubicon

There's no arguing that the Jeep Wrangler Rubicon is the most off-road-capable production vehicle ever made. Some may contest this claim, but I'm ready for the debate. Starting with a great platform like the Wrangler TJ didn't hurt its chances, as even the Wrangler SE is ready for the trail right out of the box. But with the Wrangler Rubicon, Jeep took things to an entirely new level.

It's hard to know where to start with the Wrangler Rubicon, since each of its attributes is as good as the next. The NV241OR Rock-Trac transfer case offers 4:1 low gearing and is equipped with 32-spline front and rear output shafts with a fixed rear output, a wider chain, a high-volume oil pump, and a stronger case design. The axles are also impressive and unique. There are front and rear Dana 44 HD axles, each equipped with a Tru-Lok air-actuated locking differential and 4.11:1 gears. The rear also acts as a limited-slip when the locker isn't activated. A host of factory-installed skid plates are also included, as are diamond plate steel rocker guards, four-wheel disc brakes, high-pressure gas-charged shocks, and 31-inch Goodyear Wrangler MT/R tires mounted to 16 x 8-inch cast-aluminum wheels under black fender flares. Unique "Rubicon" badges are affixed to the cowl sides.

The Rubicon is optioned very much like the Wrangler Sport and can receive essentially the same features. But with so much hardware included, most of the remaining options deal with comfort and styling. Half hard doors were standard equipment on the Rubicon until 2006, when full hard doors with roll-up windows came standard. Dual tops were optional. Air conditioning was an option in 2003, but became standard in 2004. Floor mats were optional, as was the smoker's group (ash tray and lighter), security system, and steering-wheel-mounted electronic speed controls.

Jeep's Sunrider soft top, which featured a fold back sunroof over the front seats, made its debut on the Wrangler Unlimited. Other models received the sunroof in 2005.

> ## Wrangler Unlimited Specifications
>
> 4.0L Power Tech I-6 engine
> NSG370 6-speed manual transmission ('05–'06)
> 42RLE 4-speed automatic transmission ('04–'06)
> Dana 30 front axle*
> Dana 44 HD rear axle*
> Command-Trac 4WD System (NP231J transfer case)
> *refer to Chapter 6 for available ring-and-pinion gear ratios
>
> 2004 MSRP: $24,835
> 2006 MSRP: $24,925

Extra interior space for passengers and storage is one of the biggest advantages of this model, but the lengthened wheelbase also provides more on-road stability, as well as a bit more obstacle-climbing capability on the trail. A Dana 44 HD rear axle with a Trac-Lok limited-slip differential is standard equipment, along with 30-inch tires on 15 x 8-inch aluminum wheels and four-wheel disc brakes. Only the 4-speed auto 42RLE transmission was available in 2004. Shortly after, the NSG370 6-speed manual transmission became the standard fitment, with the auto available as an option. All Wrangler Unlimiteds featured full hard doors with roll-up windows and a Sunrider soft top as standard equipment. Other standard equipment was right on par with the Wrangler Sport.

True to Jeep's tradition of providing the coolest of vehicles for the shortest amount of time, the Wrangler Unlimited LJ was only allowed three years of model year production. This is a shade less than the five years of production given to the classic Scramblers, so be forewarned that the search for these model Wranglers is sure to be arduous 20 years down the road.

Above: A Rubicon model Wrangler Unlimited was introduced in 2005 and included all of the great Rubicon features. It became a quick favorite for Wrangler fans and offered unequaled ability on the trail. (Photo courtesy DaimlerChrysler)

Left: The Jeep Wrangler Rubicon was introduced in 2003 and offered a wealth of features to further its off-road capability over other model Wranglers. Standard equipment included 31-inch Goodyear Wrangler MT/R tires mounted on 16 x 8 aluminum wheels.

Wrangler Rubicon/Rubicon Unlimited Specifications

4.0L Power Tech I-6 engine
NV3550 5-speed manual
   transmission ('03–'04)
NSG370 6-speed manual
   transmission ('05–'06)
42RLE 4-speed automatic
   transmission ('03–'06)
Dana 44 front axle*
Dana 44 HD rear axle*
Rock-Trac NV241OR transfer case
*refer to axle Chapter 6 for available
   ring-and-pinion gear ratios

Rubicon
2003 MSRP: $24,810
2006 MSRP: $28,395

Rubicon Unlimited
2005 MSRP: $28,465
2006 MSRP: $29,395

Factory-installed pneumatic lockers were installed in the front and rear Dana 44 axles, with dash-board-mounted switches for activation.

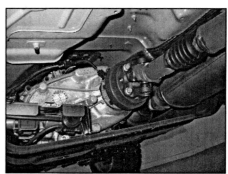

The NV241OR Rock-Trac transfer case was standard equipment on the Wrangler Rubicon and Unlimited Rubicon.

The Wrangler Rubicon Unlimited was introduced in 2005 and possessed all of the same features as the Unlimited and Rubicon models. It received the same standard equipment and options as the Wrangler Rubicon but in a longer package.

Wrangler Special Editions

2001 60th Anniversary Edition

The 2001 60th Anniversary Edition Wrangler was available in black or Silverstone Metallic. It featured specially embroidered floor mats, full metal doors, body-color fender flares, and doorsill guards. It was equipped with 30-inch tires on 15 x 8-inch aluminum wheels, fog lamps and tow hooks, air conditioning, an AM/FM CD stereo with a five-speaker system, and a dual top option.

2003 Tomb Raider Edition

The debut of this limited edition Jeep Wrangler coincided with the release of the film *Lara Croft Tomb Raider: The Cradle of Life*. It's modeled after the customized Jeep Wrangler Rubicon used by the film's title character. Just over 1,000 Tomb Raider Wrangler Rubicons were produced in 2003. They included a host of interior and exterior add-ons on top of the Rubicon features. The vehicle used 31-inch tires mounted on 16-inch Alcoa forged aluminum wheels that rest beneath graphite-painted "riveted" fender flares. Mopar accessories included a black tubular grille guard and diamond plate bumper guard, black dia-mond plate rocker rails, a windshield-mounted light bar, and fog and tail lamp brush guards. The interior included Dark Slate fabric seats with red accent stitching down the center, red seat belts, and a dash adorned with a silver-sur-round instrument panel bezel and a ser-ial-number plate. "Tomb Raider" badges on the cowl sides offset the Bright Silver exterior color.

2002–'04 Apex Special Edition

Available in Patriot Blue and black, the Apex Edition Wrangler was based on the X model, which was also introduced in 2002. The Apex special edition offered a strobe hood graphic and Ultra-hide Cognac bucket seats, as well as an AM/FM CD radio with a seven-speaker system that included a center console subwoofer and two instrument panel tweeters. The Apex edition was also equipped with 15 x 7-inch chrome wheels and P225/75R15 OWL Goodyear Wrangler A/T tires.

2004 Columbia Edition

The Columbia Edition Wrangler was part of a series that included the Grand Cherokee and Liberty. The Wrangler version featured premium graphite-painted 15-inch aluminum wheels, graphite-painted fender flares, fog lamps, a two-tone exterior treatment with "special" trim, and Columbia badges. Available colors included Patriot Blue, Flame Red, Solar Yellow, Bright Silver, and black. The interior offered khaki two-tone seats with an embroi-dered Columbia logo and silver-painted accent trim. Original purchasers of the Columbia Edition Wrangler also sup-posedly received a complimentary Columbia Bugaboo parka.

2004–'06 Rocky Mountain Edition

Based on the X model, the Rocky Mountain Edition Wrangler was equipped with a Dana 44 rear axle and 30-inch Goodyear tires on 15-inch Ravine aluminum wheels. This is another good way to score an X model with a Dana 44. Its Rocky Mountain fea-tures included center console accents, two-tone cloth seats with embroidered logos, and color-matched fender flares. A Rocky Mountain Edition decal was also part of the package, as was a seven-speaker AM/FM/CD sound system. It was available with an automatic or man-ual transmission.

2004–'06 Willys Edition

The Willys Edition was also based on the X model and included a 4.0L I-6 and a Dana 44 rear axle. These are eas-ily spotted by the "WILLYS" decal on the cowl side, a military-style star decal on the hood, water resistant camouflage or black seats, a dark green soft-top, and Moss Green paint. A "Fuel" decal was also offered and applied above the fuel-filler cap. The Willys Edition also fea-tured diamond plate sill guards painted dark green, a full-size spare tire with matching wheel, and body-color fender

A little more than 1,000 Tomb Raider edition Jeep Wranglers were produced in 2003. The vehicle is based on the Rubicon model and also incorporates a number of other features. The interior featured a silver center dash bezel and serial number plate. (Photo courtesy DaimlerChrysler)

The Rocky Mountain Edition Wrangler was based on the X model. It featured a Dana 44 rear end, 30-inch tires, and Rocky Mountain decals. (Photo courtesy DaimlerChrysler)

2005 Jeep Rubicon Unlimited Sahara Edition

This isn't the older Sahara model you're thinking of, but a limited production release of the Rubicon Unlimited Wrangler to celebrate the fabulous movie *Sahara*. The movie starred Matthew McConaughey and Penelope Cruz, who chase a treasure while being chased, but find safety and success thanks to their trusty Rubicon Wrangler Unlimited. The rig offered a Light Khaki exterior, premium cloth interior, and painted accent rims. The typical "Sahara" badging was also in place on the cowl side.

2005 Freedom Edition

The Freedom Edition Wrangler is essentially an X model with a cosmetic package. It had the full metal doors with a soft top, the 4.0L engine, 6-speed manual transmission, fog lamps and tow hooks, and Goodyear A/T tires mounted on 15-inch chrome wheels. Air conditioning and a theft deterrent system were also

flares. Tow hooks, fog lamps with mesh covers, taillamp guards, and an AM/FM stereo CD player with a seven-speaker system and a subwoofer in the center console were also part of the package.

2005–'06 Golden Eagle Edition

With an optional Golden Eagle hood decal, the Golden Eagle Edition Wrangler was for all the Daisy Dukes at heart, or anyone who wanted to give a nod to the CJ era. It was based on the Sport model and was equipped with a Dana 44 HD rear axle, 15 x 8-inch Ravine aluminum wheels with painted accents, and 30 x 9.50-inch tires. The interior offered two-tone premium seat fabric with an embroidered Golden Eagle logo and a stainless-painted center stack bezel. The Golden Eagle logo also appeared on the spare tire cover, on the fenders, and in hood side lettering. Available colors were white, green, black, and blue.

The Rubicon Unlimited Sahara Edition received extra attention due to its appearance in the action-adventure film. The Sahara star logo on the cowl side is unique to this edition.

Above: The Off-Road package was available at the dealer and included off-road bumper, rock rails, skid plates, and a Warn winch. (Photo courtesy DaimlerChrysler)

Left: The last special edition to be offered with this generation Wrangler was the 65th Anniversary Edition. It featured the Anniversary logo on the cowl side, chrome wheels, and body colored fender flares and end caps. (Photo courtesy DaimlerChrysler)

included, along with a selection of vinyl or cloth seats in Dark Slate Gray. The Freedom Edition was available outside the United States but was called the Rocky Mountain Edition in Canada, and the Red River Edition outside North America. It was offered in red, silver, blue, and black exterior colors with body-color fender flares and special side badges.

2006 65th Anniversary Edition

Based on the X model, the 65th Anniversary Edition Wrangler was offered with a selection of features and options. It was equipped with a 65th Anniversary decal, a 65th Anniversary logo on the floor mats, unique two-tone seats with an embroidered 65th logo, chrome-color center stack bezel, fog lamps, body-color fender flares, full metal doors, a seven-speaker stereo system with subwoofer, Sirius Radio, high-pressure gas shocks, Dana 44 HD rear axle, 30 x 9.5-inch Goodyear Wrangler OWL tires, 15-inch Alcoa aluminum wheels, a Sunrider soft top, and was

available in green, black, Bright Silver, and Midnight Blue.

Wrangler Sales Package Editions

A number of sales packages existed for the Wrangler over the years, with most addressing cosmetic needs. The Black Tie package included chrome tube bumpers, a chrome fuel-filler door, a decal kit, and chrome mirrors. The Travel Package offered a chrome exhaust tip, taillamp guards, rubber splashguards, seat covers, an add-a-trunk, and door entry guards. An Interior Package was also available and featured interior grab handles and a coat hook, slush-style floor mats, and interior trim. The most functional of these packages was the Off-Road Package, which included off-road style bumpers, rock rails, skid plates, and a Warn winch. These packages could be combined with most Wranglers and are yet another means of adding to the adventure of tracking down and assessing what features your used TJ possesses.

Right-Hand Drive

Not just for the overseas market, Jeep introduced a right-hand drive version of the Wrangler Sport in 2003. These models are designed primarily for fleet use but were also available to retail customers. The right-hand drive Wrangler Sport is offered with most of the same features as the left-hand drive Sport model but is limited to the use of an automatic transmission and a hard top.

Trail Rated

Beginning with the '04 model year, Jeep started its new "Trail Rated" marketing campaign to indicate a level of 4x4 capability as judged by the Nevada Automotive Test Center (NATC). This organization tests vehicles' off-road competence in a variety of off-road driving situations and assigns a score, or Trail Rating. Not surprisingly, the Wrangler Rubicon is Jeep's top Trail Rated vehicle, with the standard Wrangler just a short distance behind it.

TJ ENGINES

Jeep remained fairly consistent with its TJ engine offerings over the years, sticking with the 4.0L Power Tech I-6 for the duration of the vehicle's manufacture, and using two different four-cylinder mills: the 2.5L Power Tech I-4 ('97–2002) and the 2.4L DOHC I-4 ('03–'06). Each of the engines has its perks as well as its deficiencies, but in general all deliver sufficient power for a stock Wrangler.

The 2.5L is the slightest of the bunch, with the 1997 model delivering just 120 hp @ 5,400 rpm and 140 ft-lbs of torque @ 3,500 rpm. The 2.4L four-cylinder really stepped it up with 147 hp @ 5,200 rpm and 165 ft-lbs of torque @ 4,000 rpm. Though the 4.0L remained relatively unchanged over the years, it did benefit from increased power numbers between 1997 and 2006. The '97 4.0L produced 181 hp @ 4,600 rpm and 222 ft-lbs of torque @ 2,800 rpm. In 2001, ratings were bumped to 190 hp and 235 ft-lbs torque. Later models also received much stouter transmissions for both the four- and six-cylinder engines.

What does all this mean? Newer is better (isn't it always?). Of course, that doesn't mean that earlier TJ engines can't be built to perform at the same level and better. Aftermarket manufacturers

The 4.0L Power Tech I-6 has been a TJ mainstay through the years. Two different four-cylinder engines were also offered.

are replete with performance goodies for increased horsepower and torque. Even the four-cylinder mills can be equipped to handle up to 35-inch tires when equipped with the proper axle gearing.

4.0L Power Tech I-6

With years of experience in multiple Jeep vehicles, including the Wrangler YJ, the 242-ci 4.0L inline six-cylinder engine earned its place in the Wrangler TJ. This fuel-injected, overhead-valve mill is lightweight, powerful, and can effectively spin 37-inch tires through the gnarliest terrain. The 4.0L engine also has great potential for increased performance, which means aftermarket upgrades are aplenty.

The engine features a cast-iron cylinder block, cylinder head, camshaft, and connecting rods. It also has a cast nodular-iron crankshaft (clockwise rotation) and aluminum pistons. The crankshaft spins on seven main bearings and the camshaft rides on four. The 4.0L engines uses a six-quart stamped-steel oil pan with a one-piece gasket, and is cooled by an aluminum water pump, a mechanical cooling fan, and a downflow radiator with an aluminum core and plastic side tanks. The engine build date code number is located on the right side of the cylinder block and can be used to determine engine type, and the day, month, and year of manufacture.

Only slight variations exist in the overall 4.0L engine design. The early model Wrangler 4.0L engines were equipped with a distributor and a crack-prone tubular exhaust manifold. In 2000, the 4.0L received a few upgrades. The distributor was replaced in favor of a one-piece coil rail assembly, and the

The 2.5L Power Tech I-4 was the base model engine in '97–'02 Wranglers. Variations of this motor were also used in the previous model Wrangler and other Jeep vehicles.

This 4.0L tubular exhaust manifold was standard until 2000. It was prone to cracking around the welded seams, and was replaced by a two-piece cast-iron exhaust manifold.

potentially troublesome exhaust manifold was replaced with two intertwining front and rear exhaust manifolds made from high-silicone molybdenum cast iron.

2.5L Power Tech I-4

The 2.5L Power Tech I-4 was available from '97-2002. This 4-cylinder engine came mated to the AX-5 manual transmission or the 30RH auto. The 150-ci mill is a lightweight overhead-valve engine with a pressure-feed full-flow filtration lubrication system and a 9.2:1 compression ratio. It features a cast-iron cylinder block, cylinder head, connecting rods, camshaft, a cast nodular-iron crankshaft, and aluminum alloy pistons. The crankshaft rotates clockwise on five main bearings, while the camshaft spins on four bearings.

Introduced in the '84 Cherokee, multiple versions of the 2.5L I-4 have been installed in Wranglers since 1991. The earliest examples were equipped with carburetors, with subsequent models receiving throttle body injection systems. However, all TJ 2.5L four-cylinder engines are multi-point fuel injected and use a mechanical distributor with an internal camshaft-position sensor. A single ignition coil is secured to a bracket on the side of the engine. The spark plug firing order is 1-3-4-2. This engine can be identified using the seven-digit build date code, which is stamped on the right side of the engine block between the number three and number four cylinders. The fourth and fifth digits should be HX to signify that it is a 2.5L engine.

One of the most common questions about this engine is: "will it hold me back on the trail." You won't win any drag races with the 2.5L, but there's no reason it won't work well on the trail, so long as it's matched up with the correct axle gearing.

2.4L DOHC I-4

The 2.4L four-cylinder DOHC 16-valve engine was introduced in the '03 model year. It's a dual overhead cam engine with four valves per cylinder. The 148-ci cast-iron cylinder block is actually a two-piece assembly that uses a separate bedplate to incorporate the main bearing caps. It bolts in to the cylinder block for much better block strength. A full-flow filtration, pressure-type oiling system is employed, with the oil pump being driven by the crankshaft. The rear oil seal retainer is integral to the block. The 2.4L is the only Wrangler engine to use an electric cooling fan.

The later 2.4L I-4 engine was the standard Wrangler engine from 2003–'06. It presented 4-cylinder TJ owners with more power and torque than the 2.5L I-4 ever produced.

Early TJ 4.0L engines used a distributor and spark plug wires in its ignition system. The distributor does just what its name says: distributes spark energy through the spark plug wires to the spark plugs. The distributor cap and rotor, spark plug wires, and spark plugs can all be replaced as part of a routine tune up.

The 2.4L engine does not use a distributor, but rather has a split coil that fires two spark plugs at the same time—one half fires cylinders one and four and the other half fires two and three. The firing order is 1-3-4-2, with the cylinder arrangement numbered front to rear.

As with the 2.5L, the 2.4L isn't your best bet for setting land-speed records, but with some lower (numerically high) gears, you can do okay on the trail. Besides the different ignition system, you can identify the 2.4L by its electric fan.

Ignition System

The 4.0L engines used in Jeep Wrangler TJs can be classified in two categories: those that use a distributor, and those that do not. The '97 to '99 models fall in to the first category, as do all 2.5L four-cylinder engines. These engines are equipped with a camshaft-driven mechanical distributor that includes a shaft-driven rotor and a camshaft position sensor. The distributors are not equipped with built-in centrifugal- or

vacuum-assisted advance since base timing and advance are controlled by the Powertrain Control Module (PCM), so base ignition timing is not adjustable.

The 4.0L went distributor-less in the 2000 Wrangler, and instead received a one-piece coil rail assembly that bolts to the cylinder head and uses three separate coils with integral spark plug boots in the bottom coil. All TJ 4.0L engines have the same cylinder firing order (1-5-3-6-2-4), though the later ignition system fires the spark plugs during the compression and exhaust strokes. Ignition timing for these later 4.0Ls is controlled by the PCM and is not manually adjustable. The PCM sets the base timing and adjusts ignition timing advance through the coil ground circuit.

Powertrain Control Module (PCM)

All Jeep Wrangler TJs utilize a Powertrain Control Module (PCM) to operate the majority of engine functions by monitoring multiple sensors and

A one-piece coil-rail assembly with integral spark plug boots was introduced in the 2000 model year 4.0L engine. It replaced the distributor and the ignition coil. The spark plug firing order remained the same for all 4.0L engines.

The 2.4L four-cylinder engine uses a one-piece coil rail like the 4.0L engine, an electric cooling fan, and dual overhead camshafts.

The Powertrain Control Module (PCM) is situated under the hood and mounted to the firewall above the battery. A 32-way connector and wiring harness lead to a myriad of sensors throughout the vehicle to monitor its functions.

switches installed throughout the vehicle. The PCM is mounted in the engine compartment on the passenger-side firewall, just above the battery. Jeep refers to the PCM as JTEC (Jeep Truck Engine Controller) and it is also used by other Jeep and Dodge vehicles. Among the PCM's duties are the management and regulation of ignition timing, coil dwell, air-fuel ratio, idle speed, and the charging system, to name a few. The system is also fully adaptable to meet various operating conditions. It receives input signals and reacts by sending an output signal to make adjustments as needed. For example, the PCM will adjust idle speed using information gathered from sensors that respond to vehicle speed, transmission gear, engine coolant temperature, throttle position, and even the air-conditioning clutch and brake switches. JTEC also provides the necessary sensor and functional analysis data to the OBD II diagnostic system.

Charging System

A 117-amp alternator was factory installed on the 2.5L and 4.0L engines in most model year Jeep Wrangler TJs, though some did end up with an 81-amp unit. Starting with the 2000 model year, a 124-amp alternator was added to the lineup and was typically part of a tow package or other package options. The only change after this came in 2003 with the introduction of the 2.4L I-4, which used 124- and 136-amp alternators. In 2.5L and 4.0L engines, the alternator is mounted to the front passenger side of the engine and is pulley-driven by the crankshaft using a serpentine belt. The 2.4L alternator is also a pulley drive, but is mounted to the front driver's side of the engine.

The charging system also incorporates a factory-installed 500-cold-cranking-amp battery and a battery temperature sensor. The sensor is installed in the battery tray beneath the battery and is used to gather data for the PCM, which actually varies the battery charging rate and alternator output. This affect may be witnessed during colder weather when the voltage gauge in the dash cluster reads higher than it does in the summertime.

TJs came with 117-amp alternators, but 124- and 136-amp alternators were also installed.

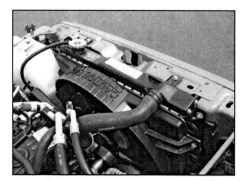

The Wrangler TJ uses similar cooling systems for the 2.5L and 4.0L engines (shown), but the 2.4L uses an electric cooling fan.

Cooling System

The Wrangler cooling system consists of many components that all share the same goal: to aid the engine in maintaining optimum operating temperature for all driving situations. This means adjusting the rate of coolant flow to efficiently cool the engine in hot climates so it won't overheat, and stabilize the temperature in colder climates, so the engine maintains its normal operating temperature. The cooling system must complete these tasks regardless of whether you're driving down the highway at 40 mph or scaling a 60-degree incline in 4-Low, relying on the engine to produce massive amounts of torque and running high RPM. It's a good idea to keep a careful watch on the temp gauge, as well as properly maintain your engines' cooling system.

The TJ cooling system is a forced circulation system that includes a thermal viscous fan drive and a reverse-rotating (counter clockwise) centrifugal water pump, a mechanical cooling fan, a fan shroud, an 18- to 21-psi pressurized radiator cap, a coolant overflow tank, and, of course, the radiator. TJs with the 2.4L use an electric fan. TJs that use automatic transmissions are also equipped with a transmission cooler, which is located inside the radiator. The plastic side tanks can be problematic and if leakage occurs the entire radiator must be replaced.

Wrangler Engine Build Date Code

There are a few ways of identifying the year of the engine in your Wrangler, but the most accurate method is to use the engine build date code, which is stamped on a machined surface on the passenger-side of the cylinder block between the number two and number three cylinders. For '97–'99 models this is just forward of the distributor. It appears beneath the coil rail assembly on later model Wranglers.

Making it Run on the Cheap

It doesn't always take a whole lot to get your engine—whether four-cylinders or six-cylinders—to produce an acceptable amount of horsepower and torque. So before you go laying out your wallet for every upgrade on the market, take the time to ensure that the stock engine is operating at its peak efficiency. Your engine may under-perform for many reasons, both big and small. The following are some basic tips on how to avoid some of the smaller reasons by using preventative maintenance and common sense. If you're picking up a used TJ, it's a great idea to check all this stuff before you buy anything else.

De-Bug the Radiator

Make sure the radiator is free of debris and that nothing is restricting airflow, including bugs and insects. Use compressed air to blow out the radiator to remove any remaining debris. It's also recommended that you flush the cooling system at least once a year and replace the fluids with a good quality coolant. If you have trouble with mineral deposits/buildup, try using distilled water rather than tap water. A faulty or defective radiator cap can also cause problems if it can't hold the necessary pressure.

An 18-psi radiator cap is standard on most Jeep TJ radiators. Try to keep your vehicle's cooling system clean and free of buildup or debris. Use a mix of coolant and water for most efficient operation.

Clean Air to Breathe

Inspect and/or replace the air filter on a regular basis. I've driven my TJ to the office after wheeling, cursing its sudden lack of power, before thinking to examine the air filter. If you've been out in the mud or dirt, you can bet your filter will be coated with dirt and dust. It won't take you long to realize that this happens every time you go wheeling. I installed an air intake that used an open-element air filter on my TJ, so I'm sure to clean the air filter after each trip to the trail. On particularly dusty weekends I'd sometimes remove the filter at the first gas stop and blow it out using the onboard air compressor and an air attachment. It's not as good as a full cleaning but it certainly made a difference on the drive home.

Keep the Spark Alive

Corroded or "snow-balled" terminals, loose or over-loaded terminals, or a low water level in the battery can cause low battery draw and cranking amperage. In extremely hot and cold climates, a faulty battery temperature sensor may even give you problems. Coil and spark plug wires and boots also age over time and can eventually fail. This happened to a Ford truck I had, and I was worried

Even an open-element air cleaner collects dust. After trail runs, do a quick clean by removing it and blowing out the dust and dirt. This makes your engine much happier for the run home, especially after idling dutifully all the day.

The stock paper air filter is a dirt and dust magnet. Look into replacing it with an open-element filter, or at least inspect and/or replace it on a regular basis. A common misconception is that the stock filter will stay cleaner than an open-element filter. This is untrue—the stock airbox just hides the dirty filter.

that the transmission was slipping for months. I eventually discovered the source after the engine completely shut down on the road. A partially severed coil wire had been grounding out, particularly during hill climbs when increased torque would rock the engine, which explained the transmission fade. Examine and replace your spark plug and coil wires on a regular basis to avoid a situation such as this.

Nasty battery terminals will affect the charging system. The stock battery cables offer weak terminals that loosen up after a while and can't handle multiple electrical accessories.

Tighten Up

Loose lips sink ships? Well, loose bolts can sink your TJ. Loose intake and exhaust manifold bolts can decrease performance and lead to parts failure. This goes for nearly every nut and bolt on your vehicle—loose suspension and steering components can decrease fuel economy and be dangerous. It's a good idea to invest in a torque wrench and use it when tightening factory bolts. This isn't entirely necessary if you think you can restrain yourself from over tightening, but for my knucklehead strength and luck (I've snapped the head off my fair share of bolts) I find this to be a much more efficient means than using a simple ratchet, and it's typically a bit faster since the click of the torque wrench tells you when to move to the next bolt. Most nuts and bolts on Wranglers have gobs of thread sealer on them from the factory. This can sometimes make them very, very hard to remove—so hard that it's amazing that they were ever able to loosen up on their own. Take care when removing or tightening the bolts and use the torque wrench to avoid using too much force. This shouldn't be a task you tackle after every time you use your TJ off-road, but it's a good idea to at least inspect and tighten bolts as needed on a somewhat regular basis.

Re-Gear to Go

Swap on some big tires and engine performance will suffer. This is because your engine has to work much harder to turn the bigger tires. Installing lower (numerically higher) axle gears can help improve performance by restoring some of that low-end power. Fuel economy may take a bit of a dive if you go too low, but that's often the price of power. Find a good compromise between new axle gears and lower gears in the transfer case. This allows you to run a higher axle gear ratio and still have plenty of low-range gearing when you put the transfer case into 4-Low.

Fuel Economy

TJs have a flat windshield and most owners slap on big tires, which pushes everything even higher into the air stream. What else can I say about fuel economy? If MPG is your chief concern, I suggest you buy a commuter car and save your Wrangler for weekend fun. Fuel economy ratings for Wrangler TJ engines have varied only slightly over the years, with slight increases coming as the 4.0L engine was refined and the 2.4L four-cylinder introduced. In stock form, you can expect to almost achieve the rated numbers, which range from 17 to 20 mpg for the four-cylinder engines and 14 to 18 mpg with the six-cylinder. Manual transmissions produce the higher numbers in both engines. I can say from experience in driving daily a 4.0L-equipped TJ on 6 inches of lift and 37-inch tires that the lowest number is most realistic. The auto trans likely brings it down a bit as well, but I'm lucky to get 14 mpg on a good day, and I'm usually in the 10 to 12 range.

There are more ways than you might think to increase your TJ's fuel economy. Most of the methods don't cost much money, if any at all, and are pretty easy steps to add to your regular maintenance routine. First off, heed the earlier mentioned engine tips to ensure that your engine is operating at its peak efficiency.

Removing extra weight from your vehicle can give a slight improvement. Do you really need your full-size spare for skipping around town? Consider keeping a skinny spare around that will

Big tires are a good way to lower your fuel mileage, but they're definitely more fun. Try running topless around town or on the trail. It saves a bit of weight for more power and better fuel economy.

work in a pinch if you get a flat close to home. Take out your tools and spare parts for daily driving. Removing your hard top in the summer months also shaves a great deal of weight. Invest in a soft top if you're worried about your hair getting messed up or the occasional rain shower.

Running trails kills gas mileage due to the excessive idling necessary for slow crawling. This is most apparent in the six-cylinder. Installing lower gears in the transfer case helps maintain better fuel economy on the road since you won't have to gear your axles as low (numerically high). Also, don't forget to air up each tire to the proper capacity before hopping on the highway. This helps mileage and assures a longer service life for your tires.

Make certain to use the proper viscosity and grade motor oil for your engine. Some synthetic oils promise increased fuel economy and they aren't always blowing smoke. Don't expect a huge gain from going synthetic, but every bit helps. Don't forget to check your air filter. Fuel economy suffers greatly if the engine can't breathe. There's also car-pooling. Leave your rig at home for a couple days per week and catch a ride with whomever you can.

When all else fails, stop pretending you're launching off the starting line every time a light turns green. You can save some money by laying off the loud pedal and taking time to smell the flowers along the way. Observing the posted speed limit is one easy method of improving your gas mileage — it's as simple as that.

Engine Performance Upgrades

There are many schools of thought on adding traditional performance parts to the TJ. Some say to leave the engine alone and re-gear the axles and transfer case to compensate for larger than stock tires. Others say to hell with that and use

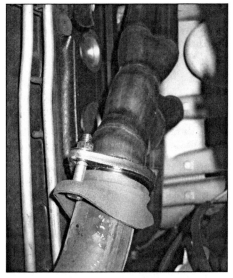

I have a bunch of engine upgrades on my own rig. So far, I've gotten the most benefit from the free-flowing exhaust and header. This shot shows where the tubular exhaust headers mate to the exhaust pipe.

every engine hop up part you can imagine. I tend to fall somewhere in the middle. Fact is, a stock engine can benefit from quite a few of the available performance parts. But even stock TJ engines, particularly the 4.0L, are decent on the

trail when paired with optimum gearing. The decision to modify your engine is strictly up to you.

Air Filters and Intake Systems

Replacement air filters and complete intake systems are available for all TJ engines. Some are basic kits that simply use an open-element air cleaner, while others include new intake pipes, as well as computer-tuning modules and larger throttle bodies. The idea for each is to increase horsepower and torque by decreasing the resistance of intake airflow. Ideally, this translates to increased acceleration and improved overall drivability.

I installed the AEM Brute Force intake kit on my personal TJ, and it produced noticeable improvements. I've also personally tested and been impressed with the Airaid Cold Air Dam intake system and Poweraid throttle body spacer. I especially like the heat shield provided with the Airaid kit, as it's a good fit next to my aftermarket onboard engine-driven air compressor,

The Airaid Cold Air Dam intake system is designed to isolate engine heat away from the air inlet and seek out cool outside air. The kit includes the air dam, a full-length air tube, and an open-element filter. The system is said to offer an additional 14 ft-lbs more torque at low RPM, which is where you'll need it for navigating difficult trails.

ARB and other companies produce air intake snorkels for those who venture into water that flows over the hood line. If you experience multiple water crossings in your off-road adventures, a snorkel may be in order. Personally, I see the tube getting crushed up against a rock or tree and possibly tearing off half of the fender with it, but they do allow for an efficient cool-air supply to the engine.

it's easy to install, and it seems to better isolate the air cleaner from engine heat.

One good thing about intake systems is that you aren't going to lose anything by installing one. Whether or not you feel a big seat-of-the-pants improvement, the engine will still be breathing (hopefully) more efficiently. In the event that performance is decreased, pull the system off and put it back to stock. They can't all be winners.

Throttle Bodies and Spacers

The 2.5L and 4.0L engines come with 60-mm throttle bodies. A larger opening is capable of delivering increased airflow, which theoretically translates into an increase in power and fuel economy. Performance throttle bodies feature up to a 62-mm inlet. Some are based on a stock throttle body that has been bored out to remove the taper in the inlet, but new aftermarket throttle bodies are also available. If you go with too big an inlet, especially with the 2.5L, your increased horsepower may come at the cost of torque. This is probably not a tradeoff you should make for an off-road vehicle.

Throttle body spacers raise the throttle body higher above the manifold to increase the amount of air in the intake manifold plenum and decrease heat transfer from the manifold to the throttle body. Some throttle body spacers have a smooth center bore, while others use straight or angled vanes or circular screw patterns (Poweraid calls this its "Helix-Bore"), which are said to provide more efficient fuel atomization. The manufacturers of each style boast higher dyno numbers, so it's hard to say which is better. I've used the AEM smooth style and the Poweraid Helix-Bore and the latter seemed to provide just a bit more acceleration. Both spacers were also paired with cold air intake kits from the respective companies. Spacers also usually include riser spacers for the throttle linkage, as well as a new gasket and longer bolts. Some spacers are ⅜-inch thick, while others measure up to 1-inch thick.

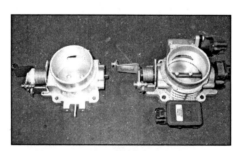

Replacement throttle bodies are available from many aftermarket suppliers and feature a larger center diameter to increase air speed and volume, which will increase horsepower. Here the stock 60-mm throttle body (right) is compared to an Edge machined 62-mm throttle body.

Headers and Exhaust

A less-restrictive exhaust system, like a free-flowing intake system, is a great way to improve performance. The stock system is restrictive because it has to meet emissions and noise standards, and power is limited as a result. Aftermarket exhaust companies push the power envelope, and many are 50-state legal. The faster air goes into your engine, the faster it will need to come out, which is why intake and exhaust upgrades work best when paired together.

Many aftermarket exhaust kits are sold as "after-cat" systems, meaning they utilize the stock catalytic converter and only replace the stock tailpipe and muffler. These systems increase exhaust flow with larger diameter piping and free-flowing mufflers. Many systems also use mandrel-bent exhaust pipes, which keep a consistent diameter through the bends for increased flow. Besides the free-flowing muffler and tailpipe, cat-back systems usually include all the installation hardware necessary for the system to be installed using the factory hangers.

The mufflers included with the aftermarket systems vary in design. The most common styles are straight-through, chambered, glass-wrapped, and more. Some mufflers are louder than others, so if you want power, but not too much rumble, you should listen around before you choose. Many manufacturers even offer sound clips of their exhaust systems so you can hear before you buy. I've used DynoMax, Flowmaster, Banks, and Magnaflow mufflers and have been pleased with the performance gains, but many other brands offer comparable results.

An exhaust system's exterior durability should also be considered, especially for a trail-ready TJ that meets rocks and other harsh obstacles on a regular basis. Exhaust system material is also important. Take a look at your factory system and note the heavy rust. Many aftermarket

Free-flowing aftermarket exhaust systems, like the stainless-steel Monster system from Banks, create a noticeable power gain and a more pronounced exhaust note. You may also get a slight improvement in fuel economy.

This is the DynoMax Blackjack header for the 4.0L. The headers feature high-temp black paint and mandrel-bent primary tubes. (Photo courtesy DynoMax)

exhaust systems are constructed from stainless steel and won't rust after one water crossing or mud puddle. The stock catalytic converter can be as restrictive as the rest of the system. High-flow style units are available from most aftermarket exhaust manufacturers and should be considered for a maximum increase in performance.

Exhaust shops can also create custom piping for those in need. This can be a big help when you combine a lot of aftermarket suspension and drivetrain components. Universal mufflers come in many sizes and shapes, so you can choose whether an oval or skinny unit will free up much-needed space so other vehicle components can operate without obstruction.

A header is a great way for early TJ owners to get rid of the crack-prone factory exhaust manifolds. They're also great for anyone eager to further open up the exhaust system. Power increases can be expected for all of the TJ engines.

GASKET

DynoMax and others offer headers for the 2.5L 4-cylinder. These headers create more power by improving exhaust scavenging and flow. (Photo courtesy DynoMax)

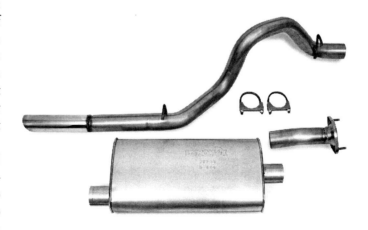

The DynoMax Super Turbo cat-back exhaust system is available for Wrangler and Wrangler Unlimited 4.0L engines. This, and other cat-backs on the market, include a high-flowing muffler and tailpipe. (Photo courtesy DynoMax)

Headers are less restrictive than the stock exhaust manifolds, offering increased flow and efficiency.

There are many header designs available from aftermarket manufacturers, each offering a list of features. They all claim great benefits and power improvements, but there are other features to take into consideration. Material is one element—stronger is typically better, as you don't want any cracks. Look at the welds around the flanges—a more complete weld will prevent leaks. Make sure you get the correct header for your year, engine, and transmission combo to ensure the best fit. I have used the Banks Torque Tube Headers on my '01 TJ for about four years now and have been quite impressed. I have used Edelbrock and JBA headers on other 4x4s with great results.

Ignition and Charging Systems

If your TJ is powered by an early 4.0L or 2.5L engine, you can upgrade the ignition system with a performance distributor, cap and rotor, new spark plug wires, and a performance coil. At this point, these early TJs are old enough that they'd likely benefit from these upgrades whether the parts are "performance" units or not. I guess this means you can think of it more as a tune up than a performance upgrade.

Performance or "hot" ignition coils provide more spark in the combustion chamber. Many are also more vibration and shock resistant than the factory units because they're sealed in epoxy or other material. Crisper throttle response is the main improvement, but you might also notice more high-end power. Aftermarket spark plug wires likely won't offer any noticeable increase in performance, unless your current wires are worn out. If your wires are old and cracked then you should see some positive results. Also, stock terminals in the coil are aluminum and don't conduct as well as copper or brass. Most aftermarket coils and plug wires use copper or brass terminals so you'll be gaining efficiency at the least. Ignition upgrades such as these will cost you less than $200 and are a great way to bring an older 2.5L or 4.0L engine back to life.

Ignition control units are also an option but will run you a bit more money. I've read all about ignition boxes, but I'm not certain they're a great fit on Jeep Wranglers. For one, many aren't watertight, making installation problematic if you plan on encountering water on any of your trail runs. Some companies, such as MSD, offer completely sealed, water- and vibration-proof ignition control boxes, but the price and difficult install tend to keep most Jeep owners away.

Spark Plugs

A buddy of mine recently told me that he changed the spark plugs in his '01 TJ for the first time with nearly 90K on the odometer. The factory-installed plugs were still sparking away, though not very efficiently. The charred remains of the electrodes were coated in soot but had somehow kept firing, but I can't imagine how much more life they had in them.

The moral to this story is to change your spark plugs on a regular basis. Had my buddy pulled the spark plugs after just a thousand miles or more and they were carbon soot-coated then it would have been a sign of a possible engine malfunction. Spark plugs last a few years—up to 30,000 miles in some cases—if all things are kosher internally.

Alternators and Starters

With additional off-road lights, power-hungry winches, and stereo systems, you may find that your TJ could use a bit more charge. A higher-output alternator can be installed to maintain the proper electrical charge and provide additional amperage output for accessories. High-amp alternators are offered in a variety of amperage ratings to suit many needs. Powermaster has units capable of 170 amps, while Mean Green can supply up to a 220-amp unit. This doesn't mean you'll burn up accessories that require less amperage, just that you'll have amperage on reserve for when it's really needed. If a 20-amp load is put on the alternator, a built-in regulator will output just that amount. If you notice your headlights dimming when electrical accessories are overloading the alternator, then you're in need of an upgrade.

Starter upgrades include high-torque or gear reduction units. These are usually smaller and lighter than the stock starter, plus they offer faster starts and easier starts on hill climbs after stalling. Mean Green starters are said to be capable of providing up to 35,000 starts compared to an average of 5,000 starts of the factory starter.

High output alternators such as this Mean Green unit are great additions to a TJ engine burdened with multiple electric accessories like stereo systems and winches.

Dual Batteries

Dual battery setups are just like they sound—two batteries instead of one. Most available dual battery kits for TJs are designed to use Optima deep-cycle batteries, which offer 800 cold cranking amps compared to 500 amps of the stock battery. These batteries are more shock and vibration resistant than regular-style

The Kilby Enterprises dual battery tray is a great fit in the Wrangler and offers secure mounting for two Optima batteries. A dual-battery setup can come in handy when you need some extra juice for powering accessories like a winch.

Cooling Upgrades

I gotta tell you, I haven't had one cooling issue with my Wrangler. The engine has not over-heated, the side tanks have not leaked, and even with very infrequent flushes, the cooling system continues to keep the 4.0L operating in its optimum temperature range (210 degrees F). This is true whether I'm rolling 75 mph down the highway at 3,500 to 4,000 rpm with the A/C blasting, or creeping along a trail at 1,000 to 2,500 rpm with intermittent torque loading and unloading as the rig tackles obstacles. Perhaps my situation is unique, or maybe Jeep just got this right in the first place.

Despite my good fortune, the cooling system does have a few weak links. If you only go with one cooling upgrade, it should be the radiator. The plastic side tanks of the factory radiator have been known to leak and coolant capacity is limited. A variety of manufacturers offer bolt-in aluminum replacement units. They are designed to use the factory fan shroud and hoses so that they offer a perfect fit without obstructing other engine components. Aluminum is also lighter in weight and displaces heat more efficiently than copper and brass. Most feature fully welded seams, so leaking is also no longer an issue.

The 4.0L and 2.5L engines can also benefit from an electric cooling fan, which can provide constant airflow to the radiator, even at low speeds on the trail. Electric fans are also adjustable when equipped with controls to do so. On hot days, you can even leave the fan on after the engine is shut off for increased engine cooling between trail obstacles. Personally, I like the mechanical fans because I've found that they usually do a sufficient job of maintaining the proper operating temperature, but electric fans are great for engine swaps where space is limited and a mechanical fan just won't fit.

Aluminum radiators are available for 2.4L and 4.0L engines as direct-fit units that use the stock fan shroud and hoses. Aluminum radiators increase coolant capacity, are lighter weight, and cool more efficiently than copper and brass radiators. Electric cooling fans can also be used to replace the factory mechanical fan. (Photo courtesy Novak Conversions)

batteries, are completely sealed so they won't spill, and don't require any maintenance.

Mean Green has a stacking tray that fits two Optima batteries in the stock battery location. It's fairly easy to install but you lose the use of two of the side post terminals and it's a bit cramped for when adjustments are necessary. Also, some aftermarket air intake tubes interfere with the upper battery, so make sure your air tube has necessary clearance. The better setup is the Kilby Enterprises dual tray that fits two Optima batteries side-by-side in the factory battery location by relocating the air conditioning condenser. These kits are trick and look factory, but the installation is a bit more labor intensive and requires a trip to an A/C shop for evacuation and recharge of the system (if your Wrangler is equipped with A/C).

FlowKooler offers high-flow water pumps that double water flow through the engine at low RPM and idle, but provide normal flow as RPM increases. The FlowKooler pump also increases water pressure to more efficiently cool the engine, and it uses less horsepower to turn than the stock pump, which helps lower the overall engine temperature. Installing a high-flow thermostat with a higher temperature rating is another method of increasing coolant flow and providing better temperature control. Thermostats are offered in a 160- to 195-degree temperature range and can be used to increase power and aid fuel economy. Be careful of lowering the temperature too much, however, since the engine is intended to operate most efficiently in a specified temperature range. High-flow thermostat housings are also available.

Superchargers

While I like the idea of superchargers, I just don't like the idea of them on Jeeps. It just seems like a muscle car project gone awry. Nonetheless, superchargers are available for all of the Jeep TJ engines. There's no doubt that they're capable of creating some awesome power, to which stock-engine Wranglers are not accustomed. If you're itching for V-8 power without the expense of a swap, one of these units may be a good bet. Most supercharger manufacturers assure that in addition to extra power, increased fuel economy comes with the package.

Quite a few companies offer superchargers for Jeep Wranglers; many are of similar design using an Autorotor twin-screw compressor and an intercooler. The Kenne Bell twin-screw supercharger produces up to 72 percent more horsepower and torque than stock with no boost lag for instant power. In addition to the compressor and intercooler, the Kenne Bell kit includes a 70-mm throttle body, 42-lb/hr fuel injectors, and

The Avenger supercharger is available for 2.5L, 2.4L, and 4.0L engines. They use Autorotor compressors, intercoolers, and install on top of the stock manifold. Superchargers give you great low-end power for crawling and high-end power to charge through sand and mud.

a reprogrammed computer with the proper fuel and spark curves.

Engine Swaps

When all else fails to bring you to your desired power level, an engine swap may be in order. An engine swap is no easy affair for the backyard mechanic or those with little patience, but if you have the time and/or money, they aren't impossible. A V-8 swap will definitely give you more power than all the available bolt-on parts for the 4.0L.

One of the first things to consider is engine dimension. So yes, size does matter. Will the engine fit under the TJ hood? What about firewall clearance? How about the steering shaft, the frame rails, the front axle, and the front driveshaft? These are all important issues to explore.

Wiring

These days most engine swap candidates are computer-controlled, which means you'll need a new computer to go with your new engine. A 4.0L PCM won't operate a GM or Hemi engine and should go with your 4.0L engine assembly if/when you sell it. On that topic, it's a good idea to get the PCM that originally came with the engine you'll be swapping into your TJ. It's not the end of the world if you don't get it, but it can end up saving you some money in the long run and usually makes engine setup a much easier process. Painless Performance and Turbo City are good sources for engine-swap wiring harnesses, as well as PCMs.

Cooling

A V-8 engine requires more cooling than any of the factory Wrangler

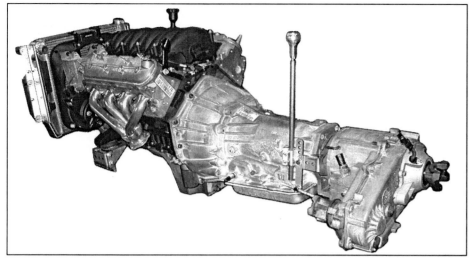

A GM Vortec V-8 is shown with a transmission and NP231J transfer case. An aluminum radiator is also a good choice when installing a V-8 engine. A two-row unit should provide sufficient cooling. (Photo courtesy Novak Conversions)

Estimated Cost of a V-8 Engine Swap

Engine: $1,000 to $4,000
Transmission: $400 to $1,400
Radiator: $325 to $700
Engine mounts: $90 to $120
Engine-to-transmission adapter: $350
Trans-to-T-case adapter: $500
Transmission oil cooler: $100
Fan and shroud: $200
Computer reprogramming: $300
Clutch: $225
Clutch release components: $175
Hardware: $100
Labor and advanced assistance: $200 to $2,000
Exhaust: $300 to $600

Low total: $4,265
High total: $11,270

*Cost estimate courtesy of Novak Conversions and includes a transmission swap. Prices are listed for information purposes only.

engines. For this reason a larger capacity and stronger radiator than the stock copper/brass/plastic unit is necessary.

Exhaust

Ever look at the factory exhaust pipe routing under your TJ? There are some pretty tricky bends to get around the oil pan and suspension components. Now imagine what type of bends must be made to clear a larger engine? A new exhaust system is necessary when completing an engine swap.

Power Steering

The Jeep power steering system is sufficient for use with most GM engines, though the appropriate GM power steering pump is required. You'll also need new high-pressure power steering lines to complete the system.

Transmission

Not all TJ transmissions have the strength to handle the torque of a V-8 engine. The AX-5 is not up to the task. The AX-15, NV3550, and others are better prepared for the increased torque and can be considered. For more transmission swap candidates check out Chapter

4. You'll also need an adapter and bellhousing if you intend to retain the stock transmission.

Emissions

Last, but hardly least, before beginning a conversion, check with your state emissions laws to make sure the swap you're considering won't keep you from passing a smog test and registering your rig.

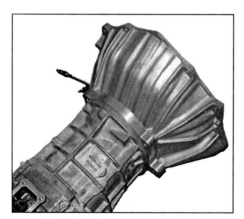

You'll need an adapter and bellhousing if you plan to retain the stock transmission with a V-8 swap. The NV3550 is a stock transmission that is worth keeping. (Photo courtesy Novak Conversions)

Cost

I've yet to come across any free lunches when it comes to building Jeeps. An engine swap will cost you, but not just in the wallet; it also might take a bit of your sanity. This occurs most frequently when proper planning measures aren't taken to ensure a smooth conversion. As I've pointed out above, it takes more than just an engine to complete a swap, and that's where most folks start pulling their hair (and their wallets) out.

Engine swaps also cost time—the "your-wife-already-gave-you-a-list-of-chores-on-a-Saturday" sort of time, as well as the more fun kind of time that is usually spent wheeling in your TJ. Don't expect to tackle such a job in a day or two, or even a week for that matter. A professional shop usually takes at least that long or longer to ensure that all of the kinks are worked out.

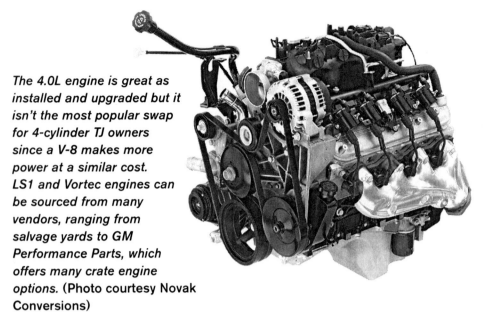

The 4.0L engine is great as installed and upgraded but it isn't the most popular swap for 4-cylinder TJ owners since a V-8 makes more power at a similar cost. LS1 and Vortec engines can be sourced from many vendors, ranging from salvage yards to GM Performance Parts, which offers many crate engine options. (Photo courtesy Novak Conversions)

The Chevy Corvette LS1 V-8 is a great fit under the hood of this TJ. It makes awesome power and is actually quite fuel efficient. (Photo courtesy Novak Conversions)

Conversion Knowledge

Some good news on the subject of engine swaps is that you don't have to go it alone. There are a number of incredible sources out there to help with either the right parts for the job or valuable advice. Novak Conversions offers its Knowledge Base tutorials and engine swapping guides. They are valuable tools that you should not go without. Advance Adapters also produces extremely helpful guides. Both companies also manufacture and sell pretty much everything you need to correctly complete an engine swap.

Engine Swap Candidates

Jeep 4.0L: For TJ owners unsatisfied with their 2.5L motor, a 4.0L engine swap might offer just enough additional power to get you through the trail. While the 4.0L is a good engine for TJs, putting one where it didn't formerly reside can be problematic. If you're going to the trouble you might as well consider a V-8. Price is comparable and the work is about the same. To do it right you need the engine, computer, wiring harness, and all of the sensors and smog equipment from the same donor vehicle. You don't want to pick all of this stuff up piecemeal because you run the risk of getting miss-matched years and it's also quite a bit more expensive.

Chevy V-8: Chevy LS1 and Vortec engines are awesome engines and work very well in TJs. One reason for this is that they're very adaptable. The LS1 uses a cast aluminum block and heads, which offer a much lighter weight than other mills—a good feature for weight-conscious trail crawlers. It also produces impressive horsepower and torque numbers, with the Corvette version offering 345 horsepower and 350 ft-lbs of torque. Fuel economy isn't lost on these powerful engines either, and 22 to 25 mpg isn't unheard of.

The Vortec series engines are based on the LS1 architecture but use a cast-iron block. These engines, in 4.8L, 5.3L, and 6.0L displacements, post similar power and fuel economy numbers and offer the same ease-of-conversion attributes as the LS1. Both engines are extremely adaptable and have great aftermarket parts support. People have swapped Chevy V-8s into almost every vehicle out there, and many have detailed their experiences in books, magazines, web-zines, web forums, and even on bathroom walls. In fact, a handful of books on building Chevy V-8s are available from CarTech.

Hemi: Hemi engines are big, powerful mills, and there are a few kits available to plant one in a TJ. American Expedition Vehicles (AEV) introduced one of the first kits and it has proven to be a plug-and-play setup. It's pretty high priced though, mainly because the engine itself is fairly costly. AEV went to great lengths and worked closely with Jeep to make this setup function properly and it appears to work well in the vehicles that I've seen. Some of the other available Hemi swap kits, though, have had some problems. Hemis make good swap candidates, but don't expect the ease of installation that comes with the Chevy engines.

The Hemi engine found in Dodge Ram trucks produces 345 hp and 375 ft-lbs of torque. This engine is also just 57 lbs heavier than the 4.0L, and is significantly lighter than other Mopar swap candidates such as the 5.2L and 5.9L V-8s. From the picture, you can see that this engine takes up some space.

TJ TRANSMISSIONS

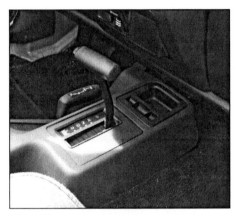

TJs with automatic transmissions feature a floor-mounted shifter. The shifter for the NP231J transfer case is also shown. There were also a variety of manual transmissions available in the TJ.

Jeep used eight different transmissions during TJ production, with each replacement offering some degree of improved performance. There were five manual transmissions employed from 1997 to 2006. The automatic transmission selection was much more stable, with the first two of the three available transmissions lasting until 2002. A 4-speed unit was introduced in 2003 and remained in use for the duration of TJ production. The majority of the TJs produced are factory-fit with a manual transmission.

Transmission selection was updated rather frequently. The NV3550 introduced in 2000 has become a desirable swap candidate for earlier TJs. 2003 not only saw the introduction of the Rubicon Wrangler, but it also brought about a new transmission offering with the 42RLE 4-speed overdrive automatic replacing the 30RH and 32RH autos. A final change to the transmission lineup came in 2005 with the release of the 6-speed NSG370 manual transmission. None of the Wrangler transmissions are so problematic that you should avoid them, but the later, beefier trannys are definitely more durable for heavy-duty use.

Manual Transmissions

Aisin-Warner AX-5

The Japanese-made Aisin-Warner AX-5 5-speed transmission was standard equipment in TJs equipped with 2.5L I-4 engines up to 2002. It was also used in Jeep Wrangler YJs and was first introduced in the 1984 Cherokee XJ. It looks very similar to the AX-15, though the bellhousing pattern and spline counts differ, so the two are not interchangeable. The AX-5 is a light-duty, overdrive (fifth gear) transmission that features a cast-aluminum split-case design halved by an iron mid-plate. It uses a special adapter to attach to the transfer case and has an integral shift mechanism mounted in the shift tower portion of the adapter housing. The AX-5 uses helically cut, fully synchronized gears and offers a 21-spline output shaft and a 14-spline input shaft that extends outward 7½ inches. It's a decent transmission for the 2.5L, but you may have problems if you add a lot of extra power or subject it to heavy-duty abuse.

The AX-5 can be identified by a series of numbers stamped at the bottom surface of the transmission case, near the fill plug, which is located on the passenger-side of the adapter housing. The

Aisin-Warner AX-5
First gear: 3.93:1
Second gear: 2.33:1
Third gear: 1.45:1
Fourth gear: 1.00:1
Fifth gear: 0.85:1
Reverse: 4.74:1
Approximate fluid capacity: 3.5 quarts (3.3 liters)
Recommended lubricant: Mopar 75W-90 API Grade GL-5

Mated to 4-cylinder engines until 2002, the AX-5 5-speed transmission is of adequate strength for mild off-road use, but won't sustain the abuse that the other available TJ transmissions will endure. (Photo courtesy Novak Conversions)

first number indicates the year of manufacture and the second and third numbers indicate the month of manufacture. The final series of numbers is the unit's serial number.

Aisin-Warner AX-15

The Aisin-Warner AX-15 is a medium-duty, 5-speed manual transmission that came in '97–'99 4.0L I-6 Wranglers. It was initially introduced in the '88 Wrangler YJ, Cherokee, and Comanche. It uses a split cast-aluminum case with an aluminum midplate. The AX-15 is fully synchronized in all five gears, features helically cut gears throughout, a 1⅛-inch, 10-spline input shaft that sticks out 7½ inches, and a long, 23-spline output shaft. This unit also uses an internal hydraulic throwout/release bearing assembly and a reverse lockout mechanism that requires the shifter to pass through neutral before it can be shifted into reverse. The AX-15 can be identified in the same manner as the AX-5 using the numbers stamped on the lower portion of the case. The fill plug is situated on the driver's side of the transmission case and the drain plug and reverse light switch are on the passenger side.

> ### Aisin-Warner AX-15
>
> First gear: 3.83:1
> Second gear: 2.33:1
> Third gear: 1.44:1
> Fourth gear: 1.00:1
> Fifth gear: 0.79:1
> Reverse: 4.22:1
>
> Approximate fluid capacity: 3.27 quarts (3.10 liters)
> Recommended lubricant: Mopar 75W-90, API Grade GL-5

The AX-15 was another holdover from the previous model Wrangler and came mated to the TJ 4.0L from '97–'99. It's a fairly stout unit and even withstands V-8 power if an engine swap is on your agenda. (Photo courtesy Novak Conversions)

NV1500

The NV1500 had the shortest run in the TJ, and was employed for just two model years ('03–'04). It replaced the long standing AX-5 as the four-cylinder 5-speed, coinciding with the introduction of the 2.4L Power Tech DOHC I-4. The NV1500 is a constant mesh, fully synchronized manual transmission with a two-piece aluminum gear housing and a detachable clutch housing. Like the NV3550, it also uses a single-shaft shift mechanism mounted outside the case to activate three shift forks for gear shifting. This transmission is easily identified by the year of vehicle and the engine installed, but it can also be identified by

---

a pair of barcode tags. The tags are located below the shift tower; the right side tag indicates the part number and the left side tag offers build sequence and manufacture date information. The fluid fill plug is located on the side of the case and the drain plug is on the bottom. The NV1500 isn't very sought after, considering it was replaced by a 6-speed, and it's only up to handling the torque load of the 4-cylinder engine.

> ### NV1500
>
> First gear: 3.85:1
> Second gear: 2.25:1
> Third gear: 1.48:1 or 1.46:1
> Fourth gear: 1.00:1
> Fifth gear: 0.80:1 or 0.83:1
> Reverse: 3.52:1
>
> Approximate fluid capacity: 4.8 pints (2.3 liters)
> Recommended lubricant: Mopar Manual Transmission Lubricant

NV3550

Jeep began using this medium-duty 5-speed transmission in the 4.0L-equipped 2000 TJ. It uses the same oblong bolt pattern as the AX-15, and is secured with nine metric bolts. With its two-piece cast-aluminum case, the

The NV3550 5-speed, used in 4.0L TJs from 2000 to 2004, is an excellent transmission that is capable of handling off-road abuse. It's also a good replacement for the earlier AX-15.

NV3550 is conservatively rated for 300 ft-lbs of torque and weighs in at just less than 100 lbs. It also features a removable clutch housing and uses a 1⅛-inch, 10-spline input shaft, a flush-mount, 23-spline output shaft that rides on roller and ball bearings, and has five fully synchronized, constant mesh gears. You can identify this transmission by the part number and identification number tags attached to the top of the transmission forward from the shift tower, or the tag attached to the front of the rear housing. The fluid fill plug is located in the front case half and the drain plug at the bottom. The NV3550 is one of the stouter manual transmissions and is a good swap candidate for TJs equipped with a failing AX-15 5-speed.

NV3550

First gear: 4.01:1
Second gear: 2.32:1
Third gear: 1.40:1
Fourth gear: 1.00:1
Fifth gear: 0.78:1
Reverse: 3.55:1

Approximate fluid capacity: 4.8 pints
(2.28 liters)
Recommended lubricant: Mopar
Manual Transmission Lubricant

NSG370

Introduced in 2005, the NSG370 6-speed overdrive transmission replaced the NV3550 and NV1550 to become the only manual transmission offered for the TJ. This was the first time the 4.0L I-6 and 2.4L I-4 engines came with the same transmission, which reduced production costs. The NSG370 features a two-piece aluminum case and uses a hydraulically actuated dual-mass flywheel clutch system with a clutch housing integrated into the transmission case. A single-rail shift system with a top-mounted shifter is employed for optimized shift quality. All gears are synchronized, with triple-cone synchronization in first and second gears, double-cone synchronization in third and fourth, and single-cone synchronization in fifth and sixth. The NSG370 was a more durable transmission for all TJs, offering improved quietness, optimal shift quality, and a wider gear range than had ever been offered (check out that 4.46:1 first).

NSG370

First gear: 4.46:1
Second gear: 2.61:1
Third gear: 1.72:1
Fourth gear: 1.25:1
Fifth gear: 1.00:1
Sixth gear: 0.84:1
Reverse: 4.06:1

Approximate fluid capacity: 1.5 liters
(3.17 pints)
Recommended lubricant: Mopar
Manual Transmission Lubricant
MS-9224

The latest TJ manual transmission selection is the 6-speed NSG370. With a first gear ratio of 4.46:1 it's the lowest-geared TJ tranny. It also offers a 0.84:1 overdrive. (Photo courtesy DaimlerChrysler)

Clutch Components

All TJ standard shift transmissions use a single disc clutch with hydraulic linkage to operate the clutch release bearing and fork. The clutch master cylinder, which is mounted to the firewall, uses an integral fluid reservoir with a line running to the slave cylinder. The slave cylinder is mounted to the clutch housing and pushes the clutch release fork for clutch disengagement when the clutch pedal is depressed. Early model Jeeps didn't benefit from this technology and instead used mechanical linkage, which becomes increasingly problematic when the vehicle is lifted.

Automatic Transmissions

30RH/32RH

The 30RH and 32RH transmissions were the only automatic transmissions available until 2002. They came mated to the 2.5L and the 4.0L, respectively. These units are also referred to as the TorqueFlite 999 or the TF904. Both of these 3-speeds use planetary gear trains, a 23-spline flush output shaft, and a round bolt pattern. At 16 inches long, these autos are relatively short as far as TJ trannys go. Identification numbers are stamped on the left (driver) side of the case just above the oil pan gasket surface.

The differences between the 30RH and the 32RH lie in the rear band, which holds the planetary gear carrier stationary during operation. The 30RH uses a single-wrap rear band, while the 32RH uses a double-wrap, which provides greater holding power. Both transmissions also use a torque converter clutch that engages in third gear via a clutch solenoid on the valve body, provided that the vehicle is cruising on a level surface. The engagement occurs upon sensor input from the PCM and is determined by coolant temperature, vehicle speed, and throttle position. The converter disengages, or unlocks, when the vehicle begins to travel uphill or if

---

the accelerator is applied. This is designed to improve fuel economy and reduce transmission fluid temperatures. These transmissions are also cooled by an integral fluid cooler mounted inside the radiator.

Though you won't hear too many people boasting about their 30RH or 32RH 3-speeds, these transmissions really aren't bad units and typically outlast other stock equipment. In fact, the majority of my TJ wheeling experiences have occurred using the stock 32RH, and I can honestly say that it has functioned well from the start. It has been right at home combined with 4:1 transfer cases, 35- to 37-inch tires, 4.56:1 gears, and Dana 60 axles.

30RH/32RH

First gear: 2.74:1
Second gear: 1.54:1
Third gear: 1.00:1

Approximate fluid capacity: 3.8 liters
(4 quarts)
Recommended lubricant: ATF+4

The 30RH was the automatic transmission that came in 2.5L I-4-equipped Wranglers and is essentially the same transmission as the 32RH. The 30RH uses a smaller rear band, but both use a cast-in bellhousing.

42RLE

The 4-speed 42RLE came along in 2003 and became the TJ automatic transmission for both the four- and six-cylinder engines. This electronically controlled transmission uses a fully adaptive control system that carries out its functions, including shift points, based on continuous sensor feedback and automatically adapts to changes in engine performance and other factors.

Inside, hydraulically applied clutches shift a planetary gear train.

The 42RLE can be identified by its barcode label attached to the upper left side of the bellhousing, or by locating the number stamped into the left rear flange of the case. The barcode label can be used to decipher unit part number, date of manufacture, manufacturing origin, build sequence number, and just about anything else you want to know about it. The stamped numbers include part number, build code, and sequence number.

The 42RLE uses a 23-spline output shaft and has a circular bolt pattern attaching it to the NP231J transfer case. It's reputedly much stronger than the earlier 3-speeds and the overdrive doesn't hurt, either. The 42RLE also features a lock-up torque converter. Input and output speed sensors and the transmission range sensor are all on the driver's side of the transmission case. The input sensor sits forward with the range sensor just aft of and below it, and the output sensor is further rearward.

42RLE

First gear: 2.84:1
Second gear: 1.57:1
Third gear: 1.00:1
Fourth gear: 0.69:1
Reverse: 2.21:1

Approximate fluid capacity: 3.8 liters
(4 quarts)
Recommended lubricant: ATF+4

Torque Converter

Wrangler automatic transmissions use a hydraulic torque-converter clutch assembly that is engaged by the clutch solenoid on the transmission valve body. It helps reduce fluid temperatures and increases fuel economy. The converter is controlled by the PCM and engages in

The 32RH 3-speed auto was offered until 2002. It's a decent transmission for a factory offering and has put up with plenty of abuse in my 2001 TJ.

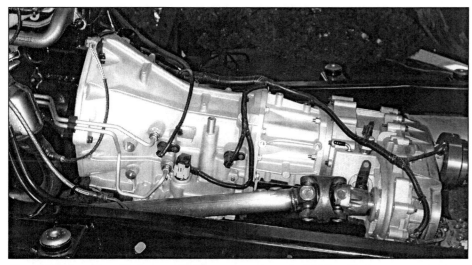

The 42RLE automatic transmission came along in 2003, offering an overdrive gear and increased strength over the 32RH.

third gear for the 30RH/32RH transmissions and in fourth gear (sometimes third) for the 42RLE. Engagement is determined by sensors that monitor coolant temperature, vehicle speed, and throttle position. The clutch is hydraulically activated and then released after the fluid pressure has dropped.

Transmission Troubleshooting

Manual transmissions tend to be somewhat noisy in general and the TJ offerings are no exception. Earlier models are usually a bit noisier, while later transmissions are more refined. Older models are simply older, too, and wear-and-tear and the level of maintenance will affect how well your transmission performs.

At any time your automatic transmission acts up with sloppy or hard shifts or other erratic behavior, your first plan of attack should be to check the fluid level and ensure that the proper fluid is being used. Low or incorrect fluid can cause a myriad of performance issues and ultimately lead to parts failure. Old or contaminated fluid traditionally has the same negative impact on internal components, so take the time to inspect your transmission fluid level on a regular

basis and change it as needed. This is especially true after wheeling, as off-road use is much harder on a unit than normal highway use. Excessive noise is typically your first indication that the fluid level is low.

Transmission Upgrades

When most TJ owners are faced with the decision to upgrade or replace the stock transmission, most do opt to replace. Not that these transmissions are useless, it's just that upgrade parts are simply not available. Since overall

The Skyjacker deep transmission pan is shown installed on a 32RH automatic trans. The deep pan holds extra fluid to alleviate the neutral drop that occurs while ascending steep inclines.

strength and gear selection are usually the biggest concerns, often the best plan of attack is to install a heavier-duty, lower-geared unit that's better suited to off-road demands.

One upgrade for the 30RH and 32RH transmissions is a deep fluid pan. Deep pans increase fluid capacity, which keeps the tranny running cooler and can also solve the neutral drop that sometimes occurs on steep inclines as the fluid sloshes to the rear of the pan. Currie Enterprises, Tri County Gear, and Skyjacker all offer deep pans. The Currie pan is constructed from heavy gauge steel, has a drain plug, and includes a new filter and gasket. The deep tranny pan may get in the way of some aftermarket engine/transmission skid plates, but the improvement in overall transmission performance is worth looking into.

Having a performance rebuild completed is one option for getting the most out of your automatic transmission. Many transmission shops can carry out such a task, or new or rebuilt performance-type units are often available from a variety of sources. High-Impact Transmission & Gear offers its 30RH and 32RH Bad Boy line of transmissions that feature upgraded heavy-duty torque converters, heavy-duty lock-up clutches,

Rubicon Express also offers a deep transmission pan for the 32RH. It comes with the filter and associated hardware. If you're flushing your tranny anyway, an upgrade like this is a great idea.

oversize springs, upgraded pressure regulators and reverse boost valves, and internal modifications for improved oiling and shifting. Transmission rebuild kits are another option for those simply seeking maximum potential from their factory gearboxes. Rebuild kits usually include a gasket and seal kit, all necessary friction clutch plates, all steel clutch plates, a flex band (as required), a filter, and bushings.

Manual transmission users can choose an upgraded clutch with greater holding capacity over stock. Centerforce offers two performance clutch kits for 4.0L TJs and one for those with the 2.5L I-4. The kits range from base model setups to dual-friction clutch disc sets that offer up to 90 percent greater holding capacity. These clutches should hold up better to a lot of feathering up and over obstacles.

Shifter upgrades are also available. Manual-transmission Wranglers can be outfitted with a performance shifter with shorter shift throws for quicker shifts. Kits usually include a new shifter base and stop collar in addition to a new shift rod and knob. Performance shifters are also available for automatic transmissions. Universal ratchet-type shifters are offered from B&M and Hurst.

Transmission Swap Options

There are a wide variety of transmission swap options for TJs. Some transmissions bolt directly to the stock bellhousing and transfer case, while others require a bellhousing or transfer case adapter. A handful of companies manufacture these adapters, including Advance Adapters and Novak Conversions. Transfer case adapters vary in length, as they not only mate the different bolt patterns of the transmission and transfer case, but also ensure proper spline engagement by accommodating the different transmission output shaft lengths. Bellhousing adapters are typi-

You can always swap in a different tranny if you don't care for the factory-installed transmissions. GM's TH350 3-speed automatic is one solid candidate for the 4.0L or GM V-8 swap. It's shown here mounted to a GM V-8 and an NP231J transfer case. **(Photo courtesy Novak Conversions)**

cally shorter—some of those used to mate the 4.0L to a GM Hydra-Matic measure just ½-inch thick.

While this certainly does not represent a list of all of the transmissions that will function in TJs, it does include some of the most common and popular swap candidates. If you're considering a transmission swap in your TJ, I highly recommend contacting Novak Conversions or Advance Adapters for additional information. Both companies can offer very valuable technical assistance as well as the parts needed to complete your swap.

To determine what transmission is best for your vehicle's setup and use, you need to decide your gearing requirements and then perform some gearing calculations. The necessary calculations include establishing the vehicle's crawl ratio and cruising RPM to find if the intended transmission will perform as expected in on- and off-road situations. A variety of online calculators are available to aid in this determination. Some of the best can be found at www.4lo.com. I've also included the formulas with some examples in Chapter 5. Additionally, some transmissions do not offer an overdrive gear, so take this into consideration if you rely on your TJ for a considerable

amount of highway use. Overdrive can be sidestepped through use of the proper axle gears, which then need to be compensated for with lower gearing in the transfer case. You can see how complicated this gets.

Manual or Auto

This is one of those long-running campfire debates that will never be laid to rest. While both offer advantages, I still believe it comes down to personal preference. There's no doubting that a manual transmission provides a somewhat greater degree of control over the vehicle, as the clutch can often be used to your advantage in many off-road situations. It's also much better for steep downhills, since the auto won't lock up to help slow you down. Automatic transmissions, however, have become increasingly popular in recent years and are being used successfully in many 4x4 applications. I've been running trails with an auto-equipped TJ for the last five years (my first 4x4 with an auto trans) and have found it to be half the work I used to put in to driving my manual-equipped CJ-5. Also, my left leg doesn't hurt at the end of the day. But like I said, transmission selection is pretty much up to you and how you use your TJ.

Manual Transmissions
NV3550: The NV3550 5-speed (detailed earlier in the chapter) is a great option. Though still a medium-duty unit, it is reputedly stronger than the previous 5-speeds. It's lightweight and is a direct fit behind any Jeep Wrangler 4.0L engine. The input splines and shaft length on the NP231 transfer case varies depending on what engine and transmission were factory installed, but it otherwise bolts to the NV3550 directly as well. This transmission is also capable of handling V-8 power and torque if you're planning on an engine swap.
NV4500: Stepping it up a big notch, the NV4500 is an awesome transmission

that can be used behind the 4.0L or for a V-8 conversion. Because of its size and weight (195 lbs, 18.9 inches long), it's probably best suited to V-8 swaps, but Advance Adapters offers kits to mate it to the 4.0L and the NP231. Since it was factory installed in both GM and Dodge trucks, the NV4500 also bolts up to powerplants from these vehicles. There are differences between the GM and Dodge versions, primarily in input shaft length, and Advance Adapters bases its available adapters and swap kits around the Dodge units. The NV4500 can also be fairly expensive compared to other transmissions, so, while it stands up to the abuse of off-road use, there are better options. It does have one advantage over transmissions with "granny" low first gears in that it offers an overdrive range for better highway performance.

NV4500	
First Gear: 5.61:1	
Second Gear: 6.04:1	
Third Gear: 1.67:1	
Fourth Gear: 1.0:1	
Fifth Gear: 0.73:1	
Reverse: 5.61:1	

T-18: The T-18 is a heavy-duty, 4-speed transmission used in ½- through 1-ton trucks. These transmissions were manufactured by Borgwarner for Ford, Jeep, and International Harvester (IH) vehicles, so many versions exist. In fact, there were 12 different versions in Jeep vehicles over the years. The Ford units generally make the best swap candidates as they are more readily available, are much more consistent in design, and have cheaper available parts. The T-18 offers a low granny first gear (6.32:1), making this an excellent choice for low-speed trail crawlers. It also features a power take-off (PTO) on the passenger side of the case that can be used to operate a winch. The T-18 is fully synchronized in second through fourth gears and uses helically cut gears, also second

through fourth. This unit is adaptable to the 4.0L engine using a custom pilot bushing and a new crankshaft positioning sensor. It's also a good fit behind GM V-8s using an adapter kit, but will bolt directly to Ford small-block V-8s. This trans also bolts to the NP231 using an adapter, a new crankshaft pilot bushing, and a conversion mainshaft.

T-18	
First Gear: 6.32:1	
Second Gear: 3.09:1	
Third Gear: 1.69:1	
Fourth Gear: 1.0:1	
Reverse: 7.44:1	

SM420: Offered in ½-, ¾-, and 1-ton GM trucks from 1947–'67, the GM Muncie SM420 4-speed manual transmission uses a cast-iron case and cover and weighs 135 lbs. Though it's been off the assembly line for a few decades, it's still a widely used standard-shift trans for Jeep conversions. SM stands for Synchro-Mesh, and the unit is indeed fully synchronized in second through fourth gears. The SM420 uses helically cut gears except for first and reverse, which are spur gears. It also features a PTO on the driver's side of the case. The transmission bolts directly to GM V-8s and also mates to a 4.0L I-6 engine using an adapter, a new mainshaft, and a crankshaft positioning sensor. Some machining may be required to the Jeep bellhousing for proper fitment. The SM420 is just 10.4 inches long, making it one of the shortest swappable transmissions. The granny-low 7.05:1 is also a huge asset.

SM420	
First Gear: 7.05:1	
Second Gear: 3.6:1	
Third Gear: 1.7:1	
Fourth Gear: 1:1	

SM465: The SM465 is a well-built 4-speed manual transmission that's usually easy to find and fairly easy to maintain. It

The SM420 is another good manual transmission that fits well in TJs. The 4-speed unit offers a granny low first gear of 7.05:1 and it is just 10.4 inches in length. Novak Conversions offers its turnkey SM420 as a bolt-in transmission for Jeep Wranglers. The trans can be mated to the 4.0L I-6 or a GM V-8. (Photo courtesy Novak Conversions)

The GM Muncie SM465 is a granny-low 4-speed used in GM trucks. It fits behind the 4.0L using adapted bellhousing or any GM V-8. (Photo courtesy Novak Conversions)

has a granny low first gear with a ratio of 6.55:1 and uses a cast-iron case and cover. 2WD and 4WD versions were used in ½- through 1-ton GM trucks from 1968 to 1991, and both work well for swapping. At 12 inches long, it's also very short, which makes it a great fit in short wheelbase Jeeps like the Wrangler. The SM465 is compatible with GM V-8 engines, as well as the 4.0L I-6 with an adapted bellhousing, a new release arm, a release bearing, clutch disc, and a crankshaft positioning sensor.

SM465

First gear: 6.55:1
Second gear: 3.58:1
Third gear: 1.7:1
Fourth gear: 1.0:1

GM/Hydra-Matic Transmissions

TH350: GM Hydra-Matic transmissions such as the 3-speed TH350 can be adapted to the 4.0L engine and also work well behind Chevy V-8s. It requires a ½-inch thick adapter plate and modified flexplate to bolt up to a 4.0L engine and allows use of a stock starter. It uses a one-piece cast aluminum alloy case and an integral bellhousing. The TH350 is the shortest auto that can be put in a Jeep and it's also one of the strongest. It's found in nearly all rear-wheel-drive GM cars and trucks through 1981, mated to V-6 and V-8 engines. 2WD and 4WD versions of this trans are available and both work well in Jeeps. They can be rebuilt affordably and many aftermarket upgrades are available. The TH350 weighs 120 lbs and is 21.75 inches long. Lock-up versions of this trans can also be used. In order to mate to the NP231, one requires use of an adapter, a new transmission output shaft, and hardware for installation.

TH350

First gear: 2.52.1
Second gear: 1.52.1
Third gear: 1:1
Reverse: 1.93:1

TH700R-4 & 4L60/4L60-E: Similar to the TH350, the 4-speed TH700R-4 also uses a cast aluminum alloy case and many of the same internal components. It is 23¾ inches long and weighs 155 lbs. This transmission mates to the 4.0L

engine in a similar manner to the TH350, and also accepts the NP231 transfer case. It features a lock-up torque converter that allows no slip between gears. Aftermarket manufacturers also offer torque converter controls that allow the converter to be turned on or off at any time so that the transmission can be tailored to the terrain. The lockup aids fuel economy, creates less heat at cruising speed, and also permits compression braking.

The TH700R-4 was redesignated as the 4L60 and later the 4L60-E in 1993 as it was converted to electronic shift. While mechanically similar to the TH700R-4, the 4L60-E is controlled by electronic actuators and sensors. For this reason 4L60 and 4L60-E are best and most simply used mated to the engine with which they were originally installed, but are excellent

The 4L60-E is a great auto trans to mate with a GM LS1 or Vortec V-8. You will probably need its factory computer for the swap. (Photo courtesy Novak Conversions)

options for those completing a GM V-8 conversion. The TH700R-4 makes for an easier and cheaper swap than the 4L60 if the 4.0L engine is retained.

TH700R-4 & 4L60/4L60-E

First gear: 3.06:1
Second gear: 1.63:1
Third gear: 1.0:1
Fourth gear: 0.70:1
Reverse: 2.90:1

TH400: The TH400 is a 3-speed transmission that came in Jeeps from 1965–'79. It was mated to AMC V-8s and even the 258 I-6, which is the predecessor to the 4.0L. It's a durable transmission capable of withstanding high-torque 4x4 use and is rated to handle 450 ft-lbs. It mates to the 4.0L and NP231 transfer case using available adapters. The TH400 is easily serviceable and upgrade parts are widely available, making it an excellent transmission option for TJ owners.

TH400

First gear: 2.48:1
Second gear: 1.48:1
Third gear: 1:1

The GM TH400 3-speed automatic transmission is an ultra-strong replacement for the factory 32RH. Of course, it also works well with GM V-8 swaps. (Photo courtesy Novak Conversions)

Other Swap Parts

As you've likely gathered, you'll need a whole mess of parts to complete a transmission swap. Not as many as

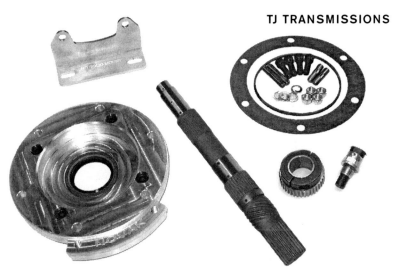

Adapters are required to mate most transmissions to the NP231 transfer case. This is an NP231 to TH700R-4 adapter kit from Novak Conversions. It includes an adapter, a 23-spline transmission output shaft, a stainless-steel base mount, and all the associated hardware. (Photo courtesy Novak Conversions)

A stock clutch pedal can be added to factory pedal arrangement if you want to convert from an automatic to a manual transmission.

you'll need to swap an engine, but plenty. Since your goal is to put a rather large object where it's not meant to go and bolt it to other components it's not designed to bolt to, you can imagine how the list of considerations expands. Swapping one transmission for another is not a bolt-in affair, but provided you approach it with careful planning and execution, it's definitely doable. Contact Advance Adapters and Novak Conversion for info on all the transmission mounts, shifters, bellhousing and transfer-case adapters, and clutch-conversion parts you'll need.

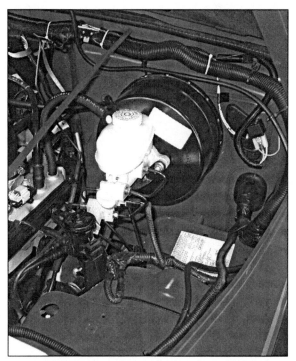

A hydraulic clutch slave cylinder and pushrod can be adapted to most bellhousings to accommodate a variety of manual transmission candidates. The kit shown also includes a mounting bracket, a fluid line, and the appropriate clutch release fork. (Photo courtesy Novak Conversions)

Since Wrangler TJs are manufactured to accept both manual and automatic transmissions, they are easily adapted to accept either. Provisions for mounting items such as a clutch master cylinder to the firewall are already in place.

TJ TRANSFER CASES

With the exception of Rubicon models, the Jeep Wrangler TJ has used only the NP231J transfer case during its production run. The NP231J is chain driven, with an all-aluminum case and a 2.72:1 low gear ratio. This model is shown with a slip-yoke eliminator (SYE) kit.

The transfer case sits behind the transmission and splits the engine's torque between the front and rear axles. In short, it's what makes a 4WD a 4WD. It has one output shaft that provides power to the rear axle, and another output shaft offset to the passenger side that powers the front axle. All Wrangler TJs are equipped with part-time 4WD transfer cases. Part-time 4WD is not meant for dry, paved roads, since the front and rear axles are basically locked together, unlike some full-time 4WD systems that vary the power from front to rear.

The NP231J Transfer Case

The NP231J transfer case benefited from nearly 10 years of experience in Jeep Wrangler YJ and Cherokee XJ before landing in the Wrangler TJ. During that reign, it was revised a number of times, with each new model receiving some improvement over its predecessor. The most notable upgrade applied to the slip yoke in the tail shaft. Prior models of the NP231J are prone to fluid loss from the rear of the case when the slip yoke pulls away and separates from the transfer case upon extreme axle articulation during off-road maneuvers (more on this later). The NP231J found in the TJ does not have this problem. Earlier models were also offered with varying input shaft lengths and spline counts. Fortunately for TJ owners, the NP231J found in the TJ has stayed somewhat consistent during its run, using the long and short style 21-and 23-spline input shafts.

The NP231J is a chain-driven, part-time transfer case using an all-aluminum two-piece case with a 3-pinion helical planetary gear assembly. It offers a low-gear ratio of 2.72:1 and is 1:1 direct drive in high range. A red and silver tag found at the rear of the case stamped "NP231J" easily identifies this transfer case. The tag notes the case model number, the assembly number, the serial number, and its low-range ratio. Aside from the Rubicon model Wranglers, which use the NVG241OR, the NP231J is the only transfer case to be used in Jeep Wrangler TJs, and is

The biggest deficiency of the NP231J is its long rear output shaft. The excessive length is due to the slip yoke assembly, which allows for driveline length variation as the suspension cycles up and down. Once a TJ is lifted, however, the slip-yoke hinders performance as it creates extreme driveshaft angles, which can cause damage to both the transfer case and the driveshaft through excessive vibration. NP231J transfer cases are easily identified by a red and silver metal tag affixed at the rear of the transfer case.

The NP231J features an oil pump and oil pump housing in the rear case half. Rock-Trac transfer cases use a slightly larger, higher volume pump for increased lubrication.

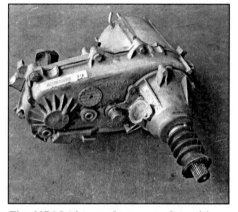

The NP231J transfer cases found in Jeep Wrangler TJs are excessively long compared to those used in other Jeep models. Notice the rear output slip yoke assembly towards the lower right.

NP231J Specifications

Low-gear ratio: 2:72.1
High-gear ratio: 1:1
Reduction type: 3-pinion planetary
Shift pattern: 2H-4H-N-4L
Torque capacity: 1,885 ft-lbs
U-joint size: 1310
Weight: 65 lbs
Length: 16 inches
Fluid capacity: 2.5 pints
Input shaft: 23-spline
Front output shaft: 1⅛-inch, 27-spline

Earlier NP231J transfers cases used input shafts that varied in length and spline count. TJ cases have stayed fairly consistent, using 23-spline and 21-spline short and long-style inputs.

also referred to as the Command-Trac Part-Time 4WD system. The NP231J was manufactured by New Process Gear, which later became New Venture Gear.

Jeep chose the NP231J as its case of choice for one of its most capable vehicle models (per the Jeep Trail Rated program), so it isn't much of a surprise that it's a fairly stout unit from the get-go.

The planetary gear assembly, drive sprockets, and chain are plenty strong and reliable for stock and mildly modified Wranglers. But that's not to say it can't benefit from the host of available upgrades. In fact, when outfit properly, the NP231J is fully capable of sustaining up to 2,300 ft-lbs torque, compared with its stock 1,885-ft-lb rating. There's a whole section on this to come. Keep an eye on your fluid level and be mindful of the rotational torque limits, and your NP231J should have a long, happy life.

The NP231J is not compatible with earlier Jeep models because Chrysler changed the offset of the front differential from the passenger side (right-hand drop) to the driver side (left-hand drop) for the Wrangler YJ. This renders the NP231J useless in earlier Jeep models without an axle swap.

Numerically Defining the NP231J

You didn't think they just pulled the "NP231" designation out of a hat did you? As with all transfer cases produced by New Venture Gear, the NP231J nomenclature can be broken down and defined. The "NP" stands for "New Process," which indicates that the unit was manufactured by New Process Gear. The first number indicates that the NP231J is a two-speed case with high and low ranges. The second number designates the strength of the case. The NP231J rates a "3" in strength, as opposed to the "4" rating given to the NVG241OR transfer case (the largest New Venture Gear transfer case is designated a "7"). The final number reveals the type of transfer case, with the "1" specifying the NP231J as a part-time 4WD case. The "J," rather obviously, stands for Jeep. Other models of the NP231 are designated "D" for Dodge and "C" for Chevrolet.

NVG241OR Rock-Trac Transfer Case

The NVG241OR Rock-Trac transfer case is also a chain-driven, planetary reduction transfer case. It uses a 4:1 6-pinion helical planetary gear assembly that offers a larger ring-gear diameter and a larger pinion size for increased strength compared with the NP231J. The 4:1 low-gear ratio is seriously advantageous to anyone who desires improved trail crawling ability. Thirty-two-spline front and rear output shafts are accompanied by larger bearings. The mainshaft, sprocket, and clutch teeth are also greatly refined over the NP231J counterparts. A wider chain is incorporated to regulate flex, and a high-volume oil pump is situated within the rear case-half to ensure thorough lubrication. Even the NVG241OR's case-halves received increased ribbing, greater wall thickness, and extra bolts to ensure that it can handle heavier torque loads.

The NVG241OR Rock-Trac transfer case was introduced with the Wrangler Rubicon in 2003. It came factory-equipped with a 4:1 low gear ratio, 32-spline front and rear output shafts, and a larger oil pump.

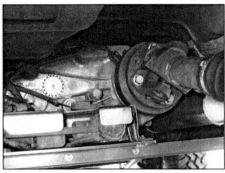

The NVG241OR also features the first factory-eliminated slip-yoke assembly making it truly off-road ready. The factory fixed yoke uses a 1330 series yoke, rather than the smaller 1310 used in the NP231J. A stronger 1350 series yoke is also compatible.

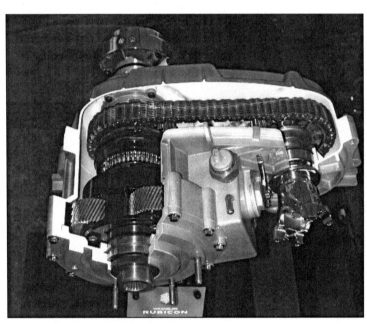

This cutaway Rock-Trac transfer case shows the wider chain and larger sprocket.

The most impressive feature of this heavy-duty transfer case is the elimination of the overly long factory slip-yoke assembly used with the NP231J. Rather, the rear output shaft and tail housing are equipped with a fixed-yoke output, greatly decreasing the overall length of this transfer case and eradicating the inherent negative issues associated with the slip-yoke-type output. This allows the Rubicon model Wranglers and Unlimiteds to use a CV driveshaft from the factory, which increases driveline length and improves U-joint operating angles. All of these performance upgrades are important factors in making the NVG241OR the most capable transfer case ever used in a production Jeep.

The NVG241OR Rock-Trac transfer case was standard equipment on Rubicon Wrangler and Rubicon Unlimited models as part of the 4:1 Rock-Trac Part-Time 4WD System. It was not offered as an available option in other Jeep vehicles. The NVG241OR case can be identified by a red and silver tag

NVG241OR Rock-Trac Specifications

Low-gear ratio: 4:1
High-gear ratio: 1:1
Reduction type: 6-pinion planetary
Shift pattern: 2H-4H-N-4L
Torque capacity: 5,555 ft-lbs
U-joint size: 1330
Weight: 97 lbs
Length: 15.24 inches
Fluid capacity: 6.5 pints
Input shaft: 23-spline
Front output shaft: 1⅜-inch, 32-spline

A slip yoke eliminator (SYE) kit, such as this kit from Advance Adapters, is designed to replace the slip yoke at the rear of the NP231J with a fixed yoke assembly. SYE kits reduce driveshaft angles by using a longer driveshaft. Most suspension manufacturers recommend using an SYE when installing a lift kit.

affixed to the rear case section. This identification tag displays the model number, assembly number, serial number, and low-range gear ratio. Since the Rock-Trac transfer case is built to withstand a good deal of abuse in its stock configuration, there are currently no aftermarket upgrades available.

NP231J T-Case Beefing Ideas

Slip-Yoke Eliminators/Tail Shaft Conversions

If you've heard or read anything about the NP231J transfer case or even just looked at it under your Wrangler, you're probably familiar with its long rear tail housing and problematic slip-yoke assembly. It's the weakest link of this otherwise reasonably strong case and can quickly lead to driveshaft and/or transfer case failure if left stock with a lifted suspension.

The design of the slip-yoke rear output on the NP231J transfer case is intended to accommodate the up-and-down motion of the Wrangler's suspension. As the suspension cycles up and down, the driveshaft must become shorter and longer by moving in and out. This necessitates the slip yoke, which features a splined shaft that slides in and out to vary driveshaft length. While this setup works fine under normal driving

The NP231J HD Super Short SYE from JB Conversions is one of the more impressive kits on the market. Its larger-diameter 32-spline output shaft is 2¼ inches shorter than most kits, assuring maximum driveshaft length.

and light off-road conditions, it can become an issue even in stock-height Wranglers once the suspension becomes fully loaded with driver, passengers, gear, and is subjected to repeated cycling.

The factory slip-yoke assembly is not recommended for use with aftermarket suspension lifts. Wranglers suffer from a

short rear driveshaft—most measure about 13.5 inches or less—because of the long tail housing. Once you lift your Wrangler, the short driveshaft is pulled farther out on its splines at static vehicle height, but it's pulled out even farther—maybe all the way—when the suspension articulates during off-road maneuvers.

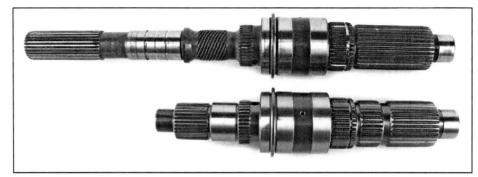

Here, a super short SYE (bottom) is compared with a stock tailshaft. The difference in length is significant and the increased strength of the new shaft is apparent.

This is the least of the slip-yoke's problems, as the real issue arises from the increased driveshaft angle. With the vehicle raised up by a suspension lift, the driveshaft must operate at a much more extreme angle, which creates a good degree of angular stress and U-joint bind, which can lead to driveline vibration and ultimately failure. Many suspension manufacturers offer a cheap remedy for this issue in the form of transfer case lowering kits, which basically consist of small spacers that drop the transfer case skid plate down lower below the framerail so the driveshaft can spin at a less severe angle. This works in theory, but it's pretty much what it's intended to be—a cheap remedy. A drop kit is essentially a Band-Aid for the bigger issue. It also robs about an inch-or-so of ground clearance beneath the transfer case, which certainly causes additional problems when negotiating difficult terrain.

Many aftermarket manufacturers offer slip-yoke eliminator (SYE) kits to solve the slip-yoke dilemma. By removing the slip yoke and tail housing assembly and replacing it with a fixed CV yoke and tail housing and CV driveshaft, you add much-needed length to the rear driveline. The CV shaft effectively decreases the operating angle of the U-joint by flattening the overall slope of the driveshaft.

Most available SYE kits add 6 inches or more to the length of the rear driveshaft. Some boast more than others, and often this measurement claim is the biggest selling point for a kit. Take your time when considering an SYE kit for your vehicle, and make sure to look at the overall design rather than simply the added driveshaft length. Some feature superior designed and constructed tailhousings and output shafts that closely match New Venture Gear engineering specifications for the best performance. In my opinion, the best SYE kits come from manufacturers like JB Conversions that specialize in this sort of conversion

SYE kits also help eliminate driveline vibration in lifted TJs by using a CV driveshaft, which reduces the working angle of the U-joints.

and can provide some degree of technical backing for the product's claimed benefits.

Needless to say, most suspension manufacturers recommend using an SYE kit when installing a lift kit. Many also package and market their own kits, all of which address the issue to varying degrees. Some kits are better than others, so be careful to find out what type of kit you're getting to make sure it's what you want. A few require modification to the stock tail shaft, while others include a new shorter shaft in the kit. Replacing the stock shaft altogether is your best bet, and most of the manufacturers recognize this and include a new tail shaft in their kits. As mentioned before, you also need to consider how much driveshaft length you gain with each kit.

Here an SYE-equipped NP231 (right) is shown side-by-side with a stock NP231J with the factory slip yoke and tailhousing in place. Even without a yoke installed, the stock unit is still longer than the SYE with the yoke installed.

Low Gears

Until the NP241OR Rock-Trac transfer case was introduced with the Rubicon model TJ in 2003, the NP231J's 2.72:1 low gear ratio was the lowest offered of all the available Jeep transfer cases to date. While this alone makes the NP231J pretty darn desirable, a 2.72:1 low still doesn't cut it when your sense for adventure and rapidly improving wheeling skills keep drawing you to more extreme terrain.

Just to clarify; lower gears, as in low range, correspond to higher numbers. So a 2.72:1 low-range gear is higher than a 4.0:1 low range. In order to completely understand the benefits of lowering

Crawl Ratio

Swapping in lower transfer case gears isn't the only way to achieve lower gearing. The final drive ratio, or crawl ratio, of the vehicle also depends on the transmission and axle gear ratios. Since most TJs use the stock transmission's first gear (unless you perform a tranny swap), the axle and transfer-case gear ratios are more commonly changed. Crawl ratio is the numerical value of how many times the engine must crank over to turn the tires. For example, a 40:1 crawl ratio would translate to 40 revolutions of the engine's crankshaft to 1 revolution of the tires. Crawl ratio can be determined by multiplying a transmission's first gear ratio by the transfer case's low-range gear ratio by the differential gear ratio. Each of the gear ratios involved in the equation will decrease the engine RPM per tire revolution and increase the torque output. Vehicles equipped with automatic transmissions receive further reduction because the torque converter nearly doubles the torque output before it even reaches the transfer case.

Lets work out an example for calculating crawl ratio using the formula and some basic stats from an '05 Wrangler: 42RLE Automatic first gear ratio: 2.84:1, NP231J low-range ratio: 2.72:1, and stock axle ratio: 3.73:1.

Transmission first-gear ratio x
T-case low-range ratio x
axle-gear ratio = Crawl ratio

$$2.84 \times 2.72 \times 3.73 = 28.81:1$$

The value is often rounded off to the nearest whole number, so our equation resulted in about a 29:1 crawl ratio. Though adequate, this isn't a very impressive number for adventurous rock crawling. Transfer cases with lower gears and lower axle gearing (both numerically higher) can substantially increase off-road capability. For example, if you were to upgrade to a 4:1 gear ratio in the transfer case and a 4.56:1 ratio in the differentials, you'd get a much more satisfying figure:

$$2.84 \times 4.0 \times 4.56 = 51.80:1$$

That makes for a difference of 23 revolutions of the crankshaft. That's a fairly substantial gain in low-speed crawling ability, and provides a noticeable effect on vehicle control and drivability while negotiating trail obstacles.

gearing, however, it's important to know what the numbers mean and how they factor into increased 4WD performance.

Tera Low231 4:1 Conversion: The only lower gearing option for the NP231J transfer case is the Tera Low231 4:1 conversion. I don't say this out of undying compassion for this particular product (though it is an impressive assembly)—this is literally the only low gearing option for this transfer case. TeraFlex, located in Sandy, Utah, manufactures a number of gearing products for many makes and models of transfer cases, as well as aftermarket axle assemblies and suspension products for the TJ and other vehicles.

Expanding on its experience in the market, TeraFlex created its Tera Low231 unit to provide a true 4:1 gear reduction in low without affecting the

The Tera Low231 4:1 conversion kit uses a replacement front case half that is constructed from strengthened aluminum with thicker walls. The new case includes a 4:1 low gear ratio and handles greater torque loads than a stock NP231J.

high gears. This means you get an improved crawl ratio, but highway fuel economy is not affected. The conversion kit consists of a brand new all-aluminum front case half with a compound 4:1

The Tera Low231's 4:1 low gear ratio is achieved through the use of a much stronger 6-pinion planetary assembly. The one-piece planetary is stuffed with thicker pinion gears and is greatly refined over the factory unit.

planetary gear assembly and a new 23-spline input shaft. The kit also includes a new front output-yoke oil seal. The Tera Low231 can easily be adapted to any NP231J transfer case.

Because of the new input shaft, the new 6-pinion 4:1 planetary assembly, and heavier-walled front case half, the TeraLow kit also increases the input torque rating of the transfer case. This makes the Tera Low231 well suited to TJs that have undergone a V-8 swap. Since the Tera Low231 conversion requires that you disassemble the transfer case, it's also a good time to install a slip yoke eliminator (SYE) kit if you haven't already.

Stronger Planetary Units and Wide Chain Kits

Just because an option exists doesn't mean you have to take it. If you're satisfied with the NP231J's 2.72:1 low gear ratio then why change anything? Many Wrangler owners wheel their rigs successfully using the factory transfer case gearing and slightly lower axle gears to accommodate a larger tire diameter. So if you don't want lower gears, can you beef up your transfer case? A larger planetary gear assembly and wider chain and sprocket should do the trick.

Many companies, such as Tri-County Gear and JB Conversions, offer heavier-duty one-piece, 6-pinion planetary assemblies that can be exchanged for the NP231J's weaker two-piece, 3-pinion units. This provides a substantial increase in strength, more than doubling the torque rating of the factory planetary. While the extra strength is nice, it's my opinion that you might as well go for the 4:1 gearing since you'll have to disassemble the transfer case either way. The Tera Low kit will run you a few more dollars, but the first time you wheel your TJ with the 4:1 kit, you'll agree that it's worth every cent.

Another means of gaining transfer case strength is to install a wider chain and drive sprocket. The NP231J uses a 1-inch-wide chain, though other models of the same case, such as the NP231D used in Dodge ½-ton pickups, use a larger 1¼-inch-wide chain that can han-

A 6-pinion planetary gear set is available to replace the stock NP231 3-pinion setup. Shown side-by-side, you can see the extra pinion gears within the 6-pinion planetary assembly on the right.

Wide chain kits are another method of beefing up the NP231 transfer case. The wider chain on the right can handle increased torque loads and won't stretch as easily, which means a longer life expectancy for the whole transfer case. A larger sprocket is also required.

dle more torque. Most good gear shops can complete this chain swap, which also requires use of the larger NP231D sprocket. According to Jason Bunch, owner of Tri-County Gear in Pomona, California, you can expect about a 25-percent increase in strength with the wider chain, which will also resist stretching and carry greater torque loads.

Achieving 2-Low Ability

Many early gear-driven Jeep transfer cases offered the ability to disengage the front axle while remaining in the lowest gear setting. This was achieved via twin-stick shifters, where you have two shifters to control transfer case operation instead of one. 2WD low gives you better steering and less driveline bind, which can help you negotiate a tight turn or continue over an obstacle. This effect can be achieved in vehicles with manual locking hubs by unlocking the front hubs and leaving the vehicle in 4WD low. However, the TJ uses automatic locking hubs, which eliminates this option. The NP231J isn't offered with this twin-stick or 2WD low-range option from the factory, though it can easily be achieved with an aftermarket kit.

The Tera 2Low231 kit from TeraFlex Manufacturing is one of the few kits for the NP231J. The kit creates a mechanical disconnect for the front and rear output shafts when the shifter is in the neutral position. This also gives you a true neutral, which can be a great aid if you flat-tow your Wrangler behind a motor home or other vehicle. The kit includes a new sector and mode fork that installs inside the transfer case. Since the installation of the 2Low kit requires disassembly of the case, it's a good idea to complete other upgrade modifications, as well as a rebuild kit (depending on necessity), at the same time.

Shifter Assemblies

Whether you've lifted your Wrangler or not, you've probably discovered that the stock transfer case shifter has a few deficiencies. The biggest annoyance I've found is that the shifter allows the transfer case to pop out of gear from time to time, particularly when set in 4-High or 4-Low. Binding between gears is another issue. While this occurs infrequently in stock Wranglers, the issue becomes worse once the vehicle is lifted. This is because the shift linkage is moved out of adjustment once the transfer case is dropped down in an effort to decrease the sharp driveline angles created by a suspension lift. Body lifts can also wreak

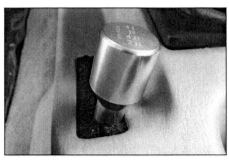

Novak Conversions offers its universal transfer case shifter for the NP231J. It is designed to replace the problematic factory Z-gate-style shifter, which is prone to binding and popping out of gear. (Photo courtesy Novak Conversions)

havoc because the stock linkage can only be adjusted so much. Some suspension companies, such as Skyjacker, provide a simple fix for this problem by offering a shifter relocation plate, which is essentially a drop-down bracket that repositions the shifter mount on the body. While this works in theory, it doesn't always work in practice, and stiff and/or sloppy shifting can still be a problem.

Novak Conversions offers one sure-fire solution to the shifter dilemma. The Novak Shifter Assembly is a universal fit to a number of Jeep transfer cases and is compatible with both the TeraLow 231 4:1 and the Tera 2Low kits. The Novak Shifter replaces the factory Z-gate shifter and the maze of linkage rods, joints, and brackets with an entirely new shifting assembly that includes a shift bracket, a shift plate, rod, lever, and shift knob. The kit is designed to eliminate the typical shifter binding issues caused by suspension flex and also addresses any problems that arise when installing a suspension lift.

Transfer Case Swap Options

Retaining the NP231J

Replacing or rebuilding your worn-out factory NP231J transfer case with a new or rebuilt unit is always an option.

After all, if it performed the intended job to some degree of success in the first place, why trouble yourself with a change that will likely require new driveshafts and possibly further modifications? Also, most drivetrain swaps can get fairly pricey once labor is factored in, so sometimes sticking with the tried and true is your best bet.

Unless your NP231J has suffered catastrophic failure such as a shattered or cracked case, it can most likely be rebuilt. To what degree you'll need to rebuild your transfer case, however, depends on the condition of the internals and the case interior once you begin disassembly. Internal components can be damaged due to a loose or worn out drive chain, which can also erode the interior case walls if it maintains continuous contact during operation. Common wear points appear on the plastic wear pads on the aluminum shift forks, but look for other irregularities as well.

One issue with a straight NP231J swap does arise, in that you can almost buy a completely outfitted NVG241OR case for what it might cost to build an NP231J to stand up to less abuse. However, if you're simply transferring components from a "built" NP231J to a new case, or already have some of the upgrade components but not all of them, then this can be an economical approach to replacing your existing transfer case while adding some improvements.

When tracking down a used or rebuilt unit, it's a good idea to look for an NP231J from a similar year and model vehicle. With the plethora of changes and upgrades applied to this transfer case over the years, later-model cases are the better choice. Also, ensure that you verify its compatibility with your transmission by checking the input shaft spline count, which varied through the years. Lastly, some NP231J cases, such as those used in Cherokee XJs were clocked differently. The general rule of

thumb is that most 4.0Ls came with 23-spline input shafts, while 4-cylinders came with 21-spline shafts.

NVG241OR Rock-Trac

Jeep sure knew what it was doing when it created the Wrangler Rubicon. Of all of its impressive features, one stands out the most: the NVG241OR Rock-Trac transfer case. Not only did it help the Wrangler Rubicon become one of the most capable production vehicles, it's also an awesome swap option for regular TJs and other Jeep models equipped with the NP231J. The NVG241OR is a direct fit to most TJ transmissions (it has a 23-spline short input and shares the NP231J's bolt pattern) and offers all the benefits of a completely outfitted NP231J. In fact, you can't build the NP231J to put up with as much abuse as the NVG241OR can take. As mentioned, it has the torque capacity of a full size truck, making it an excellent transfer case for V-8 swaps.

A number of companies offer these transfer cases ready for installation in Jeep Wrangler TJs. JB Conversions, Advance Adapters, and High-Impact Transmission & Gear are just a few suppliers of this revered transfer case. New

One of the coolest available "factory fit" transfer case swap options is the NVG241OR Rock-Trac case found in the Rubicon. It's a direct fit to most TJ transmissions and offers every imaginable upgrade over the stock NP231J.

The Atlas transfer case from Advance Adapters is a gear-driven unit available in a wide variety of low gear ratios. It's the ultimate in low-geared cases and it's shorter than the NP231 for increased driveshaft length.

driveshafts are needed for this swap (the Rubicon shafts have different yoke size on the axle ends), as well as possible modifications to the speedometer. Aside from these alterations it is essentially a bolt-in unit.

Advance Adapters Atlas Transfer Case

The Atlas transfer case from Advance Adapters in Paso Robles, California, has proven to be one of the single greatest creations of the 4x4 aftermarket. It's designed as a replacement transfer case for a wide variety of applications and it offers the ultimate in gearing and strength. These units are so popular that they can be found in everything from daily-driven vehicles such as Jeep Wranglers and full-size trucks, to full competition rock-crawling rigs where transfer case performance is paramount to a podium finish.

The Atlas transfer case uses a solid, one-piece case manufactured from 356-T6 heat-treated aluminum alloy. It's an all-gear-driven unit with helically cut gears and a twin-stick shifter with synchronized shifting. A number of models of the Atlas transfer case are available in low gear ratios of 3.8:1, 4.3:1, and 5.0:1. Another version of the case called the Atlas Highlander is offered in 3.0:1 and

2.0:1 low gear ratios. The Atlas is also 2.5 inches shorter than an NP231J equipped with a SYE, which allows for a longer rear driveshaft for less driveline vibration. At 110 pounds, the Atlas does weigh more than the NP231 (approximately 40 pounds more), but for what you gain in overall strength and gearing, the added weight is inconsequential.

Dana 300

The Dana 300 has the same six-bolt circular bolt pattern as the NP231J, but its front output is on the passenger side of the vehicle rather than the driver's side. So how does this translate as a swap option, you may ask? Well, you flip the Dana 300 upside down so the output is on the driver's side. Only a couple companies offer these "flip kits" for Dana 300 transfer cases, but they are becoming increasingly popular. If you know your Jeep history, then you're probably aware that these gear-driven cases were used in Jeep CJs from 1980–'86. They use a smaller cast-iron case than the NP231J, and are 4 inches shorter. The Dana 300 is a good swap candidate for the fact that it is gear-driven so it isn't prone to any chain stretching or wear. It can be equipped with a 4:1 low gear ratio and it offers twin-stick shifting ability. It's also usually cheaper to build up than the NP231J.

Underdrive Ability

If a 4:1 low gear ratio just isn't low enough for you, then perhaps a Klune-V Underdrive system can help you achieve that super low you've always dreamed about. A Klune-V system consists of an underdrive gearbox that bolts between the transmission and the transfer case. It's designed to multiply a transfer case's existing low gear ratio by up to four times. They're neat units that increase off-highway capability tenfold by providing a vehicle with extreme low gearing when it's needed most. Klune units do add about 6.5 inches to the rear drive-

Another TJ T-case swap option is the Dana 300. These units are 8 inches shorter than a stock NP231, and reputedly stronger when rightly equipped. It's a gear-driven case, with an available 4:1 low gear ratio. A transfer case "flip kit", such as the kit shown from Down East Offroad, is necessary for installation in the TJ. The kit also accommodates twin-stick shifters.

line length, which can be difficult for a short-wheelbase rig like the TJ. But considering the low gear crawling benefits, and the fact that it actually only adds 2.5 inches to the stock driveline length (provided that the NP231 is equipped with an SYE), Klune underdrive units are a viable means of achieving lower gearing without installing 4:1 low gearing in the transfer case.

Adapters and Rotation Rings

The NP231J and NVG241OR transfer cases can be mounted in just one position behind the transmission. This isn't a huge issue, but it means you can't rotate the cases to tuck them closer to the floor for extra ground clearance. One method of moving the transfer case up further, to make way for a flat skid plate or custom multi-link suspension, is to rotate its low end upward using a "clocking" ring to reposition the case. Clocking or rotation rings fit between the transmission and the transfer case and add

Klune-V Extreme Underdrive systems offer insane low-gearing options. The Underdrive consists of an extra gearbox that bolts between the transmission and the transfer case that is capable of multiplying the existing gear ratio by up to four times. When mated to a stock NP231J with its 2.72:1 low, the combo produces an 11:1 low ratio.

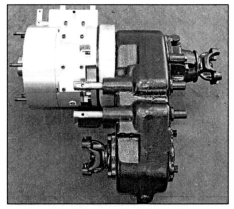

High Impact Transmission & Gear offers its Hercules Klune-V/Bronco Dana 20 combo as a popular replacement for the NP231J. Bolted together, the Klune and Dana 20 units are still 3 inches shorter than the stock NP231J and create nearly a 10:1 low range.

just a little length. Rotation rings are available from a variety of sources and are a simple means of achieving the desired positioning of the transfer case.

Should a transmission transfer swap be on your agenda, then you're going to need the proper adapter to complete the installation. Companies such as

Swapping in a transfer case other than the stock unit may require use of an adapter for proper fitment. Both Advance Adapters and Novak Conversions offer a large variety of adapters and input shafts for many popular transfer-case swap options.

Advance Adapters and Novak Conversions specialize in such transformations and can provide adapters and other necessary swap-related items to fit a number of different tranny and T-case combinations in your TJ.

Driveshaft Upgrades

Once you've installed a slip-yoke eliminator kit, you'll find that the stock rear driveshaft needs to be extended. While you can easily take measurements and order a shaft from your local driveline shop, a number of suspension companies have made it even easier than that. Provided your TJ still retains the factory drivetrain components, you can purchase an appropriate length, ready-to-install CV driveshaft from lift manufacturers such as Rubicon Express, TeraFlex, and Full-Traction. A CV driveshaft will operate more smoothly at steeper angles than a traditional two-joint shaft and is recommended when using tires taller than 35 inches. A CV driveshaft can also help eliminate driveshaft vibrations in lifted TJs. Most lift companies offer these universal fit CV driveshafts, but will also custom tailor them to accommodate any lift size. If your application calls for a specific length or feature, you can buy

Think those stock driveshafts are up to the task of extreme trails? Here a stock Rubicon driveshaft is shown twisted from torque and shock load.

TeraFlex offers this CV driveshaft with a CV yoke to fit most Wrangler NP231 transfer cases. The shaft features a long-slip spline to accommodate long travel suspensions.

Rubicon Wranglers can also benefit from a rear CV driveshaft. Rubicon Express offers a kit that will bolt right up.

directly from a driveline shop. Two shops I've used to good success are J.E. Reel Drivelines in Pomona, California, and Tom Wood's Custom Driveshafts in Ogden, Utah.

TJ AXLES

There's good and bad when it comes to the stock TJ axles, but most will find the stock axles to be of decent strength for wheeling on 31-inch tires. Rubicon model Dana 44 axles, however, are well suited for the more extreme trails. (Photo courtesy DaimlerChrysler)

Axles take a beating in any 4x4. In addition to receiving all of the horsepower and torque and distributing it to the drive wheels, the axles are also closer to the ground than any other vehicle component, making them the easiest target for rocks and other trail obstacles. Add a few water crossings and maybe some mud bogs after that, and you have an idea of what your axles must live through. Amid the axles' two basic functions—supporting the weight of the vehicle and turning the wheels—they're challenged much more with the larger tires and extra weight that come along with an upgraded Jeep.

Despite the odds, I've successfully wheeled a lot of trails in Moab, Utah, and throughout California, riding on 35-inch tires with the stock TJ Dana 30 front axle and the optional Dana 44 rear axle. I did add a few upgrades over time, including Superior Axle & Gear's Super 30 and Super 44 kits, and an OX Locker in the rear, but the front remained an open carrier. Though I did my share of backing up and making repeated attempts at some obstacles, I made it through many trails without breaking any parts. However, my stock axles are now long gone. These days, I run heavier-duty Dynatrac Pro-Rock Dana 60s to ensure worry-free excursions. I never did break those stock axles though, and I've witnessed similar results from other TJ owners' experiences with stock axles—including the begrudged Dana 35c.

Dana 30

The Dana 30 was the only front axle offered in standard model TJs. It's a full-floating unit with 27-spline inner and outer axle shafts, a 7⅛-inch ring gear, and unit bearing hubs. The axle shafts are rated to 40,000 lbs/inch. The Dana 30 axle employs one of the most common Dana differential covers ever, sharing its

Though still considered a light-duty axle, the front Dana 30 is typically more reliable than the rear Dana 35c, especially with some aftermarket upgrades. When paired with a Dana 44 rear axle, the Dana 30 front can be used effectively on trails.

Dynatrac ProRock 60 axles are a great way to go if 35-inch or taller tires and extreme trails are in your future, but the stock TJ axles can still be built to conquer trails if you outfit them properly and keep tire size down.

The Dana 35c is the TJ's standard rear axle. It's a pretty good unit for street drivers, but has earned nicknames such as "Turdy5" for its penchant for failure on the trail. To the Dana Corporation's credit, however, breakage typically occurs only after lockers and larger-than-stock tires are installed.

10-bolt pattern with the Dana 23, 25, and 27 axles, all of which served under earlier Jeep models. The Dana 30 axle itself is also no stranger to Jeeps, having been used in a variety of models, in both front and rear applications, since the 1960s. Earlier versions of the Dana 30 are not compatible with the TJ Dana 30. This includes the previous model Wrangler YJ Dana 30, which, among other reasons, is a reverse cut, high-pinion unit as opposed to the standard cut, low-pinion of the TJ

Dana 30. The Wrangler TJ and Wrangler YJ Dana 30s are both full-time unit-bearing assemblies with a fixed spindle and do not use traditional locking hubs. The use of unit bearing hubs means that the front axle components turn continuously, even when the vehicle is in 2WD.

Since the front end is rarely required to endure the weight and torque typically put upon the rear axle, the stock Dana 30 is usually up to the task of moderate to fairly extreme off-road use, depending on

Identifying Dana Axles

As I've previously indicated, all Jeep TJs use axles made by the Dana Corporation. To aid in identifying these axles, Dana stamps a complete Bill of Material (BOM) number and the manufacturing date on the axle tube. This information can often be difficult to read due to grease and dirt buildup, but if your TJ is equipped with the factory axle assemblies, it's there, so keep scrubbing the axle tubes until you see it. Dana axles also typically have the axle model number cast into one of the webs of the housing, and each axle should have a gear tag ratio attached to the diff cover bolts. This tag is often missing from many diff covers that I see, particularly if an aftermarket cover or cover skid plate has been installed. Not to worry, however, because the number stamped on the axle tube should be enough for most axle parts vendors to determine what components the factory used in the assembly of your differentials.

Upgrade or Replace: The Great TJ Axle Debate

Many opinions exist on the practicality and cost effectiveness of building up the Dana 30 and Dana 35c axles, especially since you still have no guarantee they won't break. But considering the brutal nature of four-wheeling and the toll it takes on a vehicle and all of its parts, you should know that there are no guarantees. Parts break, even in Dana 60s from time to time. If you intend on retaining the stock axles in your Wrangler, you'll quickly learn that driving over obstacles with the accelerator hammer down is a quick and easy way to break parts. The Dana 30 and 35c can take a good bit of abuse, but only so much—leave the heavy throttle to the guys with Dana 60 conversions and fat wallets. I've watched many a driver improve his driving skills by operating stock machinery that he couldn't afford to fix if it broke. Driving with finesse and consistency ensures a much longer life for all your axle and driveline components.

Those who hit it hard and break parts usually skip the 30 and 35c upgrades and swap in Dana 44s or better. But still, most of the aftermarket axle shaft manufacturers I've mentioned do warranty their products against breakage, so obtaining a replacement axle shaft upon failure isn't a huge ordeal. How many axle shafts have companies like Superior Axle & Gear had to replace due to breakage? Not many. But that still doesn't mean that other components of the factory axle assemblies won't fail. For example, both the Dana 30 and 35c use 2.5 x 0.250-inch wall axle tubes, which is also the same diameter and thickness used in the TJ Rubicon Dana 44. However, all three of these axles are prone to bending and/or spinning axle tubes in high-torque and extreme off-road situations, especially after other weak links have been eliminated.

What should you do about the axles under your TJ? That's a question you'll have to answer for yourself. First, consider how you use your vehicle: What type of driving do you do the most? Is your vehicle a daily driver? Do you drive to and from the trail? What level of trails do you anticipate tackling? And here's the biggie: What size tires do you desire?

Basically, the stock axles should hold up pretty well if you run the stock tire size. The stockers will hold up to 33-inch tires for mild off-road use. Taller tires merit a few axle upgrades, especially if you want to decrease your chances for breakage. In my opinion, you're best off replacing both the Dana 30 and Dana 35c if you want to run 35-inch tires or larger. Push your luck, and you're simply setting yourself up for some long days of fixing parts on the trail. If 35-inch tires are your goal, look into swapping a set of Dana 44 axles from a Jeep Wrangler Rubicon or other source. Custom Ford 9-inch axles are another option. For taller than 35-inch tires, you may want to consider a custom Dana 60 for even greater reliability.

It seems that for some, replacing the occasionally snapped Dana 35c axle shaft on the trail is more cost effective than a high-end replacement axle assembly. Used stock Dana 30 and 35c axle shafts are pretty easy to come by at most shops and junk yards, as other TJ owners upgrade to bigger aftermarket axle shafts and complete axle swaps. Pick up a set and carry them with you while wheeling for added peace of mind. From top to bottom (for the Dana 30): passenger-side inner shaft, assembled passenger-side inner and outer shafts, assembled driver-side inner and outer shafts, and driver-side inner shaft.

your willingness to complete trail repairs. However, its fortitude wanes the larger your tires get. A number of aftermarket parts are available for this axle, all designed to combat big-tire-related breakage and increase the Dana 30's tolerance for high-torque, high-stress driving situations.

Dana 35c

The Dana 35c rear axle has been a Jeep mainstay since 1984 when the Cherokee XJ was introduced. It was also the standard rear axle in Jeep Comanche pickups, Wagoneers, and Wrangler YJs, and continues its Jeep service as standard equipment in most

Replacement Dana 30 (foreground) and 35c (background) axle housings can usually be found cheap from 4x4 shops or a variety of web forums with classified sections. But remember that the housings are relatively weak, so inspect them carefully before purchase. Since you may not be able to discover cracks or other flaws until you get the housing home and cleaned up, you might try to get a guarantee from the seller.

Grand Cherokees and the Wrangler TJ. The "c" didn't come along until 1990, however, when Jeep began using C-clips to secure the axle shafts inside the carrier. It's a common misconception that the "c" stands for "C-clip." Rather, it stands for "custom," because the Dana Corporation ships the axles to Chrysler

The Dana 44 rear axle is one of the best optional TJ axles. Though the Rubicon Dana 44 features a locking differential, lower gears, and slightly larger axle shafts, the regular 44 uses bigger axle tubes, is equipped with a Trac-Lok limited-slip differential, and is available on standard model Wranglers.

incomplete, with final assembly taking place along the Wrangler assembly line.

The C-clips are one of the more serious drawbacks of the 35c. Since the C-clip is all that secures the axle shaft inside the carrier, if an axle shaft breaks, the outer portion of the shaft and the wheel fall off and leave you rolling on three wheels. Installing higher-strength aftermarket axle shafts is the best plan of attack in avoiding a liberated wheel on a broken shaft, but since you still have the C-clips, this will always be an issue with the Dana 35c rear axle.

The Dana 35c is a semi-floating unit with 27-spline axle shafts, a 7⁷⁄₁₆-inch ring gear, and was available with a Trac-Lok limited-slip differential. As with all TJ axles, it also utilizes a 26-spline pinion and 1310 pinion yoke. It's a bit on the light-duty side for TJ owners who yearn for big tires, a full-time locker, and extreme trails, but the majority of Jeep owners find it of adequate strength for mild off-road use, particularly if they seek out a few stronger aftermarket parts.

Dana 44

If you were wise enough to order the optional Dana 44 rear axle when you first purchased your Wrangler, or maybe lucky enough to score a used TJ equipped with one, you're a much happier camper than those dealing with the Dana 35c rear axle. Though the TJ Dana 44 uses smaller axle tubes than those used in other Dana 44 applications, it still offers a stronger carrier, bigger axle shafts, and much stronger and larger ring and pinion than the Dana 35c. It also uses 2¾-inch diameter axle tubes, which is the largest diameter of all of the TJ axle offerings, including the Rubicon Dana 44.

Numerous variations of the Dana 44 have appeared in Jeeps, beginning in the 1950s with the CJ-3A. It was used primarily as a rear application, but was also used as a front axle in some full-size

Jeeps. The Dana 44 came to the TJ in late 1997. The TJ Dana 44 uses 30-spline, 1.18-inch diameter one-piece axle shafts, and an 8½-inch ring gear. It's a semi-floating unit and is available with a 3.73:1 gear ratio. All TJ Dana 44s also come with the factory option Trac-Lok limited-slip differential.

Many aftermarket upgrades are available for the 44, including a seemingly unlimited ring-and-pinion gear ratio selection. The TJ Dana 44 fits in any Jeep TJ, regardless of whether it was originally equipped with one from the factory or not. You will, of course, need to make sure that the ring-and-pinion gears match those already in the vehicle and modify the rear driveshaft for the correct length and yoke.

The TJ Dana 44 is also the standard rear axle option for the Wrangler Unlimited. From what I've discovered, however, Rubicon 44s possess slight differences from the standard TJ Dana 44 and are more consistent with the Rubicon Dana 44. The differences lie within the center sections, as the dimensions between the carrier bearings varies, requiring the Unlimited and Rubicon Dana 44s to use more shims for setup.

This cutaway image of a Trac-Lok limited-slip differential details the arrangement of its clutch disc and plate setup. Note the sturdy one-piece case. These units are not bad for mild off-road use, but continued heavy torque loads will increase the likelihood of failure.

Not all TJ Dana 44s are created equal. This photo shows three Dana 44 differentials. The unit on the left is from an '03 TJ and uses smallish ring gear bolts and the shims are positioned between the bearing and the carrier. The carrier in the middle is from an '06 Unlimited, uses larger bolts, and the shims are set outside the bearing. The unit on the right is a Tru-Lok differential from a '03 Rubicon, also uses the larger ring gear bolts, and its shims are set outside the bearing. The varying shim arrangement between the carriers is said to be due to the dimensions between the carrier bearings.

The Wrangler Rubicon Dana 44 axles feature air-actuated lockers that can be engaged at the push of a button. The front Dana 44 is the first for the Wrangler model and is a great swap option for the Dana 30 in standard model TJs.

Trac-Lok Limited-Slip Differential

Aside from the Tru-Lok, which is only available in Rubicon TJs, the Trac-Lok is the only limited-slip differential (LSD) that came in the TJ. The Trac-Lok was available in both the Dana 35c and Dana 44 rear axles. It's a clutch-type LSD with a one-piece case and two pinion mate gears. Ring gear torque flow is transmitted from the differential case to each axle shaft through a clutch plate and disc arrangement.

Many report that the Trac-Lok begins to display signs of impending failure upon reaching 70,000 miles, which is typically when the clutch packs wear out under regular use with routine maintenance. The Trac-Lok essentially stops locking up as tight as it used to and eventually stops locking altogether. A new clutch disc kit can be installed, but if you've done it more than once you're best off looking to replace the entire LSD with an aftermarket unit. One method of determining if an installed Trac-Lok is functioning properly is to test its rotational torque. This can be completed by securing a torque wrench to the lug studs (with the wheel removed) and using the wrench to rotate the wheel. If the rotational torque reading is greater than 200 ft-lbs or less than 56 ft-lbs, the unit should be serviced or replaced.

The Trac-Lok also requires a special additive, or friction modifier, to be mixed with the gear oil in order to function properly. If the additive is not used you'll likely hear noises, or "chatter," from the LSD during operation, and performance will suffer. Note that the Tru-Lok in Rubicon Dana 44 axles does not require this additive. If you're unsure if your TJ is equipped with the Trac-Lok LSD, there may be a metal tag attached to one of the bolts securing the rear differential cover that specifies the type of limited-slip lubricant to be used. If you hit the trail frequently you'll inevitably hear TJ owners complain about the Trac-Lok, and possibly refer to it as "Trash-Lok" or other unflattering terms. The truth is it's not a bad LSD for street and mild off-road use, but once the 35-inch tires are installed and you tackle increasingly difficult trails, you're most likely going to

You can see the helical-cut gears in this cutaway image of the Rubicon TJ Tru-Lock limited-slip differential. It acts as a traditional limited-slip differential, but it can also be fully locked pneumatically by factory-installed air compressors.

want a heavier-duty aftermarket limited-slip or locking differential.

If you're looking for an inexpensive locking diff for your Dana 35c or Dana 44 rear axle, a used Trac-Lok might do the trick. Ask your local 4x4 or gear shop if they have any lying around or check out some 4x4 or Jeep-specific online forums. You'll need the whole carrier, not just the internal parts, and I suggest paying less than $50.

Bent Axle Housing = Broken Parts

You can install every upgrade imaginable in your stock axles but if your axle housing is bent, you're still going to break parts. I spent some time at Tri County Gear in Pomona, California, where I came across this tweaked axle housing that unleashed a great degree of carnage upon a Dana 44 rear axle shaft and a Trac-Lok limited-slip differential. Though irreparable damage was done to the internal components, the axle housing was not beyond repair. The crew at Tri-County Gear was able to straighten the housing and replace the broken parts to get this TJ back in action.

As shown here, the crew at Tri-County Gear used a straight steel rod secured in place by the carrier bearing retaining straps to check the trueness of this full-floating rear Dana 44 axle housing. You can see that the rod is resting firmly against one side of the inside diameter of the spindle, which indicates that the housing is in fact bent, since the rod should be centered in the tube.

Two of the casualties of this bent axle housing were this snapped Dana 44 axle shaft and these cracked side gears from the Trac-Lock limited-slip differential.

Rubicon Dana 44

The crème de la crème of the Jeep TJ axle lineup, the Rubicon Dana 44 front and rear low-pinion axles, are as good as it gets for factory TJ axles. They offer 30-spline axle shafts, a 4.11:1 gear ratio—the lowest factory offering—and selectable low-pressure pneumatic lockers. The front Dana 44 uses 19-spline outer axle shafts with a unit bearing hub design.

The Rubicon's rear Dana 44 axle uses a Tru-Lok torque-sensing helical-gear limited-slip differential that provides increased traction while driving in 2WD or 4-High. These heavy-duty gear-type limited-slip differentials typically don't wear out or lose traction with age like clutch-type LSDs. Unlike a standard limited-slip differential, the Tru-Lok also gives you the ability to

lock the rear axle shafts together at the flip of a switch—so long as you're in 4-Low. By pressing the dash-mounted rocker switch once, a low-pressure air-actuated pump mechanically locks the rear axle. Hit the switch a second time to engage the front locker.

These locking Dana 44 axles are one of the greatest attributes of the Rubicon, but since they're factory-installed, they don't come without drawbacks. For one, Tru-Lok LSDs only operate as lockers when the transfer case is set in 4-Low. While this isn't a huge problem for most off-road driving situations, it can make the difference between getting home for dinner or not confronted with deep sand or mud. Attacking this type of terrain often requires a bit more speed than 4-Low can offer, but since the Tru-Lok only engages

when the vehicle speed is less than 10 mph, it's kind of a moot point anyway.

Another drawback of the factory Rubicon lockers is that the front locker can only be engaged if the rear unit is also engaged. This won't be a huge deal for most Rubicon owners, but I've sure met a lot of them that curse this feature. Jeep presumably incorporated these features into the Tru-Lok to take away the eerie and irrational temptation to flip on the lockers at 55 mph, "just to see what would happen." There is a way to override this feature by tricking the computer into thinking that the transfer case is in 4-Low and the Jeep is traveling at less than 10 mph, and it has been employed by countless Rubicon owners eager to live life on the wild side and operate their lockers responsibly.

The Rubicon lockers can be modified to lock in any gear and at any speed by tapping an additional switch in to the locker enable signal wire in the axle lock switch pigtail. Here the pigtail is accessed behind the axle lock switch panel. Note that the color of the locker enable signal wire is red with a white stripe in 2003 models but changed to violet with an orange stripe in subsequent years. The ground wire is black in all model years.

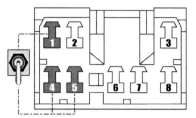

SWITCH ENABLES LOCKERS TO BE ENGAGED AT ANY SPEED WHILE IN ANY TRANSFER CASE POSITION. LOCKER ON/OFF SELECTION IS CONTROLLED BY FACTORY LOCKER SWITCH.

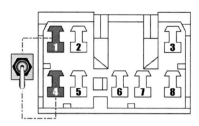

SWITCH ENABLES LOCKERS TO BE ENGAGED UNDER 10 MPH WHILE IN ANY TRANSFER CASE POSITION. LOCKER ON/OFF SELECTION IS CONTROLLED BY FACTORY LOCKER SWITCH.

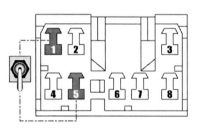

SWITCH ENABLES LOCKERS TO BE ENGAGED AT ANY SPEED WHILE IN 4WD LOW TRANSFER CASE POSITION ONLY. LOCKER ON/OFF SELECTION IS CONTROLLED BY FACTORY LOCKER SWITCH.

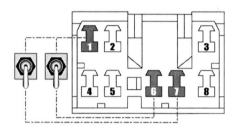

SWITCHES BYPASS FACTORY LOCKER SWITCH AND ENABLE FRONT AND REAR LOCKER TO BE ACTIVATED INDEPENDENTLY, AT ANY SPEED, IN ANY TRANSFER CASE POSITION.

The Rubicon Dana 44 can be used in any Jeep TJ as long as provisions are made to incorporate the factory air pumps and locking switches. The track width of the Rubicon Dana 44 is just slightly wider than that of the Dana 30 and 35c axles, measuring 59.5 inches compared to 58 inches.

Rubicon Lockers in Any Gear

Wish you could lock your Rubicon lockers regardless of whether your transfer case is shifted in to 4-Low or not? Well, after a bit of basic wiring, you can. You need to tap an additional switch into the locker enable signal wire and the ground wire coming off the factory locker enable switch pigtail. This switch essentially tricks the computer into thinking that the transfer case is in 4-Low when it's not. When the switch is flipped on, the lockers function in any transfer case gear range. When the switch is flipped off, the lockers only work in low range.

Though this modification requires only basic wiring skills, you should, nonetheless, acquire the proper wiring diagram for your year vehicle before attempting it, and keep in mind that

The above wiring diagrams and notes detail where the new switch should be tapped in to the Rubicon axle lock switch pigtail to achieve the desired results. In this diagram the number 1 post is the ground, 4 and 5 are the locker enable signal wires, and 6 and 7 are the rear and front locker request wires. You will need to reference the factory wiring diagrams for your year vehicle before beginning this modification. Any type of single-pole, single-throw on/off switch can be used and all connections should be soldered and properly insulated for best results. (Diagram courtesy of DaimlerChrysler and Don-A-Vee Jeep)

such a modification may affect your vehicle warranty.

Axle Upgrades

There will always be the crowd that says the Dana 30 and 35c axles aren't worth upgrading. Though they probably speak from experience, they're also likely the same guys running Dana 60s and hitting obstacles many TJ owners would rather leave to trials motorcycles or mountain goats. You do not *need* a Dana 60 to go wheeling—and don't let anyone tell you that you do. Are Dana 60s incredibly durable and wonderful in every way? You bet your ass they are. But they should be on your rig's wish list, not the *need* list. There are so many

elements of your TJ that you can build up prior to making the leap to Dana 60 axles, and you'd be wise to arrange your budget to complete these types of improvements first. I say all this with Dynatrac ProRock 60s beneath my '01 TJ, so I'm not opposed to heavy-duty axles by any means, I just don't want you to think that your stock axles can't be built to sustain some abuse.

Axle Shafts and "Super" Kits

One of the weakest links and most common breaking points of the factory Dana 30 and 35c axles are the wimpy 27-spline axle shafts. They typically break at the point just above the splines and at the yoke where the ears can become twisted. The Dana 44 shafts are

Differential Fluid Capacities

Jeep recommends using Mopar Gear Lubricant or equivalent SAE 80W-90 thermally-stable API GL-5 grade axle fluid. An SAE 75W-140 synthetic gear lubricant should be used for trailer towing applications. Axles equipped with Trac-Lok limited-slip differentials also require a friction control additive, such as Mopar Hypoid Gear Oil Additive Friction Modifier, in order to function properly.

Axle Fluid Capacity

Dana 30	40 oz/1.18 L
Dana 35c	56 oz/1.66 L
Dana 44	64 oz/1.90 L

*Dana 35c w/Trac-Lok substitute 3.5 oz/0.10 L with Friction Modifier

*Dana 44 w/Trac-Lok substitute 4.0 oz/0.12 L with Friction Modifier

a bit stronger, with 30-splines, but are also known to break. The stock axle shafts in all three of these units are constructed from 1040 carbon steel and are usually only hardened along the shafts. While this is sufficient for light-duty applications, it isn't always going to cut it when spinning big tires with a locker in difficult terrain.

Stronger material composition and an increased spline count are the main benefits of upgrading to aftermarket axle shafts. When axle spline count increases, so does the outside diameter of the shaft itself, and a fatter axle shaft of greater strength is the result. Note that you will need to upgrade your differential to match up to the spline count of your new axles.

When considering aftermarket axle shafts or an axle upgrade kit, pay close attention to advertised benefits and make sure they meet or exceed your expectations. Most offerings feature axle shafts made from higher-strength materials and incorporate design improvements such as the ability to accept full-circle C-clips at the U-joints. Many also provide preassembled components for ease of installation. Superior Axle & Gear, for example, manufactures its Super Kits for the Dana 30, 35c, and 44 axles, and each increases axle spline count, boasts greater material strength, and creates a more reliable axle assembly compared to stock. Superior's kits also include a locking differential, and both the inner and

outer preassembled axle shafts are provided with its Super 30 front axle kit.

WARN axle shafts are another good example of what you should expect from aftermarket shafts. They're made from 4340 nickel-chromium-molybdenum alloy steel and are rated at 60,000 lb/in, whereas the stock Dana 30 shafts are composed of 1040 carbon steel rated at 40,000 lb/in. For further strength, the WARN shafts also have a hardened shaft and yoke, and the yoke is machined for full-circle U-joint C-clips. Spline count is also increased and the method in which the splines are cut is said to be more efficient and to provide greater strength. These upgraded axles are better able to withstand the abuse of supporting the weight of the vehicle and turning the wheels.

Though a bent axle housing or tube certainly puts additional strain on the axle shafts, ring gear, pinion gear, and bearings, the greater durability of the new components included in upgrade kits make them more successful in resisting failure. As strong as they are, even the stoutest axle shafts will snap when used inside a severely bent or twisted axle housing. Don't risk breaking new components by installing them in a wasted housing, and have a qualified 4x4 or gear shop inspect your entire axle assembly for damage before installing any new parts. As a precautionary measure against axle housing tweaks, Superior manufactures its Super 35 truss

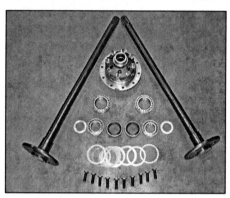

Superior Axle & Gear offers a variety of axle upgrade kits for all of the TJ axles. The Super 35 kit includes heavy-duty 30-spline, chrome-moly axle shafts, an ARB or Detroit Locker, Timken roller bearings, new seals, and Grade-8 thread-in wheel bolt studs. The Super 30 kit also includes new inner and outer axle shafts with U-joints pre-installed. Super 44 kits are also available. Yukon offers a similar concept with its Ultimate 30 and Ultimate 35 kits.

housing upgrade that bolts in place of the diff cover and lines the rear of the axle tubes with heavy-gauge steel.

Axle U-Joints

The TJ Dana 30 and Dana 44 front axles have traditionally been equipped with the Spicer 5-297X U-joint from the factory. That is, until Spicer phased out the older 5-297X and introduced the 5-760X as a replacement/upgrade. The new 5-760X has a new plastic triple lip

For ultimate axle and axle U-joint strength you can install a set of CTM Racing's massive Dana 44 U-joints, along with a set of chrome-moly axle shafts. The CTM U-joints are completely rebuildable and use greasable bronze sleeves instead of the traditional needle bearings.

seal that is said to seal better than the previous model. These two U-joints are interchangeable, and though the 760X may offer slight design improvements, it doesn't appear to be any stronger and is still usually one of the first sources of trail breakage. Add high-strength axle shafts to the big tire/high-torque equation and sooner or later you're sure to hear that familiar popping sound of the U-joint failing under the pressure.

For most, U-joints are spare parts—something you toss in the toolbox for the next time you have to change one on the trail. In recent years, however, there has been an explosion of "bulletproof" axle U-joints from the aftermarket. One of the first to appear on the scene was the seemingly indestructible CTM Racing Dana 44 U-joint, intended to replace the factory installed Spicer 5-297X/5-760X. The CTM U-joints are designed to be installed with full-circle C-clips and must be used with high-quality chrome-moly axle shafts (and don't be surprised if the shaft gives before the CTM U-joint).

After the success of the competition-proven CTM U-joint line, which also includes Dana 60 units, other aftermarket players threw their hats into the ring.

The OX U-Joint from OX Trax and the Yukon Super Joint from Yukon Gear & Axle are representative of the new age axle U-joints that have veered from traditional concept and design to increase strength. Another axle U-joint alternative is the waterproof U-joint from J.E. Reel, which is forged from high-strength alloy steel and uses high-temperature, high-pressure grease and waterproof seals.

Locking Hubs

As previously mentioned, Jeep TJ front axles use unit bearing "hubs" on the outer axle shafts that cause all of the internal components and the front driveshaft to spin continuously, even when the transfer case is not engaged in 4WD. Since the front axle assembly continues to spin, it needlessly wears the internal components, and can, in some cases, lead to greater damage if a part should fail yet go undetected. The factory unit bearings aren't serviceable, either, so replacement is the only option. When this begins to feel like routine replacement rather than scheduled maintenance, you'd be wise to look into a hub conversion. After all, why spin the whole front drivetrain when you can just as easily install a set of locking hubs to do the spinning in place of the entire assembly.

Getting rid of the needless rotation in 2WD isn't the only benefit of a front hub conversion. Manually locking hubs also allow for bigger and stronger inner and outer axle shafts to be installed, and make it easier to repair and/or install front axle shafts in the event of breakage. Also, if you do break an axle, you can simply unlock the hubs and drive the vehicle home in 2WD to inspect the damage without the worry of exacerbating the problem. Other benefits include a reduction in steering drag, which can occur in vehicles with front locking differentials, and the ability to service parts within the hub, instead of having to replace the entire unit bearing assembly. Manual hubs also allow you to put off

Factory TJ front axles feature a unit bearing hub design that keeps the internal components spinning regardless of whether 4WD is engaged.

replacing a dented or slightly bent front driveshaft that might create vibrations at highway speed but functions as intended for low-speed wheeling.

There are a few things to consider if you see a front hub conversion in your future. For one, you'll need to replace the factory composite brake rotors with full-cast rotors. You'll also probably need new wheels, unless the center diameter of your existing wheels is large enough to clear the larger hubs. Most stock wheels will not work with an aftermarket hub conversion unless the center bore of the wheel is machined out (aluminum wheels only). Mile Marker and WARN offer TJ hub conversion kits in a variety of wheel bolt patterns. A 5 on 4½-inch bolt pattern is offered for those who want to retain the factory bolt pattern. A more common and stronger 5 on 5½-inch wheel bolt pattern kit is also available, and should be considered if that's what will match your swapped rear axle.

Full-Floating Rear Axles

Jeep TJs use differently configured axles for the front and rear applications. All of the rear axles are semi-floating units, while the fronts are full floating. The difference between the two lies with how the vehicle weight is distributed. In a semi-floating axle, the weight rests

The WARN Dana 30 front hub conversion replaces the factory unit bearing hubs with manually locking hubs. Driveline wear is reduced because the front driveline can be disengaged completely, which also improves flat-towing ability. WARN's high-strength outer axle shafts are made of 4340 nickel-chromium-molybdenum alloy steel, accept full-circle U-joint C-clips, and have a hardened shaft and yoke. (Photo courtesy WARN)

upon the outer ends of the axle shafts where the wheels bolt to the axle shaft flange. In contrast, a full-floating axle uses a spindle that bolts to the housing tube end flange, while the wheel bolts to a separate internally splined hub that spins on tapered roller bearings. This effectively redistributes the vehicle weight to the hubs and bearings instead of the axle shafts, which are already dealing with extreme rotational forces channeling engine torque to the wheels.

A full-floating rear axle also helps resist internal parts failure due to a bent axle housing, but the locking hubs will take a beating. Drive flanges might alleviate some of the stress from the bent housing, but may just transfer it to the axle shafts if they are misaligned in the drive flange.

Converting your stock rear axle to a full-floating assembly is a fairly easy proposition. WARN produces two full-float foundation kits for TJs that use either locking hubs or drive flanges. The kit designed for the stock TJ 5 on the 4½-inch wheel bolt pattern is not recommended for vehicles with tires larger than 32 inches, but a 5 on 5½ kit is also offered and can handle larger tire sizes without issue.

Ring-and-Pinion Gears

If your first planned modification to your TJ is to install larger-than-stock tires, then your second mod had better be to install different axle gears. The factory axle ratios are installed to achieve the best mix of performance and fuel economy in a stock vehicle with stock components. If you install bigger tires and don't change the gear ratio, the engine is forced to turn slower to move the vehicle the same distance. As a result, both fuel economy and acceleration suffers, as does the vehicle's off-road capability, which is the reason you installed the big tires in the first place.

The Jeep Wrangler TJ employed more than a few factory gear ratios over the years, primarily to accommodate various engine sizes and axle models. Stock ratios have included 3.07:1, 3.55:1, 3.73:1, 4.10:1, and 4.11:1. The 3.07:1 is the base model ratio for most TJs, with the exception of 4-cylinder models, which use a lower 4.11:1 gear ratio. The 4.10:1 and 3.55:1 offerings are oddball factory fitments that appeared in some of the early model year Wranglers. TJs equipped with the Trac-Lok differential and 4-wheel anti-lock brakes use a 3.73:1

Semi-floating rear axles can be converted to full-floating units that use locking hubs or drive flanges. The unit shown here is a Dana 44 equipped with a WARN Full-Floater Foundation Kit and drive flanges. Locking hubs are also an option. (Photo courtesy WARN)

An open differential, or even a limited-slip, will likely leave your vehicle wanting when ultimate traction is required to tackle a difficult obstacle. As you can see here, the rear Dana 35 in this TJ can't get power to the wheel that has traction and is left to spin the wheel that has none.

axle ratio, as do all standard Dana 44 axles. The 4.11:1 ratio is also used in Rubicon Dana 44 axles.

One thing to keep in mind when changing axle gear ratios is that differential carrier cases aren't designed to fit all ring-and-pinion gear ratios. This means that in order to increase or decrease a gear ratio, you may have to replace the carrier case if the ratio you desire is beyond your carrier's break point. Car-

Gear Ratio vs. Tire Size vs. RPM

Use this table to help determine what gear ratio will work best with your desired tire size. The numbers listed inside the table represent engine RPM and are shaded according to how the corresponding tire diameter and gear ratio will affect the vehicle's performance. The RPM values highlighted in black represent the ideal tire size and gear ratio combinations for achieving the best mix of fuel economy and performance/acceleration. The yellow shaded RPM values indicate which tire size and gear ratio offer better fuel economy with diminished performance, and the blue shaded RPM values are those that will increase performance and acceleration but at the cost of fuel economy. Also, remember that this table is only designed as a guide and that you shouldn't overrule real-world driving conditions. If you frequently drive in mountainous regions or carry or tow heavy loads, then you'll want to forgo fuel economy for more consistent performance/acceleration.

GEAR RATIO

TIRE DIAMETER	3.07	3.21	3.31	3.42	3.55	3.73	3.91	4.11	4.27	4.56	4.88	5.13	5.29	5.38	5.71
26	2579	2696	2780	2873	2982	3133	3284	3452	3587	3830	4099	4309	4444	4519	4796
27	2483	2597	2677	2766	2872	3017	3163	3325	3454	3689	3947	4150	4279	4352	4619
28	2395	2504	2582	2668	2769	2909	3050	3206	3331	3557	3806	4001	4126	4196	4454
29	2312	2417	2493	2576	2674	2809	2945	3095	3216	3434	3675	3863	3984	4052	4300
30	2235	2337	2410	2490	2584	2715	2846	2992	3109	3320	3553	3735	3851	3917	4157
31	2163	2261	2332	2409	2501	2628	2755	2896	3008	3213	3438	3614	3727	3790	4023
32	2095	2191	2259	2334	2423	2546	2669	2805	2914	3112	3331	3501	3610	3672	3897
33	2032	2124	2191	2263	2349	2469	2588	2720	2826	3018	3230	3395	3501	3561	3779
34	1972	2062	2126	2197	2280	2396	2512	2640	2743	2929	3135	3295	3398	3456	3668
35	1916	2003	2065	2134	2215	2328	2440	2565	2664	2845	3045	3201	3301	3357	3563
36	1862	1947	2008	2075	2154	2263	2372	2493	2590	2766	2961	3112	3209	3264	3464
37	1812	1895	1954	2019	2095	2202	2308	2426	2520	2692	2881	3028	3123	3176	3370
38	1764	1845	1902	1966	2040	2144	2247	2362	2454	2621	2805	2948	3040	3092	3282
39	1719	1798	1854	1915	1988	2089	2190	2302	2391	2554	2733	2873	2962	3013	3198
40	1676	1753	1807	1867	1938	2037	2135	2244	2331	2490	2664	2801	2888	2937	3118
41	1635	1710	1763	1822	1891	1987	2083	2189	2275	2429	2599	2733	2818	2866	3042
42	1596	1669	1721	1778	1846	1940	2033	2137	2220	2371	2538	2668	2751	2798	2969
43	1559	1630	1681	1737	1803	1894	1986	2087	2169	2316	2479	2606	2687	2733	2900
44	1524	1593	1643	1698	1762	1852	1941	2040	2119	2263	2422	2546	2626	2670	2834

(chart courtesy Superlift)

rier cases are designated as high-ratio and low-ratio cases, and you may have one or the other based on what gears your TJ came with from the factory. The Dana 30 low-ratio case accepts 3.55:1 and down (numerically), while the high-ratio case accepts 3.73:1 and up. Dana 35c low cases take 2.73:1 to 3.31:1 gears, and high-ratio cases take 3.54:1 and up. The Dana 44 low-ratio case uses 3.73:1 and down, and the high-ratio cases work with 3.92:1s and up.

Differentials

An open differential or carrier permits speed differentiation between the drive wheels as the vehicle makes a turn. This means that the wheels on the outside of the turn are able to spin faster because its path around the corner is longer than the inner tire. This works well on paved roads, but problems arise when one of the tires loses traction and all of the power is redistributed to that tire. The result is a vehicle with one tire spinning on a surface that never gains traction (such as ice, mud, or sand) and another tire sitting idle waiting for the other to grab. It's a pretty discouraging sight to see, especially when it happens to a "Trail Rated" Jeep Wrangler. But all such woes are easily conquered with the addition of a traction-aiding device such as a limited-slip or locking differential.

Available Aftermarket Ring & Pinion Gear Ratios	
Dana 30	**Dana 44**
3.07:1	3.07:1
3.54:1	3.31:1
3.55:1	3.54:1
3.73:1	3.73:1
4.10:1	3.92:1
4.56:1	4.10:1
Dana 35c	4.27:1
3.08:1	4.55:1
3.55:1	4.56:1
3.73:1	4.88:1
3.92:1	5.13:1
4.10:1	5.38:1
4.56:1	5.89:1
4.88:1	

The full-case Detroit Locker is just about the strongest locker option available. The locker senses torque and automatically locks to spin both axles at the same rate, but still unlocks when coasting through a turn. The locking and unlocking takes a bit of getting used to on the street, as vehicle handling is affected, but the rewards on the trail will be great.

ARB Air Lockers are an absolute blessing to any axle. The push-of-a-button nature of these lockers is ideal for any 4x4, and more than likely led to the inception of the Wrangler Rubicon air-actuated lockers. Setting up these units is a bit more labor intensive since you need to drill a hole in the housing for a copper air line to pass through. With proper maintenance, you should enjoy years of trouble-free use.

Limited-Slip Differentials

A limited-slip differential (LSD) provides greater traction than an open differential using clutch packs that press together to lock the axle shafts together.

The factory LSD is the Dana Trac-Lok, which uses friction discs to lock the spider gears, but gear driven units, such as the Detroit Truetrac, are also available. LSDs are also often referred to as "posi-traction" or "posi," after the Chevy factory LSD.

Lockers

Lockers are a completely different story. With a locker, both wheels turn all the time, so as long as one wheel has traction, you're going places. This makes them the end-all-beat-all of traction devices for the trail. For this same reason, however, lockers are not the best choice for front axles since they can seriously affect steering and handling as they lock and unlock. This isn't to say that lockers aren't widely used in front axles under many 4x4s, just that care should be taken in learning to drive your vehicle after a front locker is installed. If you must run a locker in front, the issues can be minimized by unlocking manually locking hubs.

Lockers are categorized as automatic and selectable units. Automatic units, such as the Detroit Locker, are designed to keep both wheels in a constant drive mode, but also allow wheel speed differentiation when required. Under power, a Detroit Locker supplies 100 percent of the torque to both drive wheels, but it unlocks once you let off the gas, allowing the outer tire to turn faster.

Another type of locker, called a "lunchbox" locker, simply consist of replacement spider gears and springs that install in the stock carrier without removing it from the axle housing. Lunchbox lockers are the quickest and easiest method of obtaining improved traction, but do so with less efficiency and strength than a full-case LSD or locker. Examples include the PowerTrax Lock-Right and the Detroit E-Z Locker.

A selectable locker, such as the ARB Air Locker, can be locked and unlocked pneumatically. When not engaged, the ARB acts like an open differential, but at the push of a button the spider gears are locked together so the axle shafts turn at the same rate. ARB Air Lockers work incredibly well in both front and rear applications. Other selectable locking differentials include: the Detroit Electrac and the Eaton E-Locker, which are both electrically engaged; the OX Locker, which is cable-activated; and the Teraflex T-Locker, which is air-actuated. Note that Rubicons come with selectable lockers straight from the factory.

Spools

Other locked options include spools, mini spools, and welded differentials. Spools and mini spools lock the axle shafts together and do not allow any

Available Lockers and LSDs

Lockers	Applications	LSDs	Applications
Teraflex T-Locker	Dana 30, 35c, 44, & 60	Powertrax No-Slip	Dana 30, 35c, 44, & 60;
ARB Air Locker	Dana 30, 35c, 44, & 60;		Ford 8.8 and 9 inch;
	Ford 8.8 and 9 inch;		Chrysler 8¼ inch
	Chrysler 8¼ inch	Detroit Truetrac	Dana 30, 35c, 44, & 60;
Detroit Locker	Dana 30, 35c, 44, & 60;		Ford 8.8 and 9 inch
	Chrysler 8¼ inch	Auburn Gear	Dana 44; Ford 8.8
Lock-Right	Dana 30, 35, 44, & 60;		and 9 inch;
	Chrysler 8¼ inch		Chrysler 8¼ inch
Dana Powr-Lok	Dana 30	PG Powr-Lok	Dana 44 & 60
Eaton E Locker	Dana 44 & 60; Ford 8.8 inch	Dana Trac-Lok	Dana 35 & 44
Detroit Electrac	Dana 44 & 60		
E-Z Locker	Dana 30, 35, & 44;		
	Ford 8.8 and 9 inch		
OX Locker	Dana 30, 35, 44, 60; Ford		
	8.8 inch		

wheel differentiation—ever. A spool replaces the entire stock differential, while mini spools install inside the stock carrier and replace the spider gears in the same manner as a lunchbox locker. A welded diff, or "Lincoln Locker," is made by welding the stock spider gears and side gears together.

All three of these more-extreme options result in greatly improved off-road traction, but the street driving characteristics leave a little to be desired. These options should be reserved for those vehicles that are dedicated trail machines that see limited or no street use. Spools, mini spools, and welded diffs are not recommended for front axle applications.

Differential Recommendations

Each of the types of LSDs and lockers discussed here alter the manner in which your vehicle steers and handles both on the street and on the trail. LSDs have less effect, but may still be noticeable as the tires grab when gaining and losing traction. Automatic lockers are much more noticeable, particularly in front axle

applications. The first thing most locker users notice is that the tires chirp when cornering. This means your locker is working properly. Since it's designed to not allow wheel speed differentiation like an open diff, the chirp is the sound of the inside tire slipping as it tries to turn the same speed as the outside tire, which is turning faster and covering more ground. Tire chirp is just the beginning of the many new sounds you'll hear after installing an automatic locker. They can be very harsh and noisy during operation and you're likely to hear loud clunks from time to time when the gears come together under power to lock the axle shafts. Selectable lockers have very few of these affects since they are only locked when you want them locked. When the situation calls for it, you can push a button to lock the axles and then push the button again to unlock the axles after the need has passed. Selectable lockers are great in this respect but they're often more expensive and require a more involved installation than a traditional locker or limited slip.

Axle Swaps Ideas

It isn't hard to beat the stock TJ axles. Sure, the rear Dana 44 option and Rubicon Dana 44 axles are plenty stout for stock, but for those with stock or even upgraded Dana 30 and 35c axles, you're going to feel the pain from time to time. Just because Jeep decided to install these axles doesn't mean you have to keep them. Yes, a Dana 60 is an option. But a variety of other viable axle swap candidates also exist. As I've pointed out, the Dana 30, Dana 35c, and even the TJ Dana 44 have their weaknesses. That's why your best bet may be to consider swapping for one of the available direct-fit or near-direct-fit axle assemblies.

One phrase you'll hear a lot in researching axle swaps, or any swap, is "bolt-on," as in "it bolted right on without a problem." While many aftermarket components designed for the Jeep TJ are bolt-on, that isn't always the case when swapping in a Ford Explorer rear axle or a Jeep Cherokee front axle. You'll have issues such as track width, brake parts compatibility, suspension mounting configuration, axle orientation, pinion and caster angle, wheel bolt pattern, and ring-and-pinion size, to name a few. Problems will certainly arise and require a remedy before the new axles will fit your rig and function properly. Most of these issues won't be a big deal if you're purchasing custom axles, since they can be set up for your vehicle, but if you're looking for a used unit to swap, take heed.

Wheel bolt pattern will come up a number of times as you upgrade your TJ, both in aftermarket wheel selection and as you consider an axle swap. Jeep TJs use a 5 on 4½-inch wheel bolt pattern, which is considered somewhat small. Conversion kits are available to switch your TJ to the more common and preferred 5 on 5½-inch pattern. The available donor axle assemblies often use a this bolt circle, which will require different wheels than your stock pattern. This means that if you swap the rear axle and not the front you'll have to carry two different pattern wheels for spare tires.

Differential offset is another important factor to consider. The TJ uses front axles offset to the driver side and rear axles with the center section slightly offset to the passenger side. This means that you're limited to axles that share this configuration, unless a transfer case swap is also part of your plan.

Other items to keep in mind are brakes, driveshafts, and suspension bracketry. A handful of companies, such as Mountain Off-Road Enterprises (M.O.R.E.), offer laser-cut suspension brackets that are ready to weld onto the axle tubes. You will, of course, have to ensure that the brackets are properly placed, but most 4x4 shops can handle it. Driveshafts will likely need to be replaced when swapping in a new axle assembly due to length variance and pinion yoke size, but you usually end up with heavier-duty equipment as a result. If the donor axle is already equipped with brakes, you may be able to modify them to function with the TJ braking system. Otherwise, a number of companies offer complete

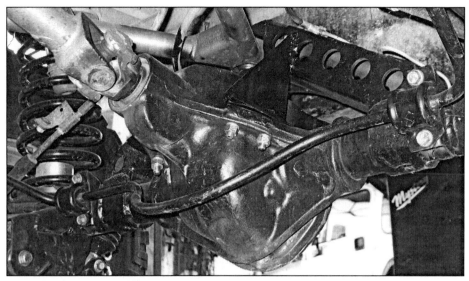

Having axles built for your rig doesn't have to be a difficult proposition. Find a reputable 4x4 shop that has experience building axles for Jeeps with coil suspensions. Ensuring that the proper suspension brackets are placed accurately on the axle tubes is paramount to maintaining the correct suspension geometry, or broken parts will result. The custom Dana 60 shown was built by Tri-County Gear in Pomona, California.

brake conversion kits, such as the Ford Explorer disc brake kit designed for Jeep TJs, available from Currie Enterprises. Lastly, note that larger or heavier-duty-than-stock differentials take up more space under your vehicle and also require more space for the suspension to fully cycle while off-road. Make sure you combine your axle swap with a proportionately sized suspension lift so that hefty new front axle won't be stuffed into the oil pan.

While performing an axle swap may be an easy proposition for some people, it's still a very involved process and requires a fair degree of mechanical skill and knowledge to complete. For example, axles of different widths may have to be widened with spacers or narrowed by cutting the axle tubes. Before beginning an axle swap, make sure you do your homework and talk to a few professionals or seek advice from someone who has completed the same or similar type of swap. By ironing out the details and knowing exactly how to set up your new axle before you begin, you'll make the conversion a much simpler and quicker

process. The following is a list of popular swap candidates.

Cherokee XJ High-Pinion Dana 30 Front Axle

The Cherokee XJ shares its front suspension configuration with the TJ. This makes its high-pinion Dana 30 front axle a perfect swap option, since all of the correct mounting brackets are already properly placed and the wheel bolt pattern and the track width are the same. The high pinion is desirable because the pinion is located above the center line of the axle. This provides a better driveshaft angle and keeps it away from rocks, but it's also much stronger for front axle applications than low-pinion assemblies because of how the gears mesh as the vehicle moves forward. You may also hear this axle and other high-pinion units called "reverse-cut" assemblies. This refers to the direction of the spiral cut in the ring gear, which is opposite of the standard-cut, low-pinion units. The gear sets used in high-pinion and low-pinion axles are not interchangeable.

The high-pinion Dana 30 front differential from a Jeep Cherokee is a great fit in the TJ.

Another benefit of the Cherokee high-pinion unit is that it uses shims for the pinion preload, as opposed to the crush sleeves used in the TJ low-pinion Dana 30. The shims last longer and make the assembly more durable. Also, if you've already equipped your TJ Dana 30 with all of the upgrades, you can easily swap all of these components (except ring and pinion) over to the high-pinion Dana 30. The strongest version of this axle is said to be from '95½ through '97½ Cherokees.

Cherokee XJ Chrysler 8¼-inch Rear Axle

Another viable Cherokee axle swap candidate is the Chrysler 8¼-inch rear axle. It came in the '91-and-up Cherokees without ABS and is also used in the Jeep Liberty. Though it still uses C-clips to secure the axle shafts in the carrier, it's a much stouter assembly than the Dana 35c. The more beefy '97-and-up units offer 29-spline, 1.21-inch diameter axle shafts and 3-inch diameter axle tubes. This isn't as easy a swap as the XJ front axle since the Cherokee uses leaf springs in back instead of coil springs like the TJ, but it can be swapped with the proper suspension mounting bracketry from your stock axle or from the aftermarket. However, the brakes cross over and the offset is the same. This axle is sufficient for light to moderate wheeling using 33- to 35-inch tires, but still doesn't offer the strength of the Dana 44.

Dana 44

The Dana 44 just keeps getting stronger as the aftermarket continually develops new products to increase its capability. One of the latest innovations is the advent of 35-spline inner axle shafts and locking diffs to match. Also, a multitude of upgrade options, including a broad range of gear ratios and locking differentials, are available for this axle. This alone gives the Dana 44 a much greater edge over other TJ axle swap candidates. It can provide nearly the strength offered by a Dana 60 but with a lighter weight and easier fit. Installing Dana 44 axles in the front and rear of a TJ offers enough strength for most vehicles running up to 37-inch tires.

Many versions of the Dana 44 exist. Jeep has employed this axle since the 1950s and it has appeared in Jeep CJs, Wagoneers, Jeepster Commandos, J-trucks, Cherokees and Comanches, Willys Wagons and trucks, and the TJ. Jeep Grand Cherokees use a version of the Dana 44, but it features an aluminum housing and isn't very desirable. Dana 44 axles can also be found under a variety of GM, Ford, and Dodge vehicles. The easiest Dana 44 axle to swap into a TJ is one from another TJ. However, the Jeep Cherokee and Comanche model rear Dana 44s are also great options since the track width is dead on and the wheel bolt pattern also matches. The Comanche Dana 44 is a particularly good find because it's said to use thicker axle tubes.

A number of companies now offer complete front and rear Rubicon Dana 44 axles, which are an easy-to-swap axle option. There are stronger Dana 44 assemblies than the Rubicon unit, but this is offset for many by the Rubicon's ease of installation.

Other Dana 44s also work, but require further modifications, particularly to the front axle. Of these other model 44s, the high-pinion units found in '70–'76 Ford F100s and F150s and the

A Dana 44 is a great upgrade for the factory Dana 30 front axle. The easiest method of swapping this axle is to use a factory housing designed for the Wrangler Rubicon since it already has the proper suspension brackets and you can use the outer axle shafts and knuckles from the Dana 30. The units shown here are Rubicon Dana 44s.

low-pinion units in '80–'86 Jeep Wagoneers are good front axle candidates. Your options are broader with the rear axle since you don't have to worry about steering, and many rear Dana 44s use a center offset. However, most of the Dana 44 axles you'll come across are wider than TJ axles, so modifications will be necessary.

Ford 8.8-inch Rear Axle

The Ford 8.8-inch rear axle out of the Ford Explorer is a very popular swap. The '95-and-up Explorers offer the best versions of this axle, featuring disc brakes and 31-spline, 1.31-inch axle shafts. The Ford 8.8-inch axle also uses 3.25-inch diameter axle tubes, has a similar track width and offset to the TJ, and has the same 5 on 4½-inch wheel bolt pattern. However, you do lose a bit of ground clearance with the 8.8, and it's not a bolt-in install by any means, requiring suspension mounting brackets. The key selling point behind the 8.8-inch is the price—a disc brake-equipped assembly can be found in a salvage yard in the $500 range. This is another axle that works great for turning up to 35-inch tires on moderate to extreme trails.

Rock Jock high-pinion 60 front and rear axles from Currie Enterprises are constructed from SAE 206-T6 aluminum castings and offer a full 60-degree cover angle, providing them with the lighter weight and ground clearance of a smaller axle.

The Dynatrac Pro Rock 60 high-pinion axle offers all of the greatness of the company's Pro 60 but with more ground clearance than a Dana 44. These axles can be used for front or rear applications and offer a tremendous degree of strength.

Ford 9-inch

The Ford 9-inch semi-floating axle is a very good swap candidate for TJs. Even in stock form, these axles are prepared for abuse and are ideal for up to 37-inch tires. Many versions of this axle were produced and most have 3.0 x 0.250-inch axle tubes and use either 1.19-inch diameter, 28-spline axle shafts or 1.33-inch diameter, 31-spline axle shafts. The 9-inch axle also features a removable third member/carrier, which eases ring-and-pinion setup since the entire carrier can be pulled and serviced on a workbench. You can find a 9-inch axle in a salvage yard, but don't expect it to bolt right in. The typical adjustments to track width, wheel bolt pattern, brake system, and suspension component bracketry still need to be carried out. These axles can be built for both front and rear applications. Also, like the Dana 60, the Ford 9-inch has served as a launching pad for aftermarket axle housing manufacturers and is constantly redesigned and improved-upon in areas of strength, ground clearance, and functionality to be one of the best off-road axles available. Currie Enterprises is one of the premier resources for Ford 9-inch axles and offers a variety of axle packages designed for TJs to handle moderate to extreme usage.

Dana 60

The Dana 60 is simply one of the best available axle swap options and can effec-tively prepare your Wrangler TJ for the extreme and beyond. It's the end-all, beat-all axle for strength and durability, and if you're building it yourself, it's not that much more expensive than any of the other viable swap options. This axle is typically found in ¾- and 1-ton GM, Dodge, Ford, International, and Jeep trucks and uses a 9.75-inch ring gear. Most Dana 60 axles offer 3.125 x 0.313-inch axle tubes and 1⁵⁄₁₆-inch diameter, 30-spline axle shafts. Some heavy-duty models are even equipped with 1⅓-inch, 35-spline axle shafts, but unless you intend to keep the axles full-width, you'll likely be ordering new axle shafts when you shorten the housing, anyway. The selection of after-market components and upgrades for the Dana 60 axle is vast and goes as far as massive 40-spline axle shafts that should definitely withstand any and all carnage you throw its way. Both standard and reverse rotation, and semi-floating and full-floating Dana 60s are available. Another key feature of the Dana 60 axle housing is that it is constructed from nodular iron, which is much stronger than the standard cast iron of most axle housings.

Custom Axle Assemblies

By far the easiest way to obtain heavier-duty axles in your TJ is to buy custom, ready-to-bolt-in units and either install them yourself or have a shop do the work. Though this can get expensive fast, you'll know exactly what you're getting and will have an excellent resource for troubleshooting and repair if issues do arise. Many companies and shops specialize in building custom axles and offer direct-fit units already equipped with the proper suspension mounting brackets, brake setup, and whatever gear ratio, locker, or axle-strengthening upgrade you may desire.

Beyond simply utilizing a factory Dana or Ford axle housing, many companies have also developed specialized axle housings to better withstand the abuse that extreme 4WD trails often dish out. Dynatrac, for example, offers its Pro Rock 60 high-clearance axle housing, which was originally designed to withstand the carnage of competition rock crawling. The Pro Rock housing is a nodular iron high-pinion unit that offers a 30-percent increase in ground clearance and features a unique dual-sump, high-pinion oiling system. The Pro Rock 60 also has extra webs cast in the housing for greater rigidity in supporting the pinion. Dynatrac also produces custom Pro 44 axle assemblies for both front and rear TJ applications. Other performance axle housings are available from TeraFlex, Currie Enterprises, Crane High Clearance, and Rockcrusher, to name a few.

COIL-SPRING SUSPENSION

It's all about suspension and the Wrangler TJ knows plenty about it. The coil suspension under Jeep TJs offers an impressive on-road ride and excellent flexibility on the trail.

Jeep has never been reluctant to produce multi-talented, useful vehicles. The Willys MB was the first to establish this tradition, serving multiple tours of duty fighting for its country. During that time it was a troop transport, an ambulance, an amphibious vehicle, an off-road hero, and whatever else soldiers asked it to be. The Wrangler TJ maintains this tradition with greater off-road capability and on-road ride and handling than the Willys MB ever offered. This is due to the Wrangler TJ's coil-spring suspension, which, in my opinion, is this vehicle's greatest attribute. It lends more off-road capability than any other vehicle component or assembly, and it's what sets it apart from the leaf-sprung Jeeps that preceded it.

Stock Suspension

Jeep marketed the TJ's Quadra-Coil 4-link suspension, which essentially means that it uses four coil springs. However, other important components work with the coil springs to complete a durable, efficient suspension system. All Wranglers, including Rubicon and Unlimited models, use this same 4-link coil suspension configuration.

The coil springs are in place to maintain the proper vehicle ride height and ride quality and are mounted between the axles and the frame. The coil springs have a number of advantages over the traditional leaf spring arrangement, including being lighter weight and having the ability to be tuned more precisely. Rubicon models use a slightly taller coil spring to help clear the 31-inch tires, as well as to accommodate its heavier gross vehicle weight rating (GVWR). The Unlimited uses longer rear control arms, but otherwise uses all of the same components.

The suspension's "links," or control arms, connect the frame and each axle and control the up and down motion of the suspension. The control arms are mounted on rubber bushings to diminish road noise. Control-arm travel is limited by the bump stops when under compression and by the shocks when fully flexed. The bump stops are mounted in the upper portion of the coil spring buckets on the frame and stop suspension compression upon making contact with the lower spring bucket on the axle. Shocks are mounted at each corner of the vehicle between the frame and axle. Besides their usual job of dampening the suspension's up and down movement, they also limit suspension droop. The front shocks mount with a bar pin through an eye at the lower mount and use a stud at the top. The rear shocks have eyes at both ends and use a bar pin at the upper mount and a bolt at the axle.

The track bar is another extremely important component of the TJ's suspension design. The TJ uses one at the front and one at the rear of the vehicle, and both secure between the axles and the frame to control lateral or sideways suspension movement. The front track bar is mounted to the frame rail using a tie-rod-style ball-joint end, and a rubber bushing at the axle end. The rear track bar is mounted on rubber bushings at both ends.

The final major suspension components are the front and rear sway bars. These are designed to keep body roll to a minimum in turns. The sway bars are mounted on rubber isolators to the upper portion of the frame rails and extend downward where they are secured by brackets on the axle tubes. You can get some increased axle articulation by disconnecting the front and rear sway bars from the axles, but they should be reconnected before returning to the pavement.

Big Tires = Mas Macho

There's more than one method to lifting a TJ. There are also a lot of different reasons to do so. Some simply want a mild tire-size increase to get them down their rain-mangled dirt driveway safely, while others are after 40-inch mud chuckers so they can dig big holes in volcanoes. Whatever lift you desire, there's a way to get it done, from using available

aftermarket kits to having a shop custom build a system to suit your needs. If you have the skills, you might even create a lift kit on your own.

Which Lift is Right for Your Rig?

There are all kinds of things I could tell you about what lift is right for your rig, but I'm still not going to tell you which one to buy. I'm not trying to be a jerk or anything, but telling someone how much they should lift their rig is like telling them what style underwear to buy. I don't know you and I don't know what makes you comfortable. Do you like stepping into your Wrangler from ground level without straining? Or do you like grabbing the roll bar and heaving your body up and into the driver's

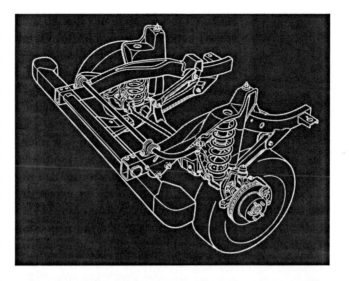

The 4-link front suspension components include coil springs, shocks, upper and lower control arms, bump stops, a track bar, and a stabilizer bar. The steering components are also crucial to an efficiently operating suspension system. (Photo courtesy DaimlerChrysler)

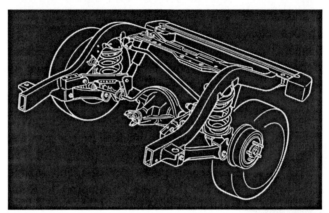

The TJ's rear suspension also features a 4-link design. The Wrangler Unlimited employs slightly longer rear control arms. (Photo courtesy DaimlerChrysler)

Front and rear track bars are part of the TJs coil suspension. Both are employed to locate the axles beneath the frame while controlling their side-to-side movement. To the lower left is an extended track bar and support bracket from Full-Traction.

Yes, I said it, big tires = mas macho. But that doesn't mean you should be stupid about it. If you want your rig to look like a monster truck, that's one thing, but if you see yourself realistically driving around and taking on trails, stop dreaming about tractor tires and start thinking 35 inch. Okay, 40-inchers tops, but you better be able to back up those 40s like a competitive rock crawler.

Many Wrangler owners get by on 32- to 33-inch tires just fine with only minor issues scaling obstacles. They might have to back up a few times or try a different line than the TJs rolling 35s, but most simply adapt to their vehicle's capabilities.

seat? That's one difference between stock height and a 6-inch long-arm system. My dad loves Jeep Wranglers and has been just shy of buying one for years, but he won't drive my 2001 Sport because it sits on 37-inch tires and he just can't climb in comfortably. I still

have a bit more leap in me, though, so it doesn't bother me so much. But I'll tell ya, sometimes it's a rough entrance.

Now that we've established that I won't be picking out your undergarments, it's time for you to ask yourself a few questions. How do you use your TJ—what type of terrain and how often? Is it a daily driver? What level difficulty of trails do you hope to traverse? Are you a beginner, intermediate, or expert driver? What size tires do you desire? What is the maximum tire size you may eventually install? How much money do you have? What size lift do you want? That last question was a trick question, but if you answered it you can probably move on to the next section.

Okay, you answered the questions above. Now I'll break it down again by repeating the most important one: What size tires do you want? The most common answer is 35s. You know, bigger is always better. But that isn't always the case when it comes to lifting a TJ. I've seen many a Wrangler happy and capable on 33s. Hell, even 31s—look at the Rubicon if you need further proof. Fact is, you can set up your TJ with any ol' tire size you want if you build the rest of the vehicle to pick up some of the slack. Lower gearing in the axles and the transfer case both aid in pushing larger-than-stock tires. Installing a limited-slip differential or a locker also helps a vehicle in navigating off-road obstacles no matter the tire size, but it's especially helpful for smaller tire-equipped vehicles that require additional traction for scaling over obstacles taller than, well, 31 inches. Installing a set of performance shock absorbers also improves suspension capability by keeping the tires on the ground where they can get some traction.

Body Lifts

When it comes to deciding on a lift kit, you'll essentially run into two

The Jeep Rubicon is a great example of how a Wrangler can be equipped with 31-inch tires and be ready to rock.

choices: body lifts and suspension lifts. A body lift is just like it sounds—it lifts the vehicle body off the frame. The kit comes in a small box and the first thing you'll think is, "how the heck is this going to help me?" The box usually contains a whole set of taller-than-stock body mounts and a bunch of longer body bolts. Some kits add spacers to the stock body mounts. Both methods do the trick.

There are other steps besides just slapping on the tall mounts. Depending on the lift size, you'll need to tweak your shifter linkages since they'll be further away from the transmission and transfer case. The radiator shroud and other engine components may require relocation as well. Most companies offer additional kits to remedy these issues, such as lifted motor mounts and shifter linkage lowering plates, so it isn't a huge problem. Ultra-tall body lifts also leave an obnoxious gap between the body and the frame rails and are most visible above the rear tires. The nasty gaps can usually be covered up by extending the factory splash guards that are installed between the body and the frame.

I'll warn you, there are body lift naysayers out there, and I was one of them for a long while. But when it came to fitting 37-inch tires where I was barely fitting 35s, that 1-inch of extra fender

Engine lift blocks are necessary to bring the engine up to the same height as the body when installing a body lift. This is because the engine mounts to the frame and the radiator and fan mount to the body. Tri County Gear and other companies produce engine lift blocks.

Body lift kits include new body mounts and bolts. Some kits use spacers and the stock body bushings.

clearance made all the difference in the world. Body lifts have their place, even on my TJ, so don't be discouraged if one of the nitpickers points a finger at you and laughs because you wanted bigger tires and didn't spring for the full suspension kit. You'll get there if/when you want to—and you'll already have that extra inch you'll need to stuff 37s.

Suspension Lifts

Suspension lifts are where it's at. Like I said, body lifts have their place, but suspension lifts raise up your Wrangler while also increasing off-road performance. Suspension systems are broken down into a few categories. Some are simply designed to increase vehicle ride

height while doing little to increase spring flex or axle articulation. Most of the budget-boost kits fall into this group. Other systems include taller springs of varying spring rates along with the minimum amount of components to effectively add a few inches of useable lift to accommodate an increase in tire size and slightly increase wheel travel. Still others are more complete and come with most everything else you need to lift your TJ correctly.

Coil Spring Spacers

Coil spring spacers are a good way to go to achieve a moderate degree of lift. The spacers are usually made from polyurethane and are offered in 1¾-inch and 2-inch lift heights. Leveling spacers in ¾-inch heights are also offered for the front springs to correct the way the front end sits lower than the rear. Coil spring spacers fit between the top of the coil spring and the spring tower and essentially move the coil spring downward to create more vertical clearance. Coil spring spacers allow use of a larger-than-stock tire but don't increase flexibility to a great degree. They are used widely as a starter lift for many TJ owners but also serve as a permanent means to fitting taller tires or to gain just a bit more clearance so you don't destroy your fenders and flares every time you compress the suspension. Coil spring spacers are also typically accompanied by longer shocks.

Partial Lift Systems

Plenty of folks are solely after the bare minimum when it comes to installing an aftermarket lift. If the ability to fit larger tires is the only goal, other handling and performance considerations are often overlooked. While partial lift systems are a good means of achieving the desired stance, they do leave something to be desired—namely, the rest of the suspension system.

Basically, the partial kits are marketed as "entry-level" systems and most

A number of manufacturers offer coil spring spacer lift kits in varying sizes, like this one from Daystar. The most common size is 2 inches to fit a 31-inch tire.

A partial lift system typically consists of the bare minimum components necessary to lift a TJ. This Rubicon Express kit includes coil springs, extended sway bar links, a track bar drop bracket, front upper shock conversion brackets, and body spacers. (Photo courtesy Rubicon Express)

offer the ability to upgrade to more advanced systems at whatever pace you and your wallet can handle. Most of these kits simply contain lifted coil springs, extended bump stops, front and rear extended sway-bar links, and a track bar relocation bracket. Some also include a drop pitman arm, brake line extension brackets and/or extended front brake lines, new shocks, a rear track-bar relocation bracket, an adjustable front track bar, replacement lower control

A complete lift system usually offers all of the components needed to lift your Wrangler. Getting a complete setup saves you the trouble of adding the other stuff later on.

Adjustable Control Arms

Why adjustable control arms? Because they allow you to tailor the length of the arm to best fit your application. This doesn't mean that you set it to whatever length you want, but rather that you set it to the lift manufacturer's recommendations. After all, they're the ones who did all the testing on the product so they should have a good idea as to how the kit should be installed. By adjusting the arm length, you can dictate how the axle moves as the suspension cycles. The longer the arm, the further rearward the axle is moved upon suspension compression. A longer arm also slightly increases wheelbase. A shorter arm moves the axle forward upon compression and shortens the wheelbase. Remember, the control arms must be installed and adjusted as a set and the lengths should be consistent with the arm on the opposite side. Adjustable arms are used with both short and long-arm systems.

Sway Bar Links and Disconnects

Extended sway bar links are included in pretty much every kit that warrants their use. Sway bar disconnects aren't always part of the deal though. You'll want to disconnect the front sway bar if you plan on traveling on moderate to extreme trails, where the extra suspension travel will come in handy. You don't necessarily have to use the "discos" manufactured by the company that makes your lift, either, as they all pretty much do the same thing. Most quick disconnect setups do not require tools, which is a big advantage over the stock parts.

A few companies produce active sway bar systems that never need to be disconnected, but still help control body roll. Currie Enterprises offers its Anti-Rock sway bar that uses two arms that attach to the stock sway bar mounts on

arms, and a transfer case lowering kit. This list varies greatly from one manufacturer to the next, so make sure you get a breakdown of what each kit contains before money exchanges hands. Partial lift systems typically max out at 2 to 3½ inches and allow up to 32-inch tires.

Complete Lift Systems

If you're truly committed to having your TJ handle as well on the trail as it does on the highway, then you'll be shopping for a complete lift system. I highly recommend a complete system if it's in your price range. There's simply no comparison to properly outfitting your vehicle the first time around. Two types of complete suspension systems are available for Jeep TJs—kits that use standard length or "short" control arms and those that use longer control arms. Complete kits usually include everything you need to lift your rig and maintain the factory handling characteristics as well. That means you get pretty much everything I mentioned above, in addition to a full set of fixed length and/or adjustable standard-length control arms. Adjustable arms typically provide a better ride and allow improved fine tuning of the suspension. Fixed arms are usually a bit cheaper and are best utilized in lower arm applications along with an upper adjustable arm. All of the available systems that utilize long control arms are adjustable. Other complete suspension system items often include an extended rear brake line, sway bar disconnects, an adjustable rear track bar, and front cam alignment bolts.

Most complete lift systems include adjustable control arms (top). Fixed-length arms are also offered and are best used for lower arm applications. A stock control arm is shown on bottom.

Most suspension systems use a track bar relocation bracket to reposition the rear track bar, causing extra stress on the factory mount on the axle. Tri-County Gear designs a rear track bar brace that features an arm that extends to the diff cover for added strength.

Tri-County Gear builds a track bar relocation kit that situates the track bar in front of the steering components and adds a brace to the frame mount that extends to the passenger-side frame rail. The lower mount extends forward from the axle tube and incorporates a skid plate to protect the Heim joint.

the front axle using steel rods with Heim joint rod ends, and rotate on a single torsion bar that fits through the front crossmember. Custom kits are also available for rear applications. One of the neat things about the rear setup is that you can preload the sway bar to correct the TJ's proclivity to squat to the passenger-side rear upon acceleration. The front end can also benefit from preloading. Teraflex and Off-Road Only also produce active sway bar systems for TJs.

Slip-Yoke Eliminators

SYE kits are a necessary item that some manufacturers package with their lift systems. If you've read Chapter 5, you know the stock rear output on the transfer case uses a long slip yoke to bolt to the rear driveshaft. The long slip yoke requires a short rear driveshaft, which quickly exceeds its maximum operating angle with even the smallest lift. The slip yoke can present quite a few problems, including driveshaft vibration, while your lifted TJ is flexing on the trail. Some lift manufacturers remedy this issue by providing transfer case drop-down brackets, which basically lower the transfer case so it's more in line with the rear driveshaft. This works for shorter lifts, but if you plan on going taller than 2 to 3 inches, an SYE kit is an absolute necessity. According to TeraFlex, vibration isn't as big an issue in TJs equipped with the 2.5L engine and they advise that the T-case lowering kit can be left off when installing their 3-inch kit. However, they do note that if vibration occurs, the lowering kit should be installed. See Chapter 5 for more info on the transfer case.

Short-Arm vs. Long-Arm Lift Systems

If you've heard anything about aftermarket TJ suspension systems, it most likely had something to do with long

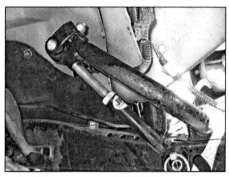

JKS Mfg. was one of the first companies to offer sway bar disconnects, but now most lift manufacturers offer their own designs and often include them with their complete lift systems. These JKS discos are unhooked and secured out of the way.

The Currie Anti-Rock sway bar system controls body roll on- and off-road and does not have to be disconnected to achieve maximum suspension articulation.

control arms. Since the introduction of the first long-arm suspension systems, "long arm" has become a TJ suspension buzzword, and everyone has an opinion on why these kits do or don't work. In my experience, they do work—very well, I might add. Long-arm systems, like lift systems with standard-length control arms, increase wheel travel and suspension flex. However, standard-length, or

A slip-yoke eliminator (SYE) is designed to replace the factory slip yoke at the rear of the transfer case so a longer driveshaft can be used to decrease the driveshaft operating angle. SYEs are essential for bigger lifts.

Short-arm lift systems are a good way to increase vehicle flex and create space for 33-inch tires.

short-arm lift kits can often limit wheel travel relative to a long-arm setup, especially with greater tire size. This is because as tire size increases so does the angle at which the control arms are forced to operate. Severe control arm angles create binding issues that limit the suspension's capability. This isn't to say that short-arm kits are a bad way to go, just that you can overdo it with tire size. This is why most short-arm kits max out at 4 inches, which is realistically only tall enough for 33-inch tires. Some lift manufacturers say you can stuff a set of 35s under a TJ with a 4-inch kit, and I've seen it done many times. But other lift manufacturers, and I agree, recommend only a 33-inch tire with a short-arm system. Any bigger and all that extra wheel travel just gets stuffed in the fender.

As with most things Jeep, there are exceptions to this short-arm rule. Some companies use control-arm drop-down brackets or offset control arms to achieve more lift and fit 35-inch tires. And of course, a 4-inch kit mated with a body lift creates enough space for 35s as well. But remember that just because you can fit them, doesn't mean you should. With 35-inch tires installed under a short-arm TJ, the vehicle's center of gravity is raised drastically, making off-camber

Long-arm suspension systems offer a great increase in wheel travel and vehicle flex and allow 35-inch and taller tires.

sections an even tippier affair. The fenders will likely wrinkle and the flares will fold in after repeatedly stuffing the tires into the fender wells, and the ride will also be a bit stiffer. Front wheel lift on sharp turns can be another issue when short arms are mixed with ultra-tall springs. Also, short-arm kits tend to have squat issues during steep vertical climbs. The rear wheels like to move forward upon suspension extension or droop, which shortens the vehicle's wheelbase

as it climbs. These issues and handling characteristics are all shared by the factory suspension setup and are partially inherent to its design. Some of the effects are much more noticeable after the installation of taller-than-stock tires.

Though I've listed a lot of negative issues regarding short-arm suspension systems, they do have a good deal of positive attributes. First off, when accompanied with the proper tire size, they offer tremendous performance on and off road,

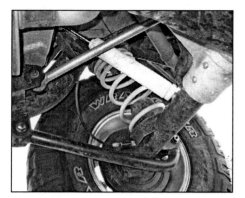

Currie Enterprises' J-Arm system represents a unique approach on the short-arm suspension design. The J-Arm provides a leverage advantage since it remains as parallel to the ground as possible by relocating the lower arm rear mounts to the rear of the axle tubes. I've seen this system in action on the company's competition TJ and watched it shatter many of the long-arm equipped TJs. The system also triangulates the rear, thus eliminating the track bar.

Short-arm lift systems like this are more easily installed than long-arm kits, which usually require a good deal of cutting and welding of the factory setup before installation can begin.

with increased flex and wheel travel from stock. These types of kits are also not as expensive as long-arm systems and their installation is much less labor intensive. Short-arm kits are also typically a more neutral suspension than long-arm systems, and they offer a good degree of mechanical traction without a lot of tire spin.

Long-arm suspension systems do a great job of maintaining the factory handling characteristics, since control arm angles are kept to a minimum. Some kits even offer an improvement over the stock ride, even with 37-inch tires. Long-arm suspension systems use a new centered crossmember to serve as an attachment point for the new longer control arms. The crossmember is also designed to support the transfer case and act as a skid plate.

Long-arm lift systems eradicate many of the negative issues associated with short-arm systems, and they also allow for much larger tires. But these benefits don't come without a price— the biggest being the actual cost of these systems. They aren't cheap by any means, but you have to consider what you're getting out of the deal. Maximum suspension articulation is one big plus, even when running 37-inch tires. Long-arm systems also mimic the factory ride and handling characteristics very closely since the long control arms better maintain the angles of the stock control arms. This is achieved by reducing the angles at which the long arms sit in relation to the chassis. The control-arm frame attachment points are relocated to a new centered transfer-case crossmember to accommodate the longer arms. A variety of Heim and flex-type joints are used to secure the arms to their attachments

Long-arm and some short-arm suspensions use Heim or flex-style joints at the control arm attachment points. These style joints are easily rebuildable and are also serviceable using the installed grease fittings.

points, which offer yet another bonus in that these joints are greaseable and typically provide an ample service life.

Issues for Lifted TJs

Pinion Angle

Pinion angle is the angle at which the pinion gear sits in relation to the driveshaft. It is the difference, represented in degrees, between pinion gear centerline and driveshaft centerline. Factory pinion angle is typically set around 1 to 1.5 degrees.

When you lift a Wrangler, essentially everything is lifted except for the axles (they do get short rise in elevation from taller tires), and every thing that's attached to the axles is forced to work at steeper angles than it's accustomed. This includes the driveshafts, control arms, track bars, drag link, brake lines, shocks, etc. Not surprisingly, most of these components make up the list of necessary swap items when installing a lift.

High-pinion axles reduce the working angle of the driveshaft and also keep it higher out of the way of rocks and obstacles. The maximum operating angle for a single U-joint driveshaft like those used on stock TJs is 3 degrees. A CV driveshaft actually offers a lower maximum operating angle, but since the pinion is adjusted to point directly at the transfer case output, the U-joint at the axle end can rotate at zero angle. For this reason, CV driveshafts are recommended for tall lifts where steep driveshaft angles are necessary.

Pinion angle can be adjusted using adjustable upper control arms. You should adjust pinion angle after installing a CV driveshaft or driveline vibration will occur. Pinion angle also affects driveshaft angle. A CV driveshaft calls for different phasing than a non CV, two-joint driveshaft. On a two-joint driveshaft, the centerline of the pinion and the transmission should be parallel. But when a CV driveshaft is installed, the pinion should be directly in line with the driveshaft. A CV driveshaft offers smoother operation at higher operating angles for longer life than conventional two-joint driveshafts, but a higher pinion angle must be maintained since a CV requires minimal joint operating angle. The more lift you install, the more you will have to adjust the pinion angle to maintain proper driveshaft alignment.

An angle finder with a magnetic base is helpful in establishing the proper pinion angle. First, find a spot on the driveshaft where the angle finder will sit flat and determine driveshaft angle from horizontal. Remove the driveshaft from the axle end and place the angle finder on the face of the yoke to find pinion angle from horizontal. The difference between the measurements will give you the pinion angle

Rear pinion angle has more adjustability than the front pinion angle since the front pinion must also maintain geometry of the steering arms. Having the pinion too high will tilt the front of the steering arm downward while adjusting it too low will have the opposite effect.

Longer upper adjustable arms allow the pinion to be rotated up or down. If the pinion angle is less than the driveshaft angle, then the upper arms can be lengthened to rotate the pinion upward. If you have a pinion angle that is too high, you need to shorten your control arms. If the pinion angle is adjusted up so high that the pinion gear and bearings don't receive any lubrication, it will cause over-heating and eventual parts failure.

Stock control arm users can install Rubicon Express TJ cam bolts at the rear upper arms, which allow for pinion-angle adjustment for proper driveline phasing (putting pinion and driveshaft at same angle). These bolts can create 2 to 3 degrees adjustment and are a cheap alternative to installing adjustable upper control arms or installing a high-pinion axle.

Steering Geometry

You'll get more of this in Chapter 8, but in short, the steering linkage includes steering gear mounted to the driver's-side frame with a pitman arm that connects to the drag link, which leads to the passenger-side steering knuckle. The tie rod leads off of the driver's-side steering knuckle and connects to the drag link just before the knuckle to create a scissor-shape linkage. The steering linkage may be forced to operate at extreme angles because of a lift, which causes stress at the system's weak points and can result in breakage. Steering issues can result in lifted TJs if steps aren't taken to prevent damage.

Next time you're standing next to a stock Wrangler TJ take a look at how the drag link and tie rod are sitting at static height. You'll notice that both are sitting parallel or near parallel to the flat ground beneath the vehicle. This is how these steering components should always sit in order to maintain proper steering geometry. When a TJ is lifted, the taller coil springs put the steering gear

Issues for Lifted TJs CONTINUED

and pitman arm further away from the axle, which forces the drag link and tie rod to sit at an increased angle to the ground. This affects steering response. It can also create wheel/tire scrub in turns, since the incorrect angle of the steering arms won't allow the inside wheel to follow a smaller radius than the outside wheel.

Lift manufacturers address this problem with a drop pitman arm, which is basically a longer pitman arm that extends to the point where the stock pitman arm would normally attach to the drag link in a non-lifted TJ. It also reduces the angle of the drag link and decreases bumpsteer. Drop pitman arms are available in different drop

heights. A 1.25-inch drop pitman arm is recommended for TJs with 1.5 inches of lift or more, while a 3-inch arm is best for TJs with 5.5 inches of lift or more.

When you install a drop pitman arm, you need to pair it with a track bar drop bracket. The track bar is also part of this equation and must maintain its position parallel to the tie rod and drag link. Most lift manufacturers address the track bar geometry using a drop-down bracket designed to position the front track bar frame mount lower. Another method is to replace the track bar with a longer adjustable track bar. An adjustable track bar is recommended in TJs with 4 inches of lift or more.

Unlike short-arm systems, long-arm systems' flex isn't limited by the length of the control arms or binding. Rather, the shocks limit travel at extension and the springs and bump stops halt the suspension compression. This abundance of flex is highly noticeable in a long-arm-equipped vehicle, not only evidenced by the addition of larger tires, but also through the increase of seemingly unrestricted axle and wheel articulation. I've seen long-arm TJs drop a coil spring from its perch before maxing out the available linear travel offered by the control arms. In these cases, a shorter shock could have been employed to avoid such a situation, but it goes to show the capability and possibilities that long-arm systems offer.

Operating a long-arm-equipped TJ on- and off-road for the past six years, I've come to discover a good deal about how this type of suspension handles in a variety of situations. For the most part, all of my experiences have indicated that long-arm systems are superior to short-arm systems. In addition to the benefits I explained above, long-arm systems also offer that decidedly "cooler" and more aggressive image that many Wrangler TJ owners desire. Remember, I'm not trying to take anything away from the benefits offered by short-arm TJ lift systems. Short-arm kits provide the majority of

Wrangler TJ owners with the added capability and increased tire size they're seeking and do so at a much lower cost. But you get what you pay for, and you will not regret splurging on a long-arm system for your Wrangler TJ.

Triangulated Rear Suspension

Triangulated 3-link rear suspension conversions are one of the more recent additions to the TJ aftermarket suspension lineup, and are becoming an

increasingly popular means of further increasing rear wheel travel. The 3-link setup gets rid of the two rear upper links and replaces them with one tri-angulated suspension link that has two attachment points at the crossmember and a single attachment point on top of the rear axle. The axle mount more-often-than-not pivots on a high-misalignment Heim joint. Suspension bind in the rear track bar is eradicated by eliminating its use altogether. True up and down wheel travel is increased as a result, which makes for less rear end squat during vertical climbs.

The Rubicon Express Tri-Link Kit eliminates the rear track bar to enhance wheel travel. On-road tracking is also improved. The kit offers a bolt-on installation for factory Dana 35c and Dana 44 rear ends.

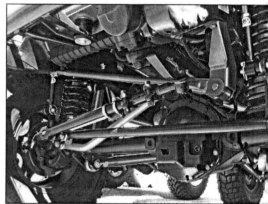

Full-Traction Suspension offers its Ultimate 4.0 lift system designed to clear 33-inch tires. The kit is bolt-on and includes a triangulated rear upper link that rides on a high-misalignment Heim joint.

Poly Performance's coil-over shock systems use coil-over hoops and include all the necessary brackets and hardware. They use 2-inch diameter, 14-inch travel shocks. (Photo courtesy Poly Performance)

The Fabtech Motorsports High Clearance Crawler suspension system features a coil-over conversion option that uses the company's Dirt Logic 2.5 remote-reservoir coil-over shocks.

Coil-Over Shock Systems

Some aftermarket suspension systems are designed to use coil-over shocks in conjunction with the link suspension. Using coil-overs gives you a more extreme degree of axle articulation and greatly improves the vehicle's off-road ability. Coil-overs replace the factory coil springs and shocks and instead use a larger-bodied shock with a built-in coil spring wrapped around the length of the shock body. Some coil-over shocks also utilize a remote reservoir to cool the shock fluid, though not all remote reservoir shocks are equipped for coil-over use. Those that are have a threaded shock body so threaded rings can locate the coil spring in place. Coil-over shocks determine vehicle ride height by using the adjustors to either compress or extend the shock and spring assembly.

A variety of coil-over shock systems are available for TJs, including kits from Poly Performance and Fabtech Motorsports. The Poly Performance kit was the first of its kind and it continues to evolve from its original design. Two versions are now available. The first requires the stock coil and shock tower attached to the driver and passenger side frame rails to be removed. The assembly is replaced with a new shock hoop that allows you to use a 2-inch diameter, 14-inch travel, remote reservoir, coil-over shock. The system also uses 4-inch stroke air bump stops and includes the necessary mounting hardware. The second Poly Performance kit leaves the factory spring towers in place to retain use of the factory bump stops. The stock shock tower is removed, however, and replaced with the company's coil-over bracket kit, which accepts 2-inch-diameter 12- or 14-inch remote-reservoir coil-overs. Both systems are reinforced by a crossmember that extends over the top of the engine and bolts to a bracket at the backside of each upper shock mount. Poly Performance also recently developed a rear coil-over kit.

Fabtech also produces a coil-over shock lift system for TJ front ends. The kit uses a new shock hoop that extends upward into the inner fender to accommodate a longer travel shock. Both the Poly Performance and Fabtech systems must be used in conjunction with a long-arm suspension system. Fabtech requires use of its own long-arm system in order to maintain proper lift geometry, but the Poly kit can be used along with both the Rubicon Express and Full-Traction long-arm systems.

Selecting the Right Shocks

Believe it or not, all shocks are not created equal. Luckily, however, most lift manufacturers have made things easier by including a properly sized set with each lift system. Manufacturers also typically have a number of shock upgrade options above and beyond the base-model units offered with their kits. Even so, you're free to explore any of the other styles available from the many shock manufacturers.

When choosing a shock for your Wrangler, you'll again need to ask yourself how you use your vehicle the most, since some shocks are better suited for one type of driving over another. I've tried quite a few of the available styles and can tell you for certain that there is a difference between them.

Hydraulic Twin-Tube Shocks

The base model shocks included with many lift systems are often hydraulic twin-tube shocks. These units work well under normal conditions but are more susceptible to fading as they heat up under use in harsh terrain. The twin-tube design makes this shock dissipate heat less efficiently since the outer tube acts like an insulator for the inner shock tube. As the shock heats up, air in the shock tube mixes with the fluid and causes foaming to the point that the fluid can't cycle through the piston at the necessary rate. This occurrence, also called "cavitation," ultimately reduces the damping action of the shock.

Many shock manufacturers reduce fluid foaming by using cellular gas or cellular foam, which is essentially a gas bag or foam cell that takes the place of the air. This method serves well where lighter damping is required, but heavier-duty use still leads to cavitation.

Twin-tube shocks run the risk of being dented by rocks or other obstacles during trail use, which might damage the inner tube and inhibit proper damping. Twin-tube shocks are also directional, meaning they will only operate in one position, usually indicated by a stamped arrow on the shock body.

I've had varying degrees of success with twin-tube shocks from one brand to the other, but in general the "good" ones

Skyjacker Softride Hydro series shocks are twin-tube hydraulic shocks.

did a decent job of holding up on the trail, only experiencing fade after a good amount of repetitive abuse. My highway experiences using twin-tube shocks have also been acceptable.

Pressurized/Gas-Charged Shocks

Shock manufacturers easily remedy the issue of cavitation by pressurizing the shock with nitrogen gas to the point that the shock fluid can't release air and cause foaming. Both low-pressure and high-pressure shocks in twin-tube and mono-tube designs are available to suit a variety of needs. Low-pressure shocks typically have 100 to 200 psi, while high-pressure units have 250 to 400 psi. Driving situations that include rapid and continuous rebound and compression shock cycles, such as hitting a whoops section in the desert or barreling down a washboard gravel road are best attacked with higher-pressure shocks. Low-pressure units fare well under trail use and produce a sound road ride as well.

I've used many different sets of gas-pressurized shocks over the years, again with varying results. I won't likely make the return to non-gas-charged dampers. The on-road ride quality is much better using gas-charged shocks and you're not as likely to run into any shock fade.

Mono-Tube Shocks

A mono-tube shock uses a single pressurized, fluid-filled tube. The single tube won't hold in heat like a twin-tube shock, but is capable of holding higher internal pressures. As a result, most race-style shocks use a mono-tube design. Mono-tubes have also proven to be my favorite style shock for the TJ. Since shock pressure varies from one manufacturer to the next, it can be difficult to

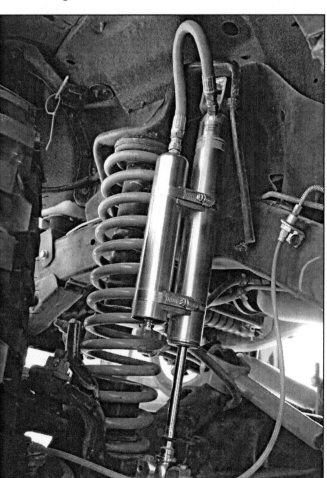

Bilstein 7100 Series shocks are gas charged and use a mono-tube design with a Schrader valve and dividing piston. They feature a 2-inch body and are available with or without remote reservoir.

Quick Lift Guide

As I previously pointed out, the best lift for you comes down to personal preference. But since you're reading this and looking for some advice, here's a general guide to get you started. I'll start with the inexpensive setups and get pricier as I break it down.

Option One

Start small if you are on a budget. 31-inch tires will fit with a bit of fender trimming. A body lift will also give you additional tire clearance, but try to keep it under 33s if you go this route because your TJ will start looking pretty goofy going any bigger. Add a set of sway bar disconnects and you'll be in business. Sway bar discos should be on your list from here on up.

Too much body lift can present transmission and transfer case shifting issues. Besides, it looks pretty kooky. Do yourself a favor and don't be this guy.

A mild body lift, like these 1-inch aluminum spacers from Tri-County Gear, is a great way to achieve some extra clearance and fit larger tires.

Option Two

"Budget boosts" are your next option. They usually consist of a set of 2-inch coil spring spacers and often include a set of longer shocks. Toss in a 1-inch body lift, and you comfortably have space for 32-inch tires, but 31s offer more space to stuff the tires and reap the most benefit from this type of lift.

Option Three

The Adjustable Coil Over Spacer (ACOS) from JKS Mfg. is another spacer option that works well on stock or lifted TJs. It's adjustable and allows fine tuning of suspension height to accommodate added weight or sagging springs, or to level the vehicle. The ACOS has 1¼-inch lift built in, so you'll be raised up a bit just installing them, and it's said to be infinitely adjustable after that, so the sky's the limit. You're still looking at 31- to 32-inch tires with the ACOS kit, but it's a neat option because you'll never need to get rid of them. You can keep them with taller springs if and when you upgrade.

Adjustable Coil Over Spacers (ACOS) from JKS Mfg. can be adjusted while on the vehicle by loosening one bolt and turning the adapter ring. ACOS are available for both front and rear applications.

Option Four

An entry-level suspension lift with new coil springs and shocks and other items comes next on the tire up-sizing train. These 2- to 3-inch kits are cool because they're easily upgraded with a set of control arms and even taller springs should you elect to go bigger. New lower control arms are also a popular add-on to this kit. Most entry-level systems offer space for 31- to 32-inch tires.

Option Five

A full suspension lift (of around 4 inches) with all-new short, adjustable control arms permits up to a 33-inch tire. Some kits fit 35s when mated with a body lift, but beware of severe control arm angles and expect a stiffer ride than with 33s.

Quick Lift Guide *CONTINUED*

Replacement control arms are usually a heavy-duty option with entry-level lift kits. They're much stronger than stock arms and some makes are even greasable.

Option Six

A 4-inch or higher long-arm suspension system offers the greatest degree of lift and permits use of the tallest tires. Kits are available to fit 33-, 35-, and 37-inch tires. It's an awesome way to go if tough trails are on your agenda.

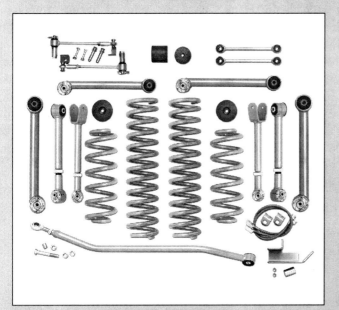

A full short-arm lift kit, like this one from Rubicon Express, includes all new control arms as well as all of the necessary components to maintain the proper suspension and steering geometry. (Photo courtesy Rubicon Express)

Option Seven

Triangulated rear suspension arms are an add-on to most long-arm systems and even to a few short-arm kits. This option won't get you much bigger tires than you already have, but wheel travel and thus off-road capability will increase.

Option Eight

For those looking for the true extreme setup, a coil-over shock system should do the trick. Some of the available kits create clearance for 37-inch and even taller tires. Coil-over systems tackle anything on the trail, but aren't as ideal for daily commuting because of their high price.

Off-road handling is at its best in a long-arm equipped TJ. Long-arm kits include all the stuff for proper installation. The plates shown with this Rubilon Express long-arm system comprise the new crossmember, transfer-case skid plate, and suspension mounts. (Photo courtesy Rubicon Express)

Option Nine

A final option is one that involves the most labor-intensive installation and a fair share of troubleshooting once installed. Air suspension systems use air bags instead of coil springs to control ride height and feel. These systems can be finely tuned to function very well on Wrangler TJs and even have the ability to force articulation to a single wheel by inflating that air bag until the tire can make traction.

narrow down what works best for your Wrangler. That's where rebuildable mono-tube shocks, such as those available from Bilstein, come into play. These shocks can be finely tuned through shock valving and piston size to achieve a desired result. Bilstein and other manufacturers have even taken a lot of the guesswork out of it by doing the testing on their own TJs and preparing shocks with a valving range that meets the needs of most TJ owners. However, if you have specific ideas on what setup will work best for your vehicle, Bilstein can also build shocks to suit you.

Adjustable Shocks

For those looking for the best of all worlds in respect to shock damping ability, an adjustable shock is a great option. A few designs exist, with some doing the adjusting internally while others use an external valve-altering knob to allow the user to adjust from one setting to the next. The Rancho RS9000 was one of the first off-road shocks to offer external adjustability. It now features nine shock settings ranging from soft to hard, and

Shock conversion kits from JKS Mfg. convert the front upper shock mount to accept a shock with an eye mount rather than a stud. This permits use of additional shock sizes and can increase suspension droop by more than 1 inch.

kits are even available to alter the damping of each shock individually using dash-mounted switches. Rancho also produces its RSX Reflex shock, which features an impact-sensing valve that tunes the shock automatically to suit the road conditions at hand. Other shock manufacturers have released similar adjustable shock designs, including Edelbrock and Explorer Pro Comp.

Shock shifter brackets from Nth Degree Mobility resituate the upper and lower rear shock mounts to create more ground clearance and to get rid of the troublesome upper bar pin mount.

Remote Reservoir Shocks

Remote reservoir shocks are widely used on off-road racing vehicles to enhance shock cooling. Since repetitive cycling heats up the shock fluid, the extra reservoir allows the shock to have a greater fluid capacity, which results in more efficient cooling to help the shock operate consistently and not succumb to heat fade. These style shocks are typically rebuildable and can be fine tuned

Suspension Tips

It's a good idea to replace the factory control arm bolts when installing an aftermarket lift kit. Many lift manufacturers do not provide new bolts with their kits and the factory bolts tend to become stripped or sheared in half over time. Use Grade 8 hardware for best results. Don't forget to use thread sealer—I've lost nuts off the control arm bolts more than a few times.

If you think your shocks are blown, they probably are. If you have the means to remove them and want to do a quick test to see how much jounce they still have, you can push the piston in and out of the cylinder a number of times to check for smoothness. If the action of the compression and rebound strokes is smooth and consistent, then the shock may still have a bit of

life. But since the shocks are already off the vehicle, you're halfway there and you might as well replace them anyway. Keep the good used shocks around though. You never know when you may need a spare in a pinch.

Stock upper control arms are prone to bending so you should consider checking them periodically. If you're still running a stock suspension then you might check with your local 4x4 shop to see if they have any straight sets of arms lying around. Most shops that work on Jeep TJs usually have quite a few after swapping them out for aftermarket equipment. Replacement factory control arms are also available from Jeep dealerships and other parts vendors.

The bump stops on my TJ tend to get pretty chewed up after being mashed into the bump stop plate over and over again. If they get too chewed up, you'll want to replace them before you blow a shock or rip off a fender.

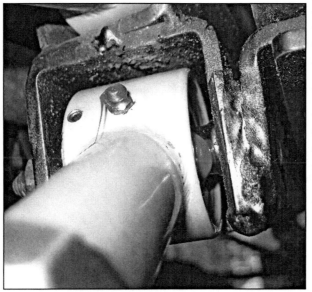

If you've installed adjustable control arms equipped with grease fittings, then you'll want to invest in a grease gun with a flexible attachment so you can lubricate the joints on a regular basis. I use a gun and kit from Green Grease that's a bit smaller and easy to fit in to tight spots.

to meet the needs of your vehicle's suspension system. Remote reservoir shocks are available in many sizes but the most common size for TJ applications use a 2-inch shock body and ⅝-inch piston rod.

Shock Extras

Once you have the right shocks for your TJ, you can use a couple different mounting methods. The factory mounts use bar-pin mounts at the front lower mount and the rear upper mount. The front shock uses a stud-style mount at its upper attachment point and the rear lower uses a simple eye mount. With the exception of the rear lower mount, all of these mounts leave something to be desired. The front upper stud mount limits the selection of shocks because longer travel shocks are usually only available for eye-style mounting. The stud mount can also bore out the mounting hole if the bolt comes loose. The factory bar-pin mounts emit a good deal of shock noise after a while as the pins wear out the center of the shock bushings. My biggest reason for disliking the bar pins is that the rear upper bar pins are a serious pain in the ass to deal with. If you've ever installed a set of rear shocks on your TJ, you know what I'm talking about. Getting a socket on the bolt heads is near impossible and getting the bolts in place without stripping the holes is another story. The

rear shocks are also situated rather awkwardly inboard on the axle tube and can be difficult to seat in the mounts without raising or lowering the axle.

JKS Mfg. offers solutions to all of these issues with a variety of products. Bar-pin eliminators and adapters replace the factory bar pins with heavier-duty units that allow the shock bushing to function more effectively by filling the eye loops completely with heavier-duty bar pins. The rear upper mounts can also receive bar-pin eliminators, which makes shock installation an easier process. The bar-pin eliminators are also offered as bar-pin adapters to allow mounting of shocks with Heim joint ends. JKS also produces shock conversion brackets that change the front upper shock mount to accept an eye mount shock.

Suspension Maintenance

The factory suspension components are a plug-and-play sort of deal. Since most of the attachment points utilize rubber bushings, lubrication isn't necessary and you pretty much just run them until they're worn out and then replace them. In fact, you'll likely shorten the bushing life if you do lubricate the bushings, since grease and oil-based lubricants like to eat rubber. Most of your

suspension maintenance comes from maintaining other vehicle components, such as the steering system and wheel alignment, to ensure that all of the vehicle components are operating in sync to achieve the best possible ride quality. This doesn't mean you shouldn't periodically inspect the suspension components for loose bolts, worn out bushings, bent control arms, or other issues, but the system itself is fairly easy to maintain.

For Wranglers equipped with aftermarket suspension, the suspension joints require the most frequent maintenance, especially if you hit trails on a regular basis. The control arm joints often feature Zerc fittings so they can be lubricated as often as necessary. I'd suggest a visual inspection of each joint after each wheeling trip at the very least, but keep the grease gun handy because you can always give it a pump on the fitting and you'll know right away if the joint is lubed or not by whether the grease purges out the sides or disappears inside the joint.

Control arm length shouldn't change on its own once it's set, but it's not a bad idea to check to be sure your arms are maintaining the proper lengths from time to time. If arm length has somehow changed, it could be an indication that another suspension component is bent or damaged.

The Bells and Whistles

Things to consider when creating a build sheet and calculating the cost of lift:

The installation of a slip yoke eliminator and CV driveshaft on the stock NP231J transfer case is recommended when installing a lift. It's an absolute requirement when lifting a TJ to use 33-inch tires or taller. The installation of a CV yoke and CV driveshaft on the stock Rubicon transfer case is also recommended when installing a suspension lift.

Most long-arm suspension systems require modification to the exhaust system. Some lift manufacturers, such as Full-Traction, offer pre-bent exhaust kits to function with their lift systems.

Skyjacker and other companies offer transfer case lowering kits to accommodate varying degrees of lift height. Spacers fit between the stock transfer case skid plate/crossmember and the frame rails.

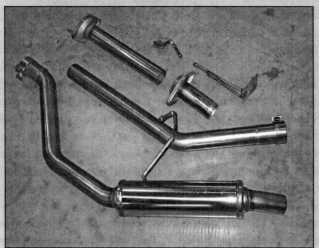

Full-Traction Suspension's Magnaflow exhaust systems offer a proper fit when installing a lift kit. The system shown is for the Wrangler Unlimited.

fit some tire and wheel combinations. The spacers will reposition the tires further outboard of the fenders.

Extended brake lines are a necessity when lifting a TJ more than 2 inches. You can usually get away with installing new front lines only, but after lifting 3 inches or more a new rear line is also recommended.

Transfer case lowering kits are included with many aftermarket lift kits with the exception of long-arm systems, which incorporate a new crossmember/skid plate to reposition and support the transfer case. The lowering kits help keep the driveshaft angles closer to stock.

You will likely need to trim the fender flares so as to limit damage that occurs once the suspension is compressed and the larger tires are fully stuffed in the fenders. Do a test run on your favorite rock pile to see where the tires rub and trim accordingly. Another option is to install a set of tube fenders for extra clearance and durability. Wheel spacers may be required to

Trimming the stock fender flares gives the tires a bit more clearance and saves their appearance. However, if 44-inch tires are in your future, you can plan on cutting up the fenders, too.

TJ STEERING AND BRAKES

Steering and brake systems remained somewhat consistent through the Wrangler TJ's production run. The steering system did receive a few updates through the years, but the overall design and setup remained the same. Power-assisted front discs and rear drum brakes were the standard brake fitment, but a number of factory brake upgrades were also available and were usually dealer packaged as part of a brake and traction group.

Steering System

All Jeep Wrangler TJs used a recirculating ball-type steering gear with a knuckle-under tie rod and drag link arrangement. The steering components include a steering wheel and column, steering shafts, a steering gear box, a power steering pump and reservoir, high pressure and return lines, a pitman arm, a drag link, a tie rod, and steering knuckles. Additional hardware items were also included in the system. A manual steering system was standard equipment until the 2000 model year when power steering was made standard.

Steering Ratio

Steering ratio is the number of degrees that the steering wheel must be

The TJ steering system is capable of handling up to 35-inch tires, but you can expect to bend a tie rod from time to time when tackling extreme trails.

turned to move the front wheels one degree. For example, a 15:1 ratio means the steering wheel can be turned 15 degrees to turn the wheels one degree. Final steering ratio is also determined by the steering linkage ratio, and is calculated using the length of the pitman arm and the steering arms on the knuckles.

Manual steering featured a 24:1 straight ratio in 1997, while the power system offered a straight 14:1 ratio. This broke down to roughly 5.1 turns from

---

lock to lock with a manual setup and 3 to 3.5 turns for the power system. The manual system remained consistent until discontinued, but in 1998, the still-optional power steering was offered with a variable 15-13:1 ratio that remained until 2003. This is to produce a quicker steering effect in the beginning of a turn and less steering effort as the wheels approach the steering stops. In 2003, the better Saginaw/Delphi steering gear was replaced with a unit made by ZF Gear with a 15:24 ratio.

Steering Gear

The TJ used two different steering gears, sometimes referred to as a steering box, over the years. The steering gears used in TJs before 2003 are Saginaw/Delphi units. Not much has changed to the overall design of the Saginaw steering gear since the introduction of the original Saginaw 800 Series in 1948. There are even parts in the original steering gears that are interchangeable with those used today. The TJ steering gear is a worm and recirculating ball gear. The balls in a recirculating ball system are ball bearings. It uses 50 ball bearings that circulate around the threads of a worm shaft inside a ball nut rack. Steering wheel motion goes to the steering shafts that lead to a worm gear shaft extruding from the steering gear. The worm-gear threads into the ball nut rack, which meshes with a sector gear that transfers the motion to the pitman arm. The ball bearings are in place to reduce friction, heat, and steering slop. GM pioneered this concept in 1940 at its Saginaw Steering Division in Saginaw, Michigan.

The ZF steering gear was introduced in 2003 model Wranglers, switching the steering system from a variable ratio to a constant ratio. Not surprisingly, this switch coincided with the purchase of Jeep by Daimler. ZF steering gears were used in most Mercedes passenger cars prior to the switch to rack-and-pinion steering systems. The ZF units are

Power steering became standard equipment on the Wrangler TJ in 2000. Jeep Wranglers used a recirculating ball steering gear made by Saginaw/Delphi from '97 to 2002.

From '03 to '06 TJs came equipped with a steering gear made by ZF Gear. A few differences are apparent, including the overall shape and the bolt pattern to the frame.

The stock 4.0L power steering pump, known as a TC-type pump, uses an external reservoir that clips to the pump body.

manufactured in India and offer a straight 15:24 ratio. There are many internal differences between the early and late-model TJ steering boxes and the two are not interchangeable. Both use a three-bolt mounting configuration, but the pattern is different, which is a helpful indicator should you receive the incorrect steering gear for your vehicle upon replacement.

Power Steering Pump & Lines

The TJ power steering pump is a vane-type hydraulic pump with a constant flow rate and displacement. This type of pump is also called a TC pump and is part of the steering system in many Chrysler vehicles. The pump is belt-driven by the crankshaft via a drive pulley pressed onto the pump shaft. Pump pressure is monitored by a pressure relief valve inside the flow control valve. The pressure relief valve is integrated into the high-pressure line fitting. On 4.0L engines, a plastic fluid reservoir is secured to the pump body with spring clips, but 2.5L- and 2.4L-engine-equipped Wranglers use a remote pump reservoir mounted to the fan shroud. A pressure switch is also part of the four-cylinder power steering systems. The switch is mounted on the high-pressure supply line and allows the PCM to monitor the steering system for incidents when load increases on the power steering pump at low RPM. In response, the PCM will turn up the idle speed via the Idle Air Control (IAC) motor to avoid engine stalling. An increased load on the power steering system may occur during tight trail maneuvering or even while navigating a parking space. Once the pump pressure decreases to an acceptable degree, the pressure switch closes and the previous idle speed is restored.

Both the 4.0L and 2.5L power steering pumps are rated at 1,400 psi and should produce a flow rate of 2.4 to 2.8 gallons per minute (GPM) at 1,500 rpm. Actual pump pressure varies with each

Power steering lines are routed between the power steering pump and the steering gear. Also shown is the pitman arm off the steering box leading to the drag link.

The stock steering linkage sits at the same angle as the track bar and should maintain this geometry for proper steering response. Keeping the correct steering geometry is essential for lifted TJs.

The steering wheel translates input to the steering gear through upper and lower steering shafts. U-joints are employed to mate the two shafts and the lower shaft has a support bearing mounted to a bracket on the frame rail (shown).

application and year and may also depend upon vehicle setup. Fluid lines are also part of the hydraulic steering system and include a high-pressure supply line and a low-pressure return. The high-pressure line moves fluid from the pump to the gear box, and the return line brings it back to the pump to loop the system. Power steering lines often deteriorate internally before they leak and can cause improper fluid flow if particles from the hose lining find their way into the pump valve and block or impede fluid flow. Adding an inline fluid filter can help avoid a disastrous situation. Old fluid can also decrease the performance of the steering system as it breaks down to a lower viscosity over time and can create sluggish steering in colder climates.

Use of the proper power steering fluid is crucial to a well-functioning steering system. Jeep recommends use of ATF+4. Synthetic fluids are another option, though they aren't manufacturer recommended. You should also keep an eye on the serpentine belt that drives the steering pump off the crankshaft. An old belt should be replaced, especially if it shows signs of age such as cracking or chipping.

Steering Linkage

The steering linkage consists of a pitman arm, drag link, tie rod, and steer-

Tie rod adjustment sleeves are used to set the toe and also to center the steering wheel.

ing dampener. Steering knuckles with steering arms are the final links between the steering wheel and the tires. The tie rod and drag link are set up in a scissor arrangement, with the drag link extending between the pitman arm on the steering gear and the passenger-side steering knuckle. The tie rod is secured to the driver's side knuckle and also bolts to the drag link. All of the drag link and tie rod connections use ball joint ends that must be greased periodically, and the steering knuckles connect to the axle tubes using upper and lower ball studs. The ball studs wear over time and can result in sloppy steering. The drag link and tie rod also feature adjustment sleeves that are used for toe and steering wheel alignment.

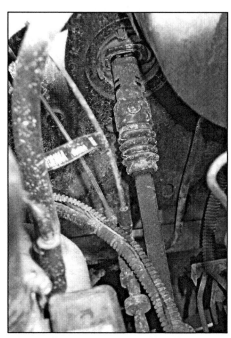

Here, the upper steering shaft passes through the firewall to connect to the lower steering shaft. The input to the upper shaft comes from the steering wheel.

Alignment

Having the proper alignment is paramount to an effective steering system and a safe-driving TJ. Assuming that your vehicle isn't plagued with any of the aforementioned steering geometry issues that can result in lifted TJs, obtaining accurate alignment isn't all too difficult. You will, however, need to know a few basic terms before you get started. Note that most people, including myself, typically have the complete wheel alignment done by a professional shop, but it's still a good idea to be familiar with the concept and terms.

Toe

An incorrect toe setting is one of the most common causes of poor steering response and uneven tire wear. Toe is visualized as the difference in the distances between the leading and trailing edges of the front tires. "Toe in" is when the distance between the centerline of the front of the tires is smaller than the distance between the centerline at the rear. Excessive toe in may produce a pigeon-toed appearance. "Toe out" is the opposite, obviously, and if set to the extreme it positions the front edges of the front tires further apart than the rear. Factory toe position specifications call for 0.15 degrees of toe in and allow for + or -0.06 degrees variance. Toe adjustment is one of the easier steps in wheel alignment. It can be completed by resetting the adjusters on the tie rod to lengthen or shorten the distance between the tie rod ends. Setting the toe is typically the final step in adjusting the wheel alignment, since it is affected by the caster and camber.

Caster

Caster is the vertical angle of the steering knuckle. It is determined by how far the front of the knuckle is tilted forward or rearward and is represented in degrees. Achieving the proper caster plays a large role in steering stability and also sees that the steering wheel returns to its center position after making a turn. Caster can be adjusted using cam bolts and rotating cams on the front lower suspension arms, and also by changing the length of adjustable control arms. Remember that caster angle also determines the pinion angle, as well as where the steering linkage sits in relation to the axle. Excessive caster in either direction can lower or raise the pinion beyond its maximum operating angle and also creates binding in the steering linkage. Alignment specifications for TJ Wranglers call for 7.0 degrees of positive caster with an allowable + or – 1 degrees of variance. Caster can be thrown out of whack by a bent axle housing or worn suspension bushings and steering-knuckle ball studs. The proper caster setting is often difficult to achieve in lifted TJs due to the low pinion front axles, but take note that the pinion angle takes priority over caster and that it should only be adjusted as far as the pinion angle permits.

Camber

The inward or outward tilt of the front tires is referred to as camber. An inward tilt (tops of the tires closer together than the bottoms) is expressed as negative camber, while an outward tilt is known as positive camber. On Wrangler TJs, camber is preset at the factory to –0.25 degrees plus or minus 0.63-degrees and is not adjustable. Incorrect camber typically results from a damaged steering component, such as a worn ball stud on the steering knuckle, and can be corrected by replacing the offending part. A bent axle housing can cause incorrect camber, among other alignment issues.

Steering Upgrades

The stock Wrangler TJ steering system is a very good area to invest time and money into if you intend to have a capable trail vehicle. Whether you consistently bend tie rods or simply desire more responsive steering, a myriad of aftermarket suppliers offer the equipment to take your TJ's steering system beyond its factory capability.

Performance Steering Gears

The Wrangler TJ is blessed with a very buildable steering system, particularly the early models that use the Saginaw/Delphi recirculating ball steering gears. The later model ZF steering gears aren't bad units for most TJ owners, but they aren't as preferred for performance applications. A handful of companies, such as PSC Motorsports, offer adapter kits to install the early Delphi steering gear in place of the ZF steering gear. This is largely due to the abundance of available parts for the Saginaw/Delphi gears, in addition to the many years of experience that the aftermarket companies have with modifying these model steering gears for performance applications.

Many aftermarket manufacturers offer quick-ratio steering gear boxes that decrease steering effort and create more responsive steering action. Quick ratio refers to the amount of turns of the steering wheel required to turn the wheels. Common quick ratio boxes are a 14:1 straight ratio compared to the 13-15:1 variable ratio of many factory steering gears. A 13-16:1 variable and custom ratios are also offered. PSC and others offer TJ performance steering gears. Most performance gears utilize a larger input shaft and a larger piston, and the cases are thoroughly machine surfaced as needed and Magnafluxed to check for cracks. Many of the flow circuits throughout the steering gear are also enhanced to tolerate an increased fluid flow rate.

The difference in steering characteristics between a performance-built steering gear and the stock unit is very noticeable, both on the road and on the trail. The effects are most apparent in big-tire-equipped TJs, but even those

Steering box skid plates are a great means of protecting the vulnerable steering gear from rocks and other obstacles.

rolling on 31s should appreciate the improved steering quality.

Rebuilding a steering box isn't something you do in your driveway. Don't necessarily trust your everyday mechanic to rebuild your steering gear, either. Most won't attempt it, which is good. Rebuilding a steering box should be done by trained professionals to achieve the best results. Typically a steering gear will be replaced with a new or rebuilt steering gear, with the old unit supplied as a core. Make sure you're getting the correct box for a TJ, since the gear could have a different or incorrect ratio or longer or shorter steering stops, all of which affect steering radius and create other issues. Other internal differences in steering gears are designed to offer varying degrees of power assist. If you get the wrong gear it could offer less power than your damaged steering gear.

Performance Power Steering Pumps

The stock power steering pump does an efficient job of circulating fluid through the hydraulic steering system, but once one element is changed, such as the addition of a high-flow performance steering gear, installation of a higher flowing pump is warranted. You have a couple of choices when seeking a performance steering pump. The first is to install a modified TC-type pump similar to that already installed on your TJ.

High flow TC-type power steering pumps such as those available from AGR Performance and PSC are modified to supply the necessary increased pressure and flow throughout the hydraulic steering system. PSC TC-type pumps create as much as 1,600 psi and move fluid at 4.5 gpm, compared to the 1,400 psi and 2.4 to 2.8 gpm offered by the stock TC pump. PSC also offers a billet power steering pulley that's smaller than stock and designed to create better low-RPM performance.

The next step up from a performance TC-type power steering pump is to use a P-type pump. Because they're larger, even in stock form, most P-pumps are capable of producing a higher flow rate than stock TC pumps. PSC and others offer kits to convert from the factory style TC power steering pump to a P-pump. Most kits require an adapter bracket and include most of the parts needed for the swap, including a P-pump, a remote-mount fluid reservoir, a new belt, fittings, and fluid lines. A P-pump swap is not a quick bolt-on affair, so allow some vehicle down time for installation especially if you're attempting it on your own. Due to the larger size of the P-pump, it also requires relocation of other under-hood items, such as the windshield washer reservoir and the radiator overflow bottle. You'll need to find space to mount the power-steering pump fluid reservoir, as well.

Improper power steering pump pressure affects hydraulic steering performance and should be monitored closely. Fluid temperature is also vital. If the fluid in your system consistently overheats then you may be over-straining the steering pump. A fluid cooler is one option employed by many with TJs turning heavy off-road tires. A fluid temperature and pump pressure gauge can also be installed for the overly concerned, but if you're still over-heating the system with all of the aforementioned components in place, it's time to break it down

The stock TJ tie rod typically breaks near the rod end along the threads, but sometimes it simply bends. Here, a bent tie rod and steering stabilizer cause the wheels to sit toe in. Larger tires are heavy and require more force to turn, which does stress the stock tie rod.

and inspect each component individually because one is likely to be faulty.

Heavy-Duty Steering Linkage

The steering linkage includes some of the most vulnerable components of the steering system. The linkage consists of a pitman arm, drag link, tie rod, and steering dampener. The tie rod and drag link are typically the biggest victims of trail damage since they reside at the front of the vehicle and are the first object to contact obstacles. Since a snapped tie rod or drag link translates into a complete loss of control, most automotive

A bent tie rod on the trail can sometimes be reshaped and sleeved for strength using a Hi-Lift jack handle. Note the bent steering stabilizer zip-tied to the track bar.

manufacturers design steering linkage to bend before it breaks, or bend to a degree anyway. Though I've witnessed a fair share of bent tie rods on the trail, I've seen just as many broken ones—usually along the threads of the tie rod end. Either way, you'll need to replace it.

The stock tie rod and drag link are constructed from hollow tube rather than solid stock, which is another reason why they fail. Though the stock setup is sufficient for stock vehicles that see minimal off-road use, it won't last long if you're slamming big off-road tires into rocks. Also, big tires and suspension lifts force the linkage to operate at excessive angles that affect the intended geometry of the system.

There are many methods of improving the stock steering linkage in your TJ and none of them are exactly cheap. Consider the cost of replacing the stock linkage after the third time, however, and price seems a moot point. Perhaps the least expensive method is to install a tie rod and ends from a '93–'97 Jeep Grand Cherokee ZJ equipped with a V-8. You'll also need the adjusting sleeves. The ZJ tie rod is made from solid stock and is much heavier duty. It's also an easy bolt-in swap to the TJ. You may find that the ZJ parts offer just a bit less ground clearance, but many find that the greater strength is worth the sacrifice. You will, however, still have to deal with the deficiencies of the stock drag link.

The tie rod from Grand Cherokee ZJ can be used in place of the stock TJ tie rod. The ZJ tie rod is solid stock and is much stronger than the TJ component.

Currie steering linkage is designed as a direct replacement for the stock setup. It's beefier than stock and has a 1.25-inch diameter solid tube with massive ball-joint tie rod and drag-link ends for a secure connection.

If you really want to extinguish any fear of trail breakage, replace the stock steering linkage with an aftermarket heavy-duty tie rod and drag link. Enough companies offer heavy-duty linkage for the TJ that it's a no-brainer install. As usual, some aftermarket steering linkage kits are better than others, so make sure the linkage you select comes from a reputable company. Currie Enterprises offers a beefy solid stock tie rod and drag link setup that also uses larger rod ends. The linkage also does a good job of maintaining the factory steering geometry. Rusty's Off-Road Products is another good source, as is Rock Krawler Suspension.

If you want to take things a step farther, there are a variety of crossover or high steering setups available to eliminate the factory scissor arrangement of the tie rod and drag link. Instead, the tie rod secures to both driver and passenger-side steering knuckles. The drag link is still fastened to the passenger side only and extends toward the pitman arm. Many of these systems, such as that available from TeraFlex, require a replacement passenger-side steering knuckle with a repositioned steering arm and tapered inserts. This is so the tie rod and drag link can install over the knuckle rather than below it. This setup creates increased ground clearance and moves these once vulnerable compo-

nents further out of harm's way. The TeraFlex kit is also designed to use Tera's heavy-duty 1½-inch aluminum tie rod and drag link, which are not only lighter than steel, but can also yield away from an obstacle when under pressure without bending.

Another option is the U-Turn crossover steering system from Off-Road Only. This system uses custom hubs that bolt to the stock steering knuckles and offer tapered mounts for a new heavy-duty 4130 chrome-moly tie rod and drag link. This is one bolt-on method of achieving a crossover steering system. Many 4x4 shops can also design and fabricate custom systems to meet your particular needs. Either way, you're sure to find that heavy-duty steering systems are not cheap.

A dropped pitman arm is often used to address steering linkage issues in lifted TJs. The overall steering ratio is altered upon installation and problems will arise if you don't take steps to address the position of the track bar. Most aftermarket suspension manufacturers take on this responsibility and supply the necessary components so that the factory steering geometry isn't too greatly altered. Along with a drop pitman arm, this is achieved through use of a track bar drop bracket so that the track bar remains parallel with the drag link. If these two compo-

The TeraFlex aluminum tie rod and drag link are designed to deflect away from rocks and then straighten once the pressure is released. The system requires the use of Tera's passenger-side high-steer knuckle.

A drop pitman arm (S-shaped arm) is used to alleviate steering linkage issues in lifted Wranglers.

nents are not mounted in a consistent plane, then an effect called "bumpsteer" may occur.

Bumpsteer is essentially when the vehicle steers itself without input from the driver. It typically occurs in vehicles with incorrect steering and suspension geometry where the suspension cycles further than the steering linkage can accommodate. Bumpsteer can create a dangerous situation to say the least, but it isn't too difficult to avoid. Maintaining a proper steering geometry is the easiest way to avoid bumpsteer. It can also occur due to worn or blown control arm bushings, but one of the biggest causes is a loose track bar.

One item to note: I haven't had a steering stabilizer installed on my daily driver '01 TJ for well over a year. Do I need one? Possibly. Has it worked just fine with minimal consequence? Bet your ass it has. I may have increased tire wear and likely caused an excessive degree of vibration in the steering linkage, but I haven't experienced the dreaded "death wobble" once. However, frequent alignment jobs after trail use are necessary in order to maintain acceptable street driving characteristics.

Cylinder-Assist Steering Systems

Cylinder-assist steering systems, also referred to as ram-type hydraulic assist systems, are very beneficial for those running big tires. A hydraulic cylinder mounts between the axle and the tie rod in place of a steering stabilizer and offers hydraulic assistance to the tie rod as it moves the tires. The power steering system already offers some degree of hydraulic assistance by improving fluid flow through the steering gear and decreasing steering effort at the wheel, but cylinder assist systems offer even more aid in turning big tires using a hydraulically operated dampener to move the tie rod from side to side. Power steering pumps, such as those available from PSC and others, can be modified to better accommodate a hydraulic assist setup. This is done internally by modifying the unit for optimum fluid flow. A high-performance steering gear is also required, as is a remote fluid reservoir to house the additional fluid that pumps through the complete system. Cylinder-assist steering systems do work well on many TJs, but proper setup of such a system is crucial to its performance. Both PSC and AGR offer complete cylinder-assist steering systems for TJs.

Full Hydraulic Steering Systems

Full hydro systems, in effect, do the same job as a cylinder assist system, but they eliminate a few of the regular steering components and take on the majority of the steering duties. Items not used in a full hydro system include the lower steering shaft, steering gear, and pitman arm. Instead, the steering column shaft secures to a hydraulic steering control box, and steering input is applied in fluid form to dual steering cylinder rams that turn the wheels. These setups get very expensive and should be reserved for those who have exhausted all other steering possibilities, and custom applications where traditional steering arrangements won't produce the desired steering force.

Aftermarket steering stabilizers are typically larger than the stock unit and are better prepared for increased vibration from larger tires and additional stress from maneuvering up and over obstacles.

Cylinder assist steering systems use high-pressure fluid from the power steering pump to help the tie rod turn the tires.

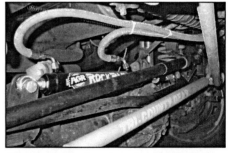

Many professional rock crawling rigs use full hydraulic steering systems. A cylinder-assist steering system is shown here mounted between the axle and the tie rod. A Tri County Gear relocated track bar is also shown.

Power-assist front disc brakes and rear drums were standard equipment on the Wrangler TJ. This setup is up to the task of stopping larger-than-stock tires.

Brake System

The standard equipment brake system uses power assist front disc and rear drum brakes. Four-wheel disc brakes were also offered as optional equipment when accompanied by a Dana 44 rear axle and Trac-Lok LSD. The system uses single-piston calipers and ventilated rotors. The drum brakes are dual shoe with cast brake drums. An Anti-lock Brake System (ABS) was also an option

Four-wheel disc brakes were available with the Dana 44 rear axle. They offer improved stopping power over rear drums and also dissipate heat more efficienty.

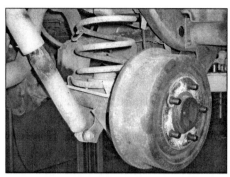

The rear drum brake setup is shown here with stock shocks and coil springs. Also note the 5 on 4½ lug nut bolt circle. The drums offer sufficient stopping power for TJs with mild lifts.

on the Wrangler TJ. In vehicles with automatic transmissions, ABS was always paired with a Trac-Lok limited-slip differential and a 3.73:1 axle gear ratio. ABS was available for both Dana 44 and Dana 35c rear axles and relies on sensors at each wheel for activation. Four-wheel disc and ABS were not offered on SE model Wranglers.

Other components of the Wrangler's brake system include a power booster, an aluminum master cylinder, a combination valve, a brake pedal, a parking brake, and brake lines. The master cylinder mounts to the brake power booster and features primary and secondary pistons that provide hydraulic pressure to the front and rear brakes. A nylon fluid reservoir is mounted to the top of the master cylinder. A combination valve with a pressure differential valve and switch, and a fixed-rate rear proportioning-valve are mounted beneath the master cylinder. Steel lines run between the combination valve and the master cylinder and also out of the combination valve to the front and rear brakes. A brake hard line runs along the driver's side frame rail to the rear brakes, and one crosses over the front crossmember to supply the passenger-side front caliper. A flexible rubber hose runs from the hard line on the frame to a union block on the rear axle that splits to two

hard lines that feed each rear drum or caliper. Flexible rubber hoses are also installed at each front wheel between a frame-mounted hard line bulk-head fitting and the front calipers.

The power booster supplies vacuum assistance to the braking system. The booster receives its vacuum supply from an outlet on the engine intake manifold and uses two internal pushrods to connect the brake pedal to the booster and the booster to the master cylinder. The booster itself features dual internal diaphragms that house vacuum pressure and atmospheric pressure to create the power brake assist when the brake pedal is applied.

The parking brake is operated by a ratcheting hand lever that sits on the transmission tunnel between the front seats. When the lever is engaged, it pulls a cable that activates the secondary brake shoes in the rear brakes. Tension in the parking brake cable is pre-adjusted from the factory but requires readjustment upon replacement or if it's disconnected to service the brake system. If the parking-brake lamp on the dash remains on after the parking brake is released, the tensioner and cable may be out of adjustment.

The brake power booster relies on a vacuum feed from the intake manifold to help it provide additional stopping power.

A cable and tensioner connected to a cab-mounted ratcheting lever is used to engage the parking brake.

Brake Upgrades

Rear Disc Brake Conversion

If you're not lucky enough to own a Wrangler equipped with the optional four-wheel disc brakes, then you'll probably tire of the factory drum brakes. Never fear—the aftermarket is here. With plenty of companies offering rear disc brake conversions, you don't have to live with drum brakes anymore. Most conversion kits are fairly basic and can be installed by a home mechanic capable of turning wrenches and bleeding brakes. It is necessary to pull the rear axle shafts for installation, which requires removing the C-clips in Dana 35c rear axles. This is good practice in case you

Installing a rear disc brake conversion is a great way to increase braking ability.

ever have to do it on the trail. This also gives you an opportunity to change the rear diff fluid. You'll also find improved braking ability as one of the rewards.

Stainless Steel Brakes Corporation (SSBC) is one supplier of rear disc brake conversions and can also supply vented rotors to further increase braking performance. The SSBC kit uses single-piston cast-iron calipers with a built-in parking brake. It includes caliper mounting brackets, brake splash shields, brake lines, and necessary installation hardware. Kits are available for both Dana 35c and Dana 44 rear axles. Currie offers a bolt-on rear disc brake conversion that uses factory Ford Explorer rotors and calipers, and custom mounting hardware. Teraflex produces yet another conversion kit that is also bolt-on.

Similar to how a ZJ tie rod can replace the stock TJ component, the Dana 35c rear disc brake assembly from '95–'98 Grand Cherokee ZJs can also be used on the TJ. This is almost a bolt-on affair for the TJ Dana 35c and works on rear Dana 44 axles with modifications to the ZJ caliper bracket center hole. The parts are available new from Jeep dealers and other parts sources, such as NAPA, or can also be sourced used from a salvage yard.

Hydroboost Brake Systems

For those seeking the ultimate in braking performance for their TJ, a hydroboost brake system should do the trick. Vanco Power Brake Supply offers a hydroboost system that produces 2,500 to 2,700 lbs of braking pressure. The system uses a hydraulic unit that replaces the stock power booster and is driven by the power steering pump to create more clamping force/pressure to hold the brake pads on the rotor. The system also incorporates a high-capacity, high-flow master cylinder with either a 1⅛-inch or 1⁵⁄₁₆-inch bore. A shaft in the hydroboost operates the master cylinder so the required braking pedal force is decreased

to a point that the pedal need only move ⅟₁₆-inch to apply braking force. Full stroke of the hydroboost is 2.5 inches, which means your vehicle will come to a full stop after applying just 1 inch of pedal stroke. The design of the shaft that activates the master cylinder means you'll still have braking force even if the hydroboost should fail for some reason, and a nitrogen chamber is also incorporated to provide stopping power if the engine stalls. The Vanco system also alters the pedal force. The feel is firm and not sensitive to exaggerated braking force unless the pedal is completely applied. The more pedal pressure applied, the more braking force produced.

A high-flow power steering pump is also necessary to operate the hydroboost brake system. The Vanco unit requires a steering pump capable of producing 1,500 psi in order for the system to function properly and to achieve the desired braking effects. An external fluid reservoir is also a good idea in order to further increase fluid volume and lessen the strain put on the power steering pump. It may also be required to relocate various smog equipment items on some model year TJs. The hydroboost works well with hydraulic clutch-equipped TJs and can accommodate disc/drum and disc/disc brake setups.

A PSC Motorsports external fluid reservoir is used to hold additional fluid so that the Vanco hydroboost brake system won't strain the power steering pump. Most reservoirs also incorporate a built-in fluid filter. The Vanco setup creates significantly more braking power than stock.

TIRES AND WHEELS

You don't get this big overnight, but 37-inch tires are possible for any Jeep Wrangler TJ with the right combination of parts.

OE Tire Fitments

The Wrangler TJ was equipped with a variety of tire and wheel packages throughout its production run. Standard equipment tire availability varied by model, but the tire size remained somewhat consistent. The smallest tire sizes appeared on early SE model Wranglers, which were standard-equipped with P205/75R15 Goodyear radials up to 2001. After that, a P215/75R15 Goodyear Wrangler RT/S RBL All-Terrain became standard on the SE, as well as the X and Sport models. Another standard fitment tire used on the Sport was the P225/75R15 Goodyear Wrangler GS-A OWL All-Terrain, which was also available to X model Wranglers equipped with the optional tire and wheel group package.

Long serving as the flagship model of the Wrangler fleet, the Wrangler Sahara was accustomed to receiving better standard equipment and available options. The Sahara tire fitments were no exception. Early Sahara models were equipped with a P225/70R16 Michelin tire mounted to a 16-inch wheel, though this was soon replaced by a 30x9.50R15LT Goodyear Wrangler OWL All-Terrain. This light truck tire also became available to Sport models and was packaged with an upgraded tire and wheel group. It was also standard fit on Wrangler Unlimited models.

The final Wrangler tire offering is the LT245/75R16 Goodyear Wrangler MT/R. This tire is often referred to as a 31-inch tire, which is its converted flotation size. It was standard equipment on Wrangler Rubicon and Rubicon Unlimited and is one of the greatest tire fitments in Wrangler history. Not only did the size better reflect the Wranglers 4x4 nature by offering increased ground clearance, it also provided increased traction by way of its aggressive tread pattern.

OE Wheels

A 15 x 6-inch styled steel wheel was standard on the SE until 2003 when it was

The standard tire and wheel package typically included a 27-inch passenger car tire on a 15 x 7-inch steel wheel.

A 30 x 9.50-inch tire and 15 x 8-inch alloy wheel were available as part of the Brake and Traction Group or standard equipment on higher-optioned Wrangler models, such as Sport and Sahara.

The Rubicon offered the largest tire size, an LT245/75R16 (31 x 10.50). The beefy Goodyear MT/R was mounted to a 16 x 8 Moab alloy wheel with 5-inch backspacing.

The 15 x 8 Ravine aluminum wheel was shod with 30-inch tires. The Ravine wheel style replaced the Canyon style in 2004 and was available on all models but the Rubicon.

replaced by a 15 x 7-inch styled steel model. The styled wheel went away altogether in 2005, when SE Wranglers received 15 x 7-inch full-face steel wheels. X and Sport model Wranglers also received the 15 x 7-inch full-face steel wheels as standard equipment for most years.

The 15 x 7-inch ECCO cast-aluminum wheel upgrade was offered on many model year Wrangler Sport models, as well as special edition X models. This wheel package was typically teamed with P225/75R15 tires and was also sporadically available to some SE model Wranglers. Wrangler Sport models might also be equipped with optional 15 x 8-inch Canyon cast-aluminum wheels fit with 30-inch tires. This was also the standard fitment on Sahara and Unlimited Wranglers.

The Canyon wheel was replaced by a new Ravine wheel in 2004. The 15 x 8-inch cast-aluminum Ravine wheel was equipped with 30-inch tires and used as standard fitment on Sahara and Unlimited, as well as Sport models and special edition X models. Some special edition X model Wranglers, including the

APEX and Freedom editions, used a 15 x 7-inch chrome wheel. The final Wrangler wheel offering was the 16 x 8-inch cast-aluminum Moab wheel, which was available on Rubicon and Rubicon Unlimited Wranglers.

There's also the consideration of wheel bolt circle. The TJ uses a 5 on 4½-inch bolt circle, which means it uses 5 lugs on a 4½-inch diameter imaginary circle. While you can install aftermarket wheels of varied backspacing and offset, you can only fit wheels with this 5 on 4½-inch bolt pattern.

Tires Upgrades

There are no two ways about it—tires are paramount to winning off-road desert races. I've witnessed meticulously built race trucks campaigned by the most calculating and equally meticulous drivers fall victim to a blown tread and then lose a race. That's one of the reasons companies like BFGoodrich have spent countless hours over the last 30 years or so developing off-road performance-type treads to better put up with the abuse of off-road use. I'm not saying

Bigger tires and wheels can greatly improve a Wrangler's off-road capability. On-road benefits can include better vehicle stability and handling, mostly due to the wider track.

that the tires on your Wrangler will see the same abuse experienced by a Trophy Truck, but it's good to be prepared for the worst. BFGoodrich isn't the only company that has done its homework over the years, as a variety of off-road treads are available from many tire manufacturers. From a simple upgrade to a light truck tire to a set of 37-inch mud terrain treads for your lifted TJ, you'll find that tires do more than win races, they also ensure you'll make it home.

Performance-type treads, such as the BFG Krawler T/A^{KX}, are designed to maximize off-road capability. The Krawlers offer a soft and flexible carcass with a deep lug tread design and beefy 4-ply sidewalls.

Reading Sidewalls

Before you leap into purchasing new tires for your Wrangler, it's a good idea to familiarize yourself with what exactly all of those numbers on the sidewalls mean. When reading metric tire sizes, you'll be looking at three sets of numbers. The numbers represent a tire's section width, aspect ratio, and rim size. Take a common Wrangler metric tire size of P225/75R15 as an example. The "P" stands for passenger-car, meaning it's designated as a passenger-car tire. Once you upgrade you'll likely move to LT-type tires, which are designed for light trucks.

The first number in the size listing is 225. This is the section width of the tire in millimeters. It's basically the distance between the sidewalls measured at the widest part of the tire. This shouldn't be confused with contact patch, which is the actual surface area of the tread contacting the ground. Section width actually changes slightly depending upon the size wheel to which a tire is mounted.

The 75 is the tire's aspect ratio, or the ratio between section height and section width. An aspect ratio of 75 indicates that the section height is 75 percent of the section width. To obtain the actual diameter of a metric tire, you need some basic math. The first step is to convert the 225 mm section width into inches by dividing by 25.4 (number of millimeters in an inch). Since the aspect ratio is 75, you then multiply the section width in inches by 0.75. The result of this equation is the sidewall height in inches.

Since sidewall appears above and below the wheel, this figure is then multiplied by two. Add the diameter of the wheel to the result and you'll have the actual tire height in inches. For the aforementioned P225/75R15 this figure is 28.29 inches. To avoid the math, you can check out some of the available online metric-to-flotation tire-size calculators, which can often be found along with

gear/drivetrain calculators. 4 Wheel Parts Wholesalers features calculators on its website, as does Randy's Ring & Pinion. The letter "R" is used to identify a radial tire. If there is no "R" in the size listing, then you can assume that it's a bias-ply tire. And of course, the 15 indicates that the tire is meant for a 15-inch rim.

As overall tire diameters increase, sizes are often indicated in flotation sizes. Flotation sizes are much easier to understand for the not-so-metric, not-so-mathy crowd, since they basically offer the essential information in a form that doesn't take a calculator to understand. A 30 x 9.50R15 tire is 30 inches tall, has a 9.50-inch width, it's a radial, and it fits a 15-inch wheel. That's it; you've got your size without any of the math. Flotation sizes are actually used for a fairly large range of tire diameters, but as wheel diameter increases, some tire manufacturers resort back to metric sizing.

Radial vs. Bias-Ply

You'll run into two types of tires as you seek out more aggressive treads for your TJ: radial and bias-ply. Bias-ply refers to the biased angle at which the nylon plies are layered across the tread area of a tire. Radial tires also get their name from the fashion that the plies cross from bead to bead. They run in a straight line at a 90-degree angle to the bead. These plies make up the body of a tire. On a radial tire, steel belts are wrapped around the inner plies before the rubber tread is molded on top. Some bias-ply tires also use steel belts like a radial, but many are constructed by simply molding the rubber tread directly over the angled plies. Both types of tires offer pros and cons, but radials are the likeliest option since they offer better street performance while still providing ample off-road capability.

Radial tires use plies constructed from polyester. Bias-ply tires use more layers of nylon plies, which is considered to be stronger than polyester. The bias-plies

A bias-ply tire such as this 37 x 12.50-15 Maxxis Creepy Crawler uses angled or biased nylon plies in its construction. Bias-ply tires are often more durable than radials, but don't have as good of street manners.

are in place to reinforce one another and result in a more durable tire capable of supporting greater loads than a radial. The angled nylon plies also help reinforce the sidewall area and allow the tread lugs to extend further down the sidewall toward the tire bead. Ply separation in a bias-ply can occur from excessive heat or when the tire becomes overloaded. You've likely seen this occur to a tractor trailer tire on the highway. Bias-ply tires are also affected by extreme temperatures, becoming stiff in cold climes, while radials operate as intended in many climates. The polyester used in the construction of radial tires is more flexible, which helps absorb shock from the roadway and also distributes the vehicle and load weight more evenly across the tread area. Bias-ply tires, however, transfer the shock from the roadway to the suspension, making for a bumpier ride.

Which one is better? I hate to do it, but this one is on you again. My first instinct is to go with the radial, but aggressive bias-ply tires still have a defi-

nite allure. There's also a bit of speculation as to how radial some radial tires are said to be. This typically applies to the more aggressive-tread radial tires with tread blocks on the sidewalls. I haven't cut one of these tires apart to examine the arrangement of the plies, so for now you'll just have to believe the tire manufacturer's claims and say it's a radial. The radial is the tire of choice for most, but those dedicated to running extreme trails on a regular basis, with little pavement driving in the interim, find the bias-ply to be a damn fine tire.

Sizing Up

The time will inevitably come when you desire larger tires for your Wrangler. Some are happy with 32-inch treads, while others are drawn to massive 40-inch swamp-ready tires. Your TJ will, of course, require an appropriate degree of lift to accommodate larger-than-stock size tires. You can look to the Quick Lift Guide in Chapter 7 to help you determine how much lift your Wrangler will need to fit your desired tire size. As a basic guide, however, you can figure on

Chris Durham's TJ runs 40-inch Goodyear MT/Rs with just a 1¼-inch body lift. You might note that the front fenders have been removed completely and replaced with a fiberglass hood and fenders.

fitting a maximum of a 31-inch tire under a stock Wrangler (with the fenders trimmed for clearance), a 31- to 32-inch tire with two to three inches lift and a body lift, a 32- to 33-inch tire with 4 inches of lift, 35s with more than 4 inches of lift, and so on. This won't hold true for every application, so be sure to have a plan before making the leap to larger tires. And you can always consult the lift manufacturer on its recommended tire size for the lift in question.

Tires are essentially what lifts a vehicle. Suspension helps, of course, but if you're willing to carve up your Wrangler's front and rear fenders rather significantly and add about a 1-inch body lift, you can fit 40-inch tires. Compared to a set of 32s, which you could run with the 1-inch body lift and stock fenders, the 40-inch tires give you about 8 inches of lift. Not bad for just a set of tires. Cutting up your TJ is, of course, a fairly drastic measure to take with your prized possession, especially when an off-the-shelf

Wider-than-stock tires help increase the track width and provide better stability on the road. A wider tread is also beneficial on the trail and requires a wider wheel for proper fitment. Here a 36 x 15.5-inch Mickey Thompson Baja MTZ is shown mounted on a 15 x 12-inch wheel.

suspension system can do the same job. But if you're up for it, it works. Really, I've seen it done.

You have other options to consider beyond just going to a taller tire. Like the height, you can also adjust tire width or even move to a larger wheel diameter. Wider tires increase the vehicle's track width for better stability and help create a larger footprint on the trail. But while some of a good thing is great, don't get out of control with tire width. I ended up with a set of 36 x 15.50s on 16 x 10-inch wheels at one point, and while it was great on the road, I hated it on the trail. I was too wide and I kept clipping obstacles along the side of the trail. Also, really wide tires may require extreme custom wheel backspacing that puts the wheel and tire so far outboard of the vehicle that it can wreak havoc on wheel bearings and overload lug studs.

Sidewalls are also important elements to tire selection. I like tall sidewalls, so I say more is better than less, but it's really up to each individual's driving style. Like most, I started out with 15-inch wheels and had a hard time moving away from the tall and flexy sidewalls. I switched to 17s after a while and haven't really gone back. The loss of sidewall is minimal and comes primarily from the more vulnerable areas around the tire bead, since the Nitto Mud Grapplers I'm currently running offer ample shoulder lugs that extend over much of the sidewall. Less sidewall gives you quicker steering response and improved lateral stability. That's why you see sports cars with 18- and 20-inch wheels. Bigger wheels also allow for bigger brakes, but remember that larger wheels also translate into more weight for the engine to push.

What's in a Tread Pattern?

Choosing new tires for your Wrangler can be a daunting task if you're unsure about what style tread you desire.

Tire size can be deceiving, so you need to think about it in relative terms. Take a look at how a 31-inch tire (left) compares to 33-inch (middle) and 35-inch (right) tires.

Now here's a 35-inch tire (right) shown alongside 37-inch (middle) and 44-inch (left) tires.

A good off-road tire should have a flexible enough sidewall to conform to the obstacle at hand. Sidewall strength is also important, especially if you like playing in the rocks.

Mickey Thompson's Baja Claw tread pattern leaves a unique footprint. This directional-tread tire functions well in a variety of terrains but sidewall biters make it work especially well in the rocks. The 6-ply sidewalls are also very resistant to tears.

With the immense variation in available designs, you really need to establish how you use your vehicle the most: street versus trail, do you use your TJ as a daily driver, do you drive on snow, mud, rocks, or sand? Even if your TJ isn't a daily driver, some aggressive tires may have adverse affects to on-road handling. If you require a smooth and consistent highway ride, then stick to more street-oriented tires. Some TJ owners go so far as to maintain two sets of tires and wheels for their vehicle in order to achieve the greatest performance both on the highway and on the trail.

All-Terrain

All-terrain-type treads are great, but they aren't always up to the task of tackling "all terrains." They leave a bit to be desired in overly muddy situations and sand can also be an issue (though I find sand to be an issue for many tread styles). The "all-terrain" term gets thrown out pretty loosely sometimes, too, which can be deceiving if you were seriously expecting what the sidewall promised. For the

Tire treads are made up of rubber tread blocks organized to create biting edges. Some tread designs extend downward across the sidewall. This ia a Mickey Thompson Baja MTZ LT375/65R16 (36 x 15.50 inch).

most part, all-terrain tires provide increased traction over stock tires through most terrain without the big increase in road noise that's typical of tires with larger tread blocks. They also look cooler than basic light truck tires. All-terrains are a great option for the daily driver crowd and also for those who spend limited time off the pavement. Some all-terrain tread designs are more aggressive than others, so don't expect the same performance from every all-terrain you see. All-terrain designs like those available from Nitto and BFGoodrich fall on the more aggressive side, while some of those available from Goodyear and others are more street-oriented.

Mud Terrain

With a significantly more aggressive tread, mud terrain tires can handle quite a bit more than their name implies. You typically get a wider spread, deeper lug pattern capable of tackling rocky terrain, loose dirt and sand, and even snow. The wider lugs are in place to give the tire greater self-cleaning ability and provide continued traction through mud and the like. There are trade-offs when moving to a larger lug tread design, such as the fact that mud terrains tend to wear more rapidly than all-terrain treads, and that they also emit more tire hum on the road. Many mud terrain designs are bias-ply tires, which adds to the rapid wear, but wear can also be attributed to the softer rubber compounds used in their construction, which can help aid traction. Before the emergence of professional rock crawling and more performance-oriented tread designs, mud terrain tires were the end-all-beat-all for any trail. Even today, they're one of the most popular tread designs available. The release of hard core performance-oriented tires moved mud terrains to the middle ground between the extreme and all-terrain designs. Not surprisingly, the middle ground—i.e., not too easy, not too hard core—is exactly the type of wheeling that most Wrangler owners enjoy.

Rock Crawling

"If you build it he will come," is a memorable line from *Field of Dreams*, but it's also a good characterization of how rock crawling tire treads came to be. When the sport of competitive rock crawling began to take shape in the late 1990s, most competitors used mud terrain and all-terrain tires, doing their best to make them work by siping and grooving the treads to create more biting edges to grab the rocks and hang on. However, it didn't take the tire manufacturers long to figure out that the tire market was expanding before their very eyes. After extensive testing by BFGoodrich, along with the expertise of multiple competitors, the first rock crawling-specific tread went into production as the BFG Krawler T/A^{KX}. Many other tire manufacturers answered the call and released a variety of rock crawling treads of various designs. Most follow similar design cues and involve a soft rubber compound,

The Goodyear MT/R is a great mud-terrain and all-around tire. It's also standard fitment on Wrangler Rubicons.

BFG's Mud Terrain T/A^{KO} is a standby for many. I used a set of these in a 37-inch size and enjoyed the road manners as much as I did its trail abilities.

The Super Swamper TSL Bogger is a popular mud-terrain tire for heavy mud use; they're even used by many professional mud-bog racers. Bias-ply and radial versions are available in a wide variety of sizes.

multiple-staggered deep tread lugs, large shoulder lugs, and reinforced sidewalls. Some are also bias-ply tires.

While the mud-terrain tread was once king, the rock-crawling tread now reigns. These tires are typically only available in taller sizes, with most starting at 35 inches. Some are only offered for 17-inch wheels. Increased off-road ability is achieved through the use of rock crawling type treads, but expect your on-road handling to take a bit of a hit. I personally didn't mind the move, even for daily driving, but be forewarned that tire wear will be greater with the more pavement these tires see. A second set of tires and wheels for the street are a good investment for those that want the best of both worlds.

Tire Tuning

Balancing

If you wheel your TJ across tough terrain on a regular basis, then tire balancing can become a repetitive task. You don't necessarily need to have your tires balanced after each run, but at least have it done on a somewhat regular basis. This helps your tires last longer and helps provide a consistently smooth highway ride. It can also help lengthen the life of steering and suspension components, since out-of-balance tires can create excessive vibration that is transferred to these areas.

Larger tires are often more difficult to balance and require more weights. Some tire shops have trouble with them because their machines don't work with 35-inch tires. Bias-ply tires are harder to balance and may even require ballast, such as the granular ballast from MRT.

Tire Siping and Grooving

Those that can't leave anything alone will be glad to know that even tires can be modified. As previously mentioned, many rock crawling competitors add sipes or grooves to the tread to enhance traction. Sipes are small lateral cuts in the lugs that create more forward biting edges. Grooves are similar but on a larger scale. They involve using a hot knife to section the tread blocks, again so more biting edges can be exposed to the rocks beneath. Tire siping is typically completed by a tire shop using a special machine, but grooving can be carried out by anyone skilled enough (or possibly brave enough) with a hot knife. It

Tires can be machine-siped to offer enhanced traction for many driving situations. Notice all the extra horizontal sipes cut in the tread blocks.

Multi-terrain type tires are another advancement in off-road treads. This Nitto Mud Grappler is a good example. It excels in many terrains, particularly on rocks and even in sand.

The larger the tire, the larger the balancer required to properly balance it. Many tire shops balance larger tires with the balancing machine's cover up. Other tire shops just use larger balance machines.

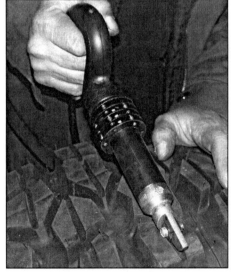

Grooving a tire is an old racer trick to gain more forward biting edges and a tread pattern unique to the track or obstacle at hand. Tire-grooving tools like this one are available from MRW Racing Wheels.

can be disconcerting carving up a brand new set of tires, but when a few seconds worth of traction can be achieved as a result, most competitors don't give it a second thought. Though you don't really fight for seconds on the trail, siping and grooving tires is still a great means of obtaining the upper hand against troublesome obstacles, and it's a great means of creating more traction where an unmodified tire finds none.

Air Pressure

Air pressure is just about the single most important factor in how well the tires on your Wrangler will perform. On the trail, most drivers run too much air, causing a loss of traction and capability. By lowering the air pressure in the tires, the tire's contact patch becomes wider and is therefore better able to conform to rocks and other trail obstacles. You also run much less risk of damaging a sidewall with lower tire pressure. I've found that many folks even run too high an air pressure on the road. Wonder why your suspension doesn't handle as well as the manufacturer claimed it would? Try dropping a few psi from the tires and try it again. It took me a couple weeks to dial in a set of 37-inch BFG Krawlers before I finally settled on 28 psi up front and 26 psi in the rear—for highway use. For the trail I'd go much lower, usually in the 8 to 10 range up front and about 6 to 8 in the rear. This is nothing, really, considering I wheel with guys from time-to-time who are most satisfied rolling in the 2 to 5 psi range. A good set of beadlock wheels are necessary if you intend to drop lower than 10 psi, but slipping a tire bead can be somewhat situational, so you can get away with less air if the terrain permits.

Tires vs. Gearing

Another factor to keep in mind when installing larger-than-stock tires is how the vehicle's gearing will be affected. Minor changes in size have little effect, but a big-

If you run too low of air pressure in your tires without beadlocks, you run the risk of slipping the tire bead off the wheel.

ger leap, such as from a stock 28-inch tire to a 33- or 35-inch tire, requires a ring-and-pinion swap to maintain optimum acceleration and fuel economy. This is also important to successful off-road use since the final drive ratio is decreased because the larger tires turn slower than the stock.

Speedometer Correction

Having the speedometer tell me the exact speed at which my TJ is moving has never been too great a concern of mine. But, since I'm sure quite a few of you prefer to stay within the law, as well as keep accurate records of your fuel mileage, I should probably make you aware of the fact that equipping your Wrangler TJ with larger than stock tires and different ring-and-pinion gear ratios will affect your actual vehicle speed in respect to what the speedometer displays. Depending on tire size, the actual speed can vary from 1 to 20 percent or more, so the difference between actual and displayed speed increases as the vehicle accelerates. I can usually estimate my actual speed to within ⅕-mile or less depending on what's rattling and how loud, but I've also come to know how to read the speedo with adjusted eyeballs. When it reads 60 mph I know from what I've gathered from roadside mile markers and onboard GPS systems that I'm actually traveling at a much

faster pace, closer to the 75 to 80 mph range, to give you an idea.

This estimation of speed calculation has worked for me ever since I lifted my TJ, but there are better means of obtaining an accurate speedometer reading, even in modified Wranglers. Using some basic math, it's easy to calculate the actual speed of the vehicle with the new larger tires in place. The formula goes as follows:

$$Actual\ Speed = new\ tire\ diameter\ x\\ indicated\ speed\ /\ old\ tire\ diameter$$

$$Actual\ Speed = 37\ x\ 60\ /\ 28$$
$$Actual\ Speed = 79.2$$

The figures used in the example represent the new 37-inch tire size, an indicated speed of 60 mph, and the 28-inch diameter of the factory tires. With an actual speed of 79.2 mph, my estimation of 75 to 80 mph was pretty much on the money. Note that the most accurate figure will be obtained using actual tire measurements that you complete yourself, rather than the stated tire size on the sidewall.

If you'd rather see the correct numbers on your speedometer, there are other options. The vehicle speed sensor and speedometer drive gear are located in the tail housing of the NP231 transfer case. The speedometer can be recalibrated by replacing the gear with a gear that has a different tooth count. Factory speedometer gears varied in teeth count depending on what axle gear ratio and tire size the vehicle was equipped with from the factory. The 1999 Wrangler, for example, used 28-, 29-, 30-,and 31-tooth speedo gears to accommodate the four tire sizes used with 3.07:1 axle gears. The 3.73:1 axle gear ratio was mated with 34-, 36-, and 37-teeth gears, and TJs with 4.11:1 axle gear ratio used 39-, 40-, and 41-teeth speedo gears. As you can likely see, this creates an abundance of dealer-available speedo gears to choose from when attempting to recalibrate your speedometer. The easiest way to determine which speedometer gear your new tire size will require involves a quick equation:

$$New\ Speedo\ Gear = Old\ Speedo\ Gear \times Old\ Tire\ Size\ /\ New\ Tire\ Size$$

$$New\ Speedo\ Gear = 36 \times 28\ /\ 37$$
$$New\ Speedo\ Gear = 27.24$$

The above figures represent the stock 36-teeth speedo gear, a 28-inch original tire diameter, and a 37-inch new tire diameter. The result of the equation is that a speedometer gear with 27.24 teeth will effectively recalibrate the speedometer. Since fraction-tooth gears don't exist, the number is rounded down to 27. If you don't know the teeth count of your existing speedometer gear, remove the gear and count the teeth so you know which replacement gear to purchase. A Jeep dealership may also be able to determine the teeth count by the vehicle year, factory gear ratio, and factory tire fitment.

Because the Wrangler TJ uses an electronic speedometer, it's possible to alter the speed sensor signal so that the speedometer provides an accurate reading, even with larger-than-stock tires and a different axle gear ratio. There are a few ways to go about this, but the easiest method is through use of Superlift's TruSpeed Speed Sensor Recalibrator. TruSpeed is a tunable electronic unit that installs inline with the factory speed sensor wire to alter the signal it sends to the PCM. It's adjustable to accommodate tire size and gear ratio changes and provides an accurate speedometer reading in relation to the actual vehicle speed. Other speedo correction devices reflash or reprogram the ECM so that it knows what size tires the engine is turning. Hypertech offers its Power Programmer III to satisfy this and a variety of other PCM-related issues.

Wheel Upgrades

You need to buy new wheels if you intend to install larger than 31- to 32-

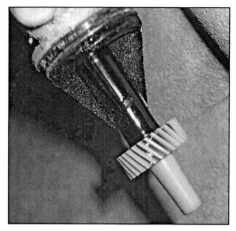

Replacement speedometer gears are fairly inexpensive and are easy to install. The speedometer gear installs in the tailhousing of the transfer case.

inch tires. It isn't so much the height as it is the width that taller tires happen to be. With the 15 x 8-inch factory wheels, you can get away with the 31s and 32s in 9.50- and even 10.5-inch widths, but the 15 x 7s won't cut it. If you want 35- or 37-inch tires, they start at 12.5 inches wide, so you'll need at least a 10-inch wide wheel. Also, the 5-inch backspacing comes into play because a wider tire will certainly contact suspension and steering components if it sits so far under the fenders.

Wheels are manufactured from steel or aluminum. Steel wheels use a steel center and barrel that are welded together to form one wheel. Aluminum wheels are made a few different ways, including a variety of casting methods, and forging, which involves high-pressure molding of a solid chunk of aluminum. The chunk of aluminum, by the way, is called a billet. It's a term that gets thrown around a lot and is often used incorrectly. A billet is just a chunk of metal, be it aluminum, steel, titanium, or other. When someone on the trail claims to have "billet" wheels it more precisely identifies the manufacturing process (forging) than what kind of material was used.

The forging process is used to manufacture complete wheels, as well as wheel pieces, such as wheel centers and barrels. The centers and barrels are then welded together in the same manner as steel wheels. Wheel manufacturers sometimes mix and match pieces as well, using forged- or cast-aluminum centers mated to steel or rolled-aluminum outers. Aluminum wheels can also be constructed using multiple pieces, where the barrel, or outer wheel, is split and welded together around its perimeter. This method is often used to accommodate custom backspacing and wheel widths. Cast wheels are often one-piece units, but as mentioned, cast wheel pieces can also be used to make up multi-piece wheels. The casting process involves use of a wheel mold that is gravity-fed or high- or low-pressure counter-fed molten aluminum. The molten aluminum then takes the wheel mold's shape as it cools and hardens.

Aluminum vs. Steel Wheels

This is one of those unending debates that almost completely relies on personal preference. There are varying benefits to aluminum and steel wheels. If we were talking performance sports cars, the answer would be aluminum hands down. Aluminum wheels offer less unsprung weight than steel wheels and will absorb more road irregularities and bumps. The lighter unsprung weight also contributes to better steering response. But do 4x4s need that much performance?

Steel wheels are also strong, but they're quite a bit cheaper than aluminum wheels. They do the same job as an aluminum wheel and do it rather well. Strength and weight are probably the biggest factors in the wheel debate, but how well a wheel holds up to 4x4 use is the greater test. As mentioned, aluminum is strong and light, while steel is strong and a bit heavier. Steel wheels bend, but they often still hold air. Aluminum wheels sometimes bend, but more often they simply break. They

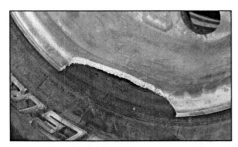

Cast-aluminum wheels can crack or chip when obstacles are hit with great force. Some forged-aluminum or steel wheels can be repaired if they are bent.

won't break completely all the time, but a piece will break off or a crack may develop. Some forged aluminum wheels can be pounded back into shape if they are bent, but cast wheels often simply crack or break. It does take a good amount of force, of course, so don't think aluminum is necessarily inferior, but keep it in mind. I currently run a set of Allied steel wheels and they have been some of my favorites.

Beadlock Wheels

If tough trails are in your future, consider running a set of beadlock wheels. Beadlock wheels are designed to keep the tire bead seated so it won't slip off the wheel when you run low air pressure in the tires. Beadlocks do more than keep the bead seated—they also function as skid plates for the wheels. Outer bead rings can be replaced if they become extensively damaged, as can bolts, but if the rim or lip of the wheel becomes damaged, you may be looking at complete replacement. The beadlock ring also provides protection to the tire's bead area.

Beadlock wheels use an extra ring welded in place around their outer circumference. This inner ring features bolt holes around the perimeter to secure an outer ring in place. The tire bead is sandwiched between the two rings so that it can't spin on or slip off the wheel. The bead rings can be bolted together using bolts, Nylok nuts, or even

threaded nut inserts that can be press-fit into the holes in the inner bead ring. A company called Hutchinson also produces internal beadlock wheels. These are two-piece wheels that bolt together with an internal beadlock device and the tire sandwiched in between, securing both the inner and outer beads. To date, these are the only style of beadlock wheels that have gained Department of Transportation (DOT) approval—all others are deemed appropriate for off-road use only. Many simulated beadlock wheels are available, but don't be fooled into thinking that these wheels do the same job. While they may look cool, the bead ring is strictly cosmetic and won't provide any assistance in keeping the tire on the wheel.

As I mentioned, beadlocks allow you to run much lower air pressure in the tires. But how low can you go? I personally like my tires filled at around 6 to 8 psi, but I know quite a few who run lower. It also depends greatly on what tires you run. Some softer compound treads can get away with higher PSI as they already conform well to rocks and other obstacles. Stiff bias-ply tires require lower air pressure than radials before becoming flexy enough for extreme trail use. No matter how low you go, beadlock wheels keep the tire securely attached to the wheel.

Wheel Size and Fitment

Wheel sizing is pretty basic—or at least you'd think so. Wheel diameter and width are listed in inches. For example, a 15 x 8-inch wheel has a 15-inch diameter and an 8-inch width. But that isn't the whole story. There's also the concern of wheel backspacing and offset, which both play an enormous role in how a wheel fits any particular vehicle. These determine where the wheel (and thus the tire) sits in relation to the vehicle.

Wheel offset is the distance from the width centerline to its mounting surface.

These aluminum OMF beadlocks keep the Goodyear MT/R securely attached to the wheel. Check out the OMF scalloped outer bead ring.

Beadlock wheels can also help prevent sidewall damage by acting as a skid plate. The outer bead ring protects the wheel rim and tire bead.

A 15-inch wheel was standard on all TJs except the Rubicon. A larger wheel can be utilized but requires less backspacing if paired with a taller or wider tire. This is a 32 x 11.50-inch Pro Comp Mud Terrain on a 15 x 10-inch wheel. It uses 3¾-inch backspacing to keep from rubbing on the aftermarket control arms.

Negative offset indicates that the wheel-mounting surface is inboard of the centerline. Too much negative offset puts extra stress on the vehicle's lugs and can overload wheel bearings. It can also create interference with steering and suspension components since the front wheels will turn wider and possibly contact the fenderwells.

Positive offset is when the wheel-mounting surface is outboard of the wheel centerline. You wouldn't want to run positive offset wheels on your TJ, since the wheels would tuck under the fenders and severely limit larger tire fitment. Zero offset, when the wheel-mounting surface is even with the wheel centerline, is also an option.

Most OE wheels use a fairly standard offset, but backspace is set at more than 5 inches. Wheel backspacing is the distance from the back edge of a wheel to its mounting surface. Backspacing can be verified by positioning a straight-edge across the back side of the wheel and then measuring the distance from the straight-edge to the wheel mounting surface. The wheel should be removed from the vehicle when completing the measurement. Stock wheels measure up as follows: Canyon and Ravine wheels have 5.5-inch backspacing, stock 7-inch-width wheels have 5.25-inch backspacing, and Moab wheels offer 5-inch backspacing. Wheels with less backspacing, say 3.75 or so, help increase track width and aid in vehicle stability. This positions the tires and wheels further outboard of the fenders, which helps increase suspension articulation since the tires will have more room to compress before damaging fenders.

Since stock wheels are designed for the stock tire application, wider tires on a stock wheel won't necessarily work. The tire may rub the coil spring bucket on the frame and other components, and may even contact the steering arms. Fronts will rub on the lower control arms, though steering stops can be adjusted slightly to address minor changes. Make sure you check with the lift manufacturer to get correct wheel size and backspacing specifications when installing a lift. Most lifts don't work with stock wheels and some require wheels with less backspacing than others. Typically, a taller than 31-inch tire necessitates use of wheels with 3.75 to 4 inches backspacing.

Installing larger wheels while maintaining the original tire diameter is called plus sizing. It's a term used more widely among the truck lowering and sports car crowds, but it can be applied to any tire and wheel package. Plus sizing results in a shorter, stiffer sidewall, and bigger wheels mean more unsprung weight, which affects the suspension and steering. Larger diameter wheels also require a tire with a higher load rating, which is a bit tougher, but also a bit heavier as a result. If you're budget minded, remember that tires designed for 15-inch wheels are usually cheaper.

Wheel Spacers

Wheel spacers can be employed to accomplish a variety of tasks. First and foremost, they enable you to use the stock wheels with larger tires, since they position the wheels further outboard of the vehicle. Some tire shops may give you grief about liability if they work on a vehicle equipped with spacers, but rest assured that you aren't putting yourself in danger, provided installation is completed correctly and doesn't go over about 1¼ inch. Wheel spacers can also be used as adapters to convert the bolt pattern to accommodate a larger and stronger bolt circle. This comes in handy—to temporarily convert wheel bolt patterns—if you want to buy new wheels to accommodate an upcoming axle swap that will employ a different, larger wheel bolt pattern, such as 5 on 5½.

Since spacers can make up for an improper backspacing on a particular application, they can be used in place of buying new wheels. Spidertrax offers quality 1.25-inch thick aluminum spacers and M.O.R.E. offers spacers available in custom widths. However, if you're thinking dollars and sense, realistically you can buy new wheels with the desired BS and sell the old ones and pretty much make up the cost of spacers. However, you can also sell the wheel spacers/adapters once you don't need them anymore.

Spidertrax wheel spacers can be used to fit wider wheels and tires, as well as to convert to a larger 5 on 5½ wheel bolt pattern. This allows a greater variety of wheels to choose from, as the 5 on 5½ pattern is widely used.

INTERIOR AND EXTERIOR UPGRADES

Much of the Wrangler TJs allure is due to its body style. It's a continuation of a tradition that started more than 65 years ago and remains largely unchanged from its original design. The TJ even went back to round headlights like the CJs before it and the front fenders have a flatter appearance, similar to many early models. And, of course, the seven-slat grille adorns the front-end, making a bold and unmistakable announcement of its arrival.

Those accustomed to civilian Jeeps had long understood that function came before form and interior amenities have traditionally been rather bleak. Many improvements were incorporated over the years, but most simply looked added on. But the TJ changed all of that. Form was finally part of the package and the TJ features one of the most enhanced and user-friendly interiors to appear in a traditional Jeep. In fact, the TJ's fancy interior was one of the bigger shocks for many upon its release. Compared to its predecessors, the TJ interior more resembled the Cherokee XJ than it did the previous model Wrangler. An actual dash was in place with a single instrument cluster (centered in front of the steering wheel no less) and a center dash bezel for stuff like the radio, A/C

Inside and out, the Wrangler TJ is a refined version of its classic brethren.

vents and controls, and ashtray. Driver and passenger-side airbags, a first for the Wrangler, also graced the car-like dash.

However, as with nearly every TJ component, there is room for improvement. In fact, you can hardly throw a stone in a 4x4 shop with out hitting

something that will bolt-on to your Wrangler. The exterior offers multiple upgrade opportunities, from bumpers to skid plates, to cargo racks and extra lighting options. The interior is equally blessed with scads of products designed to somehow improve the functionality or pleasure of your driving experience.

Year-To-Year Interior/Exterior Updates

1997: introduction

1998: new hood latches, next generation air bags and defeat switch for passenger-side (late models), new steering wheel, fold-forward easy-entry driver's seat, new bumper pads

1999: 19-gallon fuel tank, hood vent replaced with new cowl, dial climate control knobs replace slide controls, headlight switch moved to turn indicator, improved PCM, new JTEC engine controller with new engine function sensors, frame made 16 lbs lighter

2000: 4.0L engine received redesigned cylinder head, new exhaust manifold and dual catalyst 2.25-inch exhaust system, tilt steering column with leather-covered steering wheel option added in SE and Sport, standard equipment stereo upgrades, child seat tethers in rear seat

2001: new reinforced fuel tank skid plate (later models), child seat anchorage system, revised instrument cluster, new steering column with improved tilt mechanism and lighting and windshield wiper controls, intermittent wipers as standard equipment, new center console with rear seat cup holders, new soft top, new fuel filler cap, redesigned stereo and optional subwoofer, wider rearview mirror, seat material improvements

2002: full doors with roll-up windows, fog lamps, and tow hooks standard on Sport, new HVAC system, optional premium sound system with tweeters and subwoofer, 30-inch tires standard on Sahara, introduction of X model

Full doors with roll-up windows became standard equipment on the sport model in 2002. The hard top was still optional.

2003: introduction of Rubicon model, new transfer case skid plate for new auto trans, sport bar foam added, corner speaker pods with dual dome lamps on sport bar replace sound bar, additional 12V power outlet added to dash, new 4-spoke steering wheel, redesigned dashboard with oval stereo and HVAC openings, key cylinder on doors made chrome instead of black, new rearview mirror with map lights and temperature and compass displays, new shorter ratcheting side mirrors, new soft-top material, new fold-and-tumble rear seat with quick release, new taller and softer front bucket seats with tip-and-slide passenger seat, header and A-pillar trim added for increased head impact safety, new and repositioned model/edition logos ("Sport" logo moved higher on fender, redesigned Sahara logo)

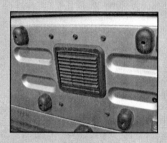

The vent in the tailgate was added in 2003, replacing the one previously placed in the rear sides of the hard top. This aided soft-top equipped Wranglers, which didn't previously have the benefit of a vent.

2004: Trail Rated badge added to all Wranglers, standard AM/FM CD stereo on all models except SE (replaces cassette), new dash storage, U.S. right-hand drive model available, wheel group upgrades with standard spare tire cover, 30-inch spare tire cover with Sahara logo, tilt steering wheel standard on SE and X.

2005: tip-and-slide driver's seat on all models with cloth seats, AM/FM stereo with in-unit six-disc CD changer, rear seat made standard on SE model, improved tailgate latches made from stamped aluminum instead of cast aluminum and feature black plastic cover, medium gray or khaki color-keyed molded-in-color fender flares and flare extensions replace black flares on SE, X, Sport, and Unlimited

The tailgate latches were improved in 2005 and received plastic latch covers.

2006: Sunrider soft-top offered on short-wheelbase Wranglers, slim-profile bumper end caps on SE and X, available factory-installed Sirius Radio, end of model production

The Sunrider soft top became available on standard model Wranglers in 2006 and features a flip-back sunroof over the front cab area.

The flat panel dash went out with the previous model Wrangler YJ to make way for an updated version that included driver- and passenger-side air bags, an efficient HVAC system, and a respectable sound system. (Photo courtesy DaimlerChrysler)

Aftermarket Tops

The ability to drop the top or pull it off and leave it home is one of the coolest things about owning a Jeep. It can become a convertible instantly with

Driving topless is one of the big thrills of owning a Jeep Wrangler. Whether simply folded back for the afternoon or removed and stored in the garage for the summer months, don't forget to let the wind mess up your hair from time to time. You can also remove your doors for trail use.

a soft top or fairly quickly with a hard top. But either way, you have the option and you should exercise it as often as you can. Since I live in Southern California, I've had my TJ topless for more than a year. I do use a bikini top the majority of the time, but I still keep a tarp and rain gear handy in the event of a downpour.

Jeep has really come a long way with its soft tops over the years. I remember seeing torn and tattered factory soft tops on Wrangler YJs, newer ones even, and had almost come to expect this as a matter of fact for Jeep-produced soft tops. But with the Wrangler TJ, all of this changed. The mounting configuration made it easier to raise and lower, and along with the vinyl material, made it quieter inside the cab when completely sealed. Though some of the early soft tops still suffer from the same issues of deterioration, 2001 and later models received a new four-ply sail-cloth top that has proven to be much more worthy of the Jeep name. The top was updated again in 2004 to use a 3-ply material that

Early Wrangler tops were more susceptible to wear damage and often develop tears over the driver- and passenger-side door surrounds and at the rear just in front of the top boom. Later-model tops are much more resistant to the elements, though color fade is still an issue.

is said to be as quiet as the 4-ply material. Some tops will fade over time and the windows will likely scratch (and more so when they aren't cared for properly), but most TJ owners will be pleased with the factory TJ soft tops for their functionality and ease of use.

Full Soft Tops

The technology behind factory and aftermarket soft tops has certainly improved over the years, from more durable materials to new and creative features, such as the factory soft top sunroof option offered on later Wranglers and the Unlimited. This type of top was initially introduced by the aftermarket company Bestop as the Sunrider top, but eventually became factory-issued under the same name. It's a neat feature that permits the top's front section to be flipped back over the rear section to create the sunroof opening. Early model Wrangler owners with the old-style factory top can still obtain this feature by installing a Bestop Sunrider top. Smittybilt also offers a similar feature on its Outland soft tops. Noise with a soft top is always an issue, but some are better than others.

Aftermarket full soft tops can be installed on any TJ. Those that came with a hard top will need to purchase a complete soft top with hardware, which is pretty easy to install. TJs that were equipped with a soft top from the factory can use a replacement soft top skin with the stock hardware. I've had great luck with my Bestops over the years. You may want to look for a top with as little hardware as possible, that way it'll be easier to remove when the sun comes out.

Full Hard Tops

The factory hard top adds quite a bit of weight to your TJ and takes a little longer to remove. And when you do go topless, you have to store it somewhere. Those are the worst things about running a full hard top on a TJ. Conversely, the pluses are huge. The cab stays cooler when the AC is pumping and warmer when the heater is on. The dust stays out, the mud stays out, and the windows will never become so scratched that you can't see through them.

Hard tops were available as an option for most models. Aftermarket hard tops are easy to come by but they aren't cheap. Figuring that the factory dual top group ran about $1,600 in 2006, you'll likely pay up to $2,000 to get an aftermarket unit—and that doesn't include shipping. Used stock tops are also pretty pricey, but are still a viable option. Bestop offers two aftermarket hard tops: a two-piece unit that features a removable front section to create an open-air sunroof, and a one-piece hard top similar to the factory hard top.

One of the bigger issues with having a hard top is where to store it when it's not on your Wrangler. A lot of people (including myself) are only dealing with a one-car garage these days, and most aren't keen on seeing that $1,600 extra sitting in the yard serving as a sun shade for the hounds. Bestop, Quadratec, and others offer neato storage caddies and such that stack the hard doors and top together on a cart that you can wheel around. These seem to minimize the space used and make things a bit more manageable.

Removing a hard top can also present problems, especially on the occasions you find yourself without extra hands. Though Jeep doesn't recommend it, I've solo-maneuvered my share of hard tops onto quite a few TJs. The Unlimited hard top is another story. It's longer and heavier and it's a bit awkward to remove, even with help. A few companies offer ceiling-mounted hoists that simply raise the hard top off the vehicle with a pulley system. The Hoist-a-Top, from a company called Lange Originals in Salt Lake City, appears to have this setup down pat. They offer manual and powered hoists, in addition to a few other Jeep top and body accessories, including quick-release latches for rapid hard top removal and installation.

Bikini Tops

A bikini top is great in the summertime, or for any time really. It can function as your primary top and it works great for keeping out excessive sun while letting the wind blow through your hair. I like running the bikini with half doors and half windows in place, and it actually makes for a great enclosure. Soft bulkheads are also available to offer a more complete seal from the elements. Bikini tops typically attach to a rail installed along the top of the windshield frame and also secure to the sport bar. They're available in a variety of configurations, including over cab and safari-style, and in many colors and styles.

Half Tops

Half tops have increased in popularity over the TJ's lifespan, and even the retro-style half hard top of the Jeep Scrambler era has made a comeback. This was largely due to the release of the Wrangler Unlimited, which had Scrambler wannabes aching for the look and

The factory hard top has seen few changes over the years. The vents in the rear sides were removed after 2002 and moved to the tailgate.

Bestop offers a soft half top that features a rear tonneau cover and a built-in mesh screen that stays in place after the rear window is removed.

function of this style top, which was a staple in the original vehicle. I gotta say, they do look cool, on the Unlimited or even a standard Wrangler. They also work great in extreme hot or cold climates since the smaller enclosed area is heated or cooled more rapidly.

Only a few half-top options are available for Wranglers. Bestop offers a soft half top that incorporates a fold-back sunroof and a rear tonneau cover for the cargo area. As far as hard half tops, Gr8tops manufactures a quality hard half top that fits both the Wrangler and Unlimited with either full hard doors or half doors. The top includes a bulkhead piece to completely seal the cab and offers a very factory fit appearance.

Doors

The style of doors on a TJ can make or break a new passenger's vehicle approval rating. Some folks just can't get used to open air, while others feel restricted by the roll-up windows on the full hard doors. I'd recommend going with whichever style best fits your weather. The full hard doors with roll-up windows help keep the cab warmer dur-

Half hard doors use soft upper doors with zip-out windows. The upper door halves are also easily removable and stowed away for a more open-air experience.

ing the cold months, while half doors keep it cool in the summer. The hard doors are also significantly more secure, especially when paired with a hard top, and the roll up windows are much more user friendly than the zipper windows that go with the half doors. If rocks are in your future, pull the doors off and leave them at home or at camp to avoid unnecessary damage. This also gives you a little better view of the trail. Any TJ can be equipped with factory TJ hard or half doors, no matter which it came with.

You'll notice that once you've removed the doors the dome light stays on. In the '01 Wrangler manual, it mentions that "Many of these vehicles do not have fully enclosed hard doors." But that's about all it mentions on door removal. Though entirely possible and traditionally practiced, taking off the doors isn't a task that Jeep necessarily endorses. They'll tell you how to lower the top and fold down the windshield, but removing doors isn't even brushed on. Therefore, the dome light stays on when the doors are off. There are a few ways around this minor issue, including installing a fused switch bypass that enables you to turn off the dome light manually, or a few companies also offer small spring-loaded clips that fit over the button on the doorjamb to keep it depressed when the doors are off. There's also the issue of side mirrors, which are mounted to the doors. Skid Row Automotive and others offer mirror relocation brackets that mount the stock mirrors to the windshield hinge so you and your TJ can remain street legal when the doors are off—another obvious indication that Jeep (or at least its lawyers) prefers that the doors stay on.

Aside from the factory doors, the aftermarket is also well stocked. A variety of half door styles exist, including steel-frame soft half doors, molded plastic half doors, and tube steel half doors. I've only sampled the latter, having had enough of the soft doors in my CJ days. Bestop's

molded plastic half doors are pretty cool for those stuck with only hard doors. They accept the factory upper doors and windows and include 400-watt stereo speakers, map pockets, and entry lights. These doors are a good fit and will stand up well to rocks and other obstacles. One drawback, however, is that they aren't paintable, so black is your only color choice.

The steel-tube half doors also work well and are right at home on the trail. These are designed to limit weight and save the factory equipment from damage in extreme wheeling situations, or just add some peace of mind that you won't fall out of your rig trying to spit tobacco. O-R Fab makes a quality set called Rock Doors that fit on the factory hinges. The doors feature arm padding, a map pocket, and a latch kit. Currie Enterprises also produces some very sturdy tube doors that are equipped with locking paddle latches. Original equipment full steel doors are available from a variety of sources, but they aren't cheap. You'll find better deals shopping for used units.

When considering half doors, you'll also want to invest in some quality door uppers/windows. The standard style is

These steel tube doors from O-R Fab are easily installed and provide for mounting the factory side mirrors.

4WD Products and others offer side mirror kits that relocate the side mirrors to a windshield hinge mount.

Color-matched fender flares look good on the street but you can expect to crease them on occasion when you fully articulate the suspension.

Bushwacker makes 4- and 6-inch width flares to provide additional coverage for wider wheels and tires.

the soft upper with a zipper window. I've been running a few sets of these since 2001. I keep the OE set that came with my Sport model for wheeling trips and save a nice set that I attempt to take care of for daily driving use. I've also used a set of slider windows. While I like the ease of opening and closing the slider window over the zipper style window, you lose the ability to hang your arm out the window comfortably. I'd also accidentally smack my head into the glass from time to time, forgetting that just because it was open didn't mean my head could fit through. However you do it, half doors and door uppers won't seal out the cold as well as full hard doors and a hard top will, but you'll always have the versatility of removing the uppers and taking in a breeze when the hard door guys are roasting.

Fender Flares

The factory fender flares will fade with time. If you stay away from car wash rags soaked with tire treatment, they may last a bit longer, but eventually they'll fade to whitish gray. This isn't a huge issue, but if you're big on appearance it will be a thorn in your side. Those of you with body colored flares don't have much to worry about, aside from the typical folding over and spider webbing that may

occur after tire contact during suspension compression. The effects will be greater with larger tires and more difficult trails. The factory color-matched painted flares aren't a very common sight on trail-equipped TJs since they're about 1-inch wider and rock scars are more visible. The color-matched crowd isn't always the most trail savvy, either, and many so-equipped vehicles remain stock. For this reason, the condition of the factory fender flares is a useful indicator of how the vehicle was used by the previous owner.

You have a fairly broad selection when you're looking to replace the factory fender flares. Your first option is to use factory replacement flares from Jeep. Some states require the flare to cover the tire, so if you have taller and wider tires or wheels with more backspacing, you might elect to use an extended-width flare to keep it legal. Legality isn't the only reason to install wider flares, since they also aid in keeping mud splatter to a minimum. But for my needs, wide flares are simply more material to hang up on rocks and other obstacles along the trail. I still have the factory rear flares in place and though well scarred and faded, they still serve the intended function.

A few things to keep in mind when shopping fender flares include the fact that most cannot be installed without modification if you have aftermarket

rocker guards. Also, pay attention to what you're getting, because flares are made from a variety of materials, including ABS plastic, polyurethane, and Polyolefin. The factory flares are made from Polyolefin and don't like paint, but the plastic flares can be easily painted if that's your goal. As I mentioned previously, flare width should also be considered. For example, a factory flare is about 3¼ inches wide. Thus, a 6-inch flare will offer 2¾ inches of increased tire coverage. Flare Manufacturers include Bestop, WARN, Xenon, and BushWacker. The OE style replacement flares are the cheapest option. Check out Quadratec or 4 Wheel Drive Hardware for good deals on these and other parts.

If you stuff the tires into your fender flares enough times, they will eventually give up. Match the right size wheels and tires with the right lift kit to avoid this problem.

Bumpers

The first thing you'll find about your factory bumpers is that the plastic bumperettes will soon disappear. It took just one wheeling trip in my TJ. If you intend to keep your stock bumpers, then you have a couple of choices. You can leave the bumperettes on and likely destroy them but maybe save the actual bumper from tweaks, or you can lose the bumperettes and run the risk of flattening a few corners. I noticed that one company now offers steel end cap inserts to replace the plastic units, but I expect that appearance is perhaps their greatest attribute. If the factory bumpers aren't up to snuff, as usual, the aftermarket is overflowing with alternatives.

Stock plastic bumperettes may help in the parking lot but they'll take little off-road abuse before becoming damaged or falling off.

The twin-tube bumper is an old stand by for many but it adds little to no functional improvements over stock. In fact, approach angle is diminished a bit and many of these designs don't have provisions for mounting a winch. (Photo courtesy DaimlerChrysler)

Bolting on a new bumper seems like it should be just about the easiest thing in the world to accomplish. For the most part it is, but that's only after you've chosen a bumper. Some aftermarket bumpers are better than others in terms of construction, material, and strength, but the variety of available styles leaves it up to you to decide which will work best for your vehicle. Styles range from your basic flat steel units designed to look factory fit, to retro twin-tube designs, to more compact units created to improve approach and departure angles and keep weight to a minimum.

Other buying considerations exist. Do you plan to install a winch? Will the rear bumper incorporate a spare tire carrier? Some bumpers can be sealed to hold air and serve as an air tank for an onboard air system. Many bumpers also have provisions for mounting D-ring shackles and might incorporate a hitch receiver. Tabs for light mounting are also common. The material should also be an important factor. While you might get away with a thin-wall steel unit to function as a light bar, it likely won't cut it on the trail scraping up against rocks or other obstacles. Heavier-duty materials mean more weight, so don't be surprised if the front end of the vehicle dips a bit with a sturdy bumper. This will be most noticeable on Wranglers with stock coil springs, since aftermarket springs are typically a bit stiffer and are better prepared for heavier loads.

Winch Mounting

If you intend to mount a winch, pay close attention to your bumper manufacturer's statement regarding winch mounting. Not all aftermarket bumpers are made with every brand and model winch in mind. Most winch manufacturers offer winch mounting plates or hardware to accommodate their specific models, and they aren't always universal. WARN and Ramsey winches are both popular brands and are often used by

Hoop-style bumpers became increasingly popular with the rise of professional rock crawling. Some will aid in preventing damage to the hood in the event of a rollover on the trail.

Some bumpers are sealed to hold air to serve as an air tank for an onboard air system. That'll come in handy when you need to air your tires back up after a day of wheeling.

Shorty-style bumpers are better for more extreme trails since there's less bumper to hang up on obstacles. This can help improve the vehicle's approach and departure angles, as well as its side-to-side clearance.

Many aftermarket rear bumpers incorporate a spare tire rack. Some are designed to only carry up to a 35-inch tire, so make sure the one you choose will work for your spare.

bumper manufacturers for designing winch mounts for their products. This isn't to say that other models won't fit, but remember to inquire about the winch you currently use, and also the one you hope to get down the road. I'll talk more about winches in Chapter 11.

Tow Hooks

Most Wranglers were factory-equipped with front and rear tow hooks that mount to the frame, but aftermarket bumpers often require these tow hooks to be removed for proper fitment. Since most quality aftermarket bumpers incorporate some sort of D-ring mount or other stable tow point, this isn't a huge deal. Some

bumpers, however, don't include provisions for such, so make sure you don't eliminate a necessary attachment point on your vehicle. D-ring mounts can be welded onto most steel bumpers by a capable 4x4 shop. Tow hooks can also be relocated to an alternate secure location.

Spare Tire Racks

The factory spare tire carrier will hold a slightly larger tire and wheel, but if you get too big, you may end up causing damage. I'd recommend upgrading to a heavier-duty aftermarket carrier once you exceed a 31-inch tire. You can get away with a taller tire (though not much wider), but you'd really just be pushing your luck. Aftermarket swing-away tire carriers are great, but you should be wary of trying to hang too big a tire at the rear of your Wrangler. I've folded in two tailgates over the years trying to carry a spare that was too big for my carrier. The added weight can be enough to alter the vehicle's driving characteristics, plus the bigger the tire, the more to hang up on obstacles during off-road maneuvers. In recent years, I've switched to keeping the spare in the cab resting between the wheel wells. A 37-inch tire just fits and provides a good deal more space at the rear of the vehicle for a tighter departure angle.

Most spare tire carriers are incorpo-

rated into the rear bumper and swing away from the vehicle on a greasable pin or spindle so you can access the rear door. You need a quality locking mechanism to ensure that the weight of the tire won't allow the carrier to swing open on its own. This happened to me a couple times. I nearly wiped out a parked car the first time and I knocked over some trash cans on the other. This is a very dangerous situation, so I promptly replaced the bumper and tire carrier for a better-built unit. This is just how it goes with aftermarket parts—every once in a while you'll get a dud. Tire carrier locking method varies from bumper to bumper. Many use cam-style locks, while others use a locking pin. The locking pin design seems the most flawless method, but does require you to insert the pin for it to work properly.

Spare tire racks can also typically be outfitted to tote other gear, as well. A Hi-Lift jack mount is almost a given on most carriers, and some can be equipped to hold GI-type gas cans, axes, and shovels. Some manufacturers also produce cargo baskets or racks that can be bolted to the tire carrier. Remember that each item you add will add weight to the rear and that vehicle handling may be affected. I actually prefer spreading out the weight and typically make do with what I can pack inside the rig.

Body Armor

If you plan to wheel your Wrangler, then plan on investing in some quality body armor. Heavy-duty body protection comes in many shapes and is available for nearly every part of your rig. The aforementioned bumpers are a great aid in withstanding damage to the lower front and rear, but more is needed to protect other vulnerable components.

Rocker Guards

The rocker panels are an easy target for rocks and will suffer greatly if

Bumpers are often used as an attachment point for a tow strap or winch line, so material strength and how the bumper is secured to the vehicle are crucial to a well designed bumper.

The factory spare tire rack can safely support up to a 31-inch tire. You can sneak a bit larger, but don't snivel if your tailgate is tweaked down the road.

Rocker guards are all designed to accomplish the same goal: protect the rocker panels from damage. Most rocker guards wrap under the body and also bolt through the floor, while others also extend further inward and secure to the frame rail. These TJ rocker guards from FourXDoctor feature a tube step.

precautionary measures aren't taken. Rubicons are pre-equipped with diamond plate rocker guards, but aftermarket units offer even greater protection. FourXDoctor makes some very sturdy and functional rocker guards, as do Currie Enterprises, JC Fab, Poison Spyder Customs, and many, many others. Each set is a variation of the same theme and they all appear to bolt on and function similarly. One of the varying points is the step design; some offer a tube step that lines the bottom edge, while others offer no step at all. How the rocker guards are mounted to the vehicle also varies and is an important design aspect. Solid mounting points should be used so that additional damage doesn't occur to the vehicle should they fail.

As with bumpers and other body protection equipment, the strength of the steel rocker panels are very important. It's likely that you'll need to trim the factory fender flares a bit for proper fitment, but most other available rocker guards will fit well. Lastly, and this may sound stupid, but be careful not to catch a toe, or worse yet, your whole foot, in the tube step offered on some rocker

guards while climbing in and out of your Wrangler. I've almost broken an ankle after my foot slipped from the step that extended outward from the rocker panel. Face-planting into the driver's seat after forgetting to wipe the mud off your boots is a fun one, too. It does a number on your shin, as well.

Steel Body Panels

Steel body plate panels can be bolted or riveted on to cover damage that previously occurred or to protect stock panels from harm. I've had a set of Warrior steel corners in place ever since some bozo "tapped" me in a parking lot, they've actually saved me from quite a few blunders. A deep scratch in the steel panel could have meant torn stock sheetmetal, had it not been for protection. Beyond rear corner guards, the aftermarket has significantly expanded its TJ steel body panel offerings in recent years. Previously, your chief option was to locate a salvage or new old stock (NOS) body component and have a body shop graft it onto your TJ. Poison Spyder Customs manufactures full rear steel body panels for TJs and LJs that can also be outfit with steel tube fender flares for additional rock protection. The panels are made from ³⁄₁₆-inch laser cut steel and install over the factory panels using ⅜-inch counter-sunk bolts. Some people use a bead of silicone sealer to prevent water from getting between the stock and aftermarket body panels.

Tube Fenders

Tube fenders are another trick piece of body armor that creates a sturdy barrier between the rocks and your stock sheetmetal. I installed a set of Poison Spyder Customs front tube fenders a few years back and am still reaping the rewards. Tube fenders install over a portion of the stock fender with the outer area cut away. This makes them somewhat of a permanent item on your vehicle, unlike a bumper that merely

Think your TJ body is torn up? Steel body corners bolt on over the factory sheet metal and provide good added protection from trail obstacles.

Poison Spyder Customs offers full steel body panels that extend from behind the door pillar and wrap around the corner of the body to the tailgate. These work well for covering up existing body damage and also protecting it from new damage.

This is a good example of what can happen to the factory sheet metal if left unprotected. Looks like it's time for a tube-fender upgrade.

Tube fenders are a great way to remove a fear of rocks. Where you used to hear "crunch," the fender will just slide on over rocks. In many situations I've witnessed minimal scarring to areas that would have been destroyed without the tube fenders.

The factory tin shield offers little protection for rocks and other obstacles. The FourXDoctor skid plate is shown. Imagine what the fuel tank would look like if it wasn't protected by a skid plate.

bolts on and off. A number of companies manufacture tube fenders for TJs, and most incorporate a welded-on flare of some sort to minimize road spray and keep it legal.

Skid Plates

Jeep finally got it right with the Rubicon by including much-needed skid plates. Though most non-Rubicon model TJs include a factory-installed transfer-case skid plate (it was an option for some SE years), the underbelly is still left largely unprotected. Predictably though, the aftermarket is well stocked with skid plates to protect each vulnerable item and help you slide over rocks when necessary.

Fuel tank skid plates are one of the more popular add-ons, as Wrangler owners quickly find that it grinds over obstacles after the rear wheels roll over them. There's a factory fuel tank skid plate in place, but it's made of tin and doesn't offer a great deal of reprieve. A variety of fuel tank skid plates are offered, including those available from FourXDoctor, TeraFlex, Tomken, and others. Another option is to replace the fuel tank with an aluminum tank and steel skid plate from Gen-Right Off Road. The 18-gallon tank is designed so that the rear axle can be

moved back, up to five inches, to allow the wheelbase to be lengthened. The Gen-Right tanks also allow another inch of ground clearance and an improved departure angle over stock.

The engine and transmission are left entirely unprotected from the factory. Skid plates are available to accommodate both areas and in many cases, are bolt-on items. Skid Row Automotive makes a quality skid plate to protect this area, as does Tri-County Gear, Teraflex, and others. Many suspension manufacturers have also taken the opportunity to incorporate protection into their suspen-

sion crossmember/transfer case skid plate by extending plates forward and securing them to the frame. Note that some engine and transmission skid plates may interfere with long-arm suspension components or the front driveshaft and may have to be modified for installation.

Other popular armor includes steering box skid plates and differential guards. Steering box skid plates are usually secured using the stock steering box bolts plus additional bolts for added rigidity. Differential guards come in a variety of forms, from basic bolt-on hoop-style skids that protect the lower part of the diff, the cover, and bolts, to the more extreme guards that replace the whole diff cover with a solid-steel unit . Rear lower shock mount skid plates are also offered, as are lower control arm skid plates, body mount skids, and lower radiator skid plates.

Replacement Body Parts

If you're restoring your TJ or repairing some damage a variety of replacement body panels and complete bodies are available. Replacement or NOS sheetmetal body and tub panels are perhaps the cheapest outright option, but consider the time and cost of installing these items. If your stock panels are rock

Skid Row Automotive offers an oil pan and engine skid plate for Wranglers. They bolt on and protect the vulnerable parts from weekend-ruining damage.

Long-arm suspension systems, like this one from Fabtech, require the factory skid plate to be removed completely. The skid plate is replaced with a new skid plate/crossmember that also serves as a mounting point for the control arms.

The AEV heat reduction hood is designed to help maintain cooler engine operating temperatures during low speed wheeling by allowing the engine heat to leave the engine compartment.

scarred, the aforementioned steel body panels typically only require some or a portion of the factory panels beneath for mounting, so they may be time and money better spent since you'll also gain much needed rock protection. The floor pans, rear floor section, inner fenders, and rusted parts are better replaced by standard sheetmetal.

Beyond body panels, complete replacement bodies are a more labor-intensive, yet enticing option. No companies currently offer steel TJ bodies, but replacement aluminum tubs are available and can be tailored for use on a TJ. You'll need to drill all the right mounting holes in all the right places, and then swap everything over to the new tub. The tubs can be mated with steel or stainless fenders. A few aftermarket hood options include the Campbell Enterprises fiberglass hood with integral fenders and the AEV heat-reduction hood.

Roof and Cargo Racks

There are some very cool roof racks available from the aftermarket for both hard- and soft-top equipped Wranglers. Racks can be used to carry all sorts of extra gear for the trail, whether you're heading off for a month long journey or simply like to be prepared for disaster.

Racks create a mounting location for off-road lighting and can also be outfit with axe and shovel mounts, spare tire mounts, Hi-Lift jack mounts, and even additional bike, kayak, ski, and snowboard racks.

The majority of the available roof racks also take into consideration that many Wranglers are factory-equipped with soft tops and mount to the vehicle at the windshield frame and the rear corners rather than the top itself. This means the roof rack can be used even when the Wrangler is topless, and also makes the racks appealing to those with hard tops because installation does not require drilling into the top. There are also a few racks, such as the Top Hat Rack and the A/T Quick Rack available from Olympic 4x4 Products, which mount to the sport cage.

There are also a number of interior mounting racks available, as well as receiver-hitch racks and spare tire carrier racks. The receiver-hitch racks are great for on-road hauling but create such a large rear overhang that they aren't the best for trail use. Spare tire carrier racks, such as those made popular on CJs for traversing the Rubicon Trail, are a better option for hauling equipment on the trail. If you don't have any rear passengers, the interior rack is also a very cool

Kilby Enterprises manufactures an interior rack for TJs that bolts to the factory sport bar and the rear tub. The rack creates an extra layer of storage above the floor.

option. A variety of manufacturers offer storage racks, including Olympic 4x4 Products, Kilby Enterprises, Garvin Industries, Bestop, and others.

Lighting

There are endless lighting possibilities available, from discreet-yet-luminous fog lamps to bright-as-day HID setups designed for off-road desert racing. Forward facing lights are a great means of lighting up the trail ahead and can be mounted in many locations. The front bumper is a common spot, especially if the aftermarket bumper you run has light tabs. Rear mounted lights on the spare tire carrier or roof rack can be used to light the camp area or in the event of trailside repairs, and rock lights (lights mounted under the vehicle to the frame or other components) are used to illuminate the trail during nighttime excursions or for the times you don't beat the sun home.

The factory headlights can also be upgraded to light the road ahead more efficiently. IPF offers its H4 headlamps, which produce a much whiter and brighter beam. Many TJs came factory-equipped with front bumper-mounted fog lamps that offer a good amount of light. A few years back I replaced the fog

Rear-mounted "Rubicon"-style racks secure to an aftermarket spare tire carrier and are a great spot for carrying an ice chest or camping equipment.

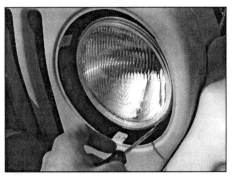

Installing a set of IPF H4 headlights is one way to get more from the factory lights. These lights produce a blue/green glow as they cool down after being turned off.

The windshield hinge light mounting brackets from 4WD Products support one light each, and are a great use of available space.

lamps with a set of driving lights and used the existing wiring that led to the factory switch. The only problem was that Jeep wired the fog lamps so they would turn off if the high beams were used. If you don't mind only running the additional lights with the low beams, then this is a good route. Otherwise, you'll want to install your own dash-mounted switch, along with a relay and inline fuse.

Chrome Extras

As with most vehicles and particularly Jeeps, many extras are available to meet a variety of owners needs. Vehicle dress-up items make up a large portion of this market and most provide little if any improvement to the Wrangler. But, they are available and if you want to lay chrome over everything in sight then that's your prerogative. Some of the available chrome items include grille overlays, headlamp rings, windshield hinges, hood latches, gas filler housings and doors, mirrors, and door hinges. You name it—if you want it to be chrome, it's likely available for the TJ. Other popular add-ons for the TJ are mud flaps, bug

deflectors, doorsill guards, headlight guards, spare tire covers, bras, doorsill paint protectors, and hydraulic hood lifts.

Interior Upgrades

The TJ interior is entirely user-friendly. I've yet to discover any major deficiencies beyond basic comfort needs and a lack of lockable security, which is pretty much the nature of a full convertible rig. Even still, a vast amount of upgrades are available for the TJ interior. From seats, consoles, and roll cages, to storage and security components, stereo and navigation, and grab handles, the aftermarket is pretty well stocked.

Seating

The TJ seats started out fairly basic, but an improved design was introduced in the '03 model year. The early seats were softer, offering less support and minimal functionality. The later designs featured a higher back and headrest, greater lumbar support, and a seat release mounted to the side of both the driver and passenger seats that make it easier to get into the back seat. For those

Many TJ owners have replaced the factory rear lamps with round LED taillights. The LEDs sit flush with the sheetmetal, so they aren't as likely to be damaged by rocks.

Entry steps are a popular add-on to Wranglers, especially after the vehicle has been lifted. These steps appear to be a dealer-installed option.

The TJ dash can be outfitted to accommodate even the biggest gear heads. This dash features a variety of CBs, speakers, flashlights, and a GPS system.

TJ seats prior to 2003 were very standard-looking front bucket seats that lacked comfort and support. Vinyl (shown) and cloth seats were available.

The later seat, which came along in 2003, was much more functional and incorporated an adjustable headrest and lumbar support.

Aftermarket rear seats are also available from sources such as Bestop. The seat fits well with either factory or aftermarket hardware in the factory location.

Bestop offers some of the most widely used seats in its TrailMax line of seats. The ones shown feature adjustable headrests and mildew-resistant fabric. A heated TrailMax seat is also available.

used to traditional Jeep seating, the higher backs may be a bit cumbersome at first, especially for shorter drivers who may have trouble seeing over their shoulders. The new seats are definitely more comfortable and make it much easier to get in and out of the back seat area.

The selection of aftermarket seats is fairly broad. I've seen many different styles of seats bolted in place of the factory seats. Some require creative mounting, but many others bolt right into the factory seat mounts and/or seat sliders. One of my favorite aftermarket seats comes from MasterCraft. I've used a set of MasterCraft Rubicon seats in my 01' TJ for nearly five years and am constantly reminded of their worth. The company's latest seat offering is its Reclining Baja RS seat, which uses the same seat suspension technology, yet incorporates a reclining back rather the traditional fixed back of a racing-style seat. MasterCraft also produces rear seat covers for the factory rear fold and tum-

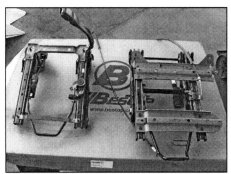

The early and late model seat frames are different and some seats may require special adapters for fitment. The later model seat slider is shown on the left.

ble seat. The slip-on covers keep the factory seat material clean and also allow you to match the front seat design and color scheme.

The Bestop TrailMax seat has been a staple to many Wrangler YJ owners for years and it also makes a good fit in the TJ. The seat can be ordered with a variety of options, including an adjustable or fixed headrest or even seat heaters. Many

material options are also available to match factory colors, and a waterproof neoprene version is also offered. Bestop also manufactures a fold-and-tumble seat that is quite similar to stock and looks factory fit. Beard, ProCarr, PRP and others also offer aftermarket front and rear seats.

Roll Cages and Safety

Driving a vehicle in any situation comes with certain dangers. On city streets, these dangers are great, since you not only have to rely on yourself but also the thousands of drivers around you. Driving off-road can also be dangerous, but in most cases the highest risks occur

It only takes one rollover to help you realize that a roll cage is a necessity. Even when you're in control. it's not hard to imagine ending up on your side or roof. See page 130. (Photo courtesy Kevin McNulty)

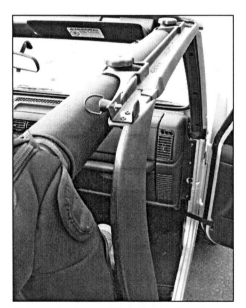

The factory sport bar that extends toward the windshield from the roll bar should not be considered adequate for rollover protection.

at a low speed in a completely controlled environment, where it's just you, your Wrangler, and the obstacle at hand. Still, this doesn't mean you shouldn't take precautionary measures to make sure you make it home in one piece.

Wearing your seatbelt at all times is the best way to increase your odds of staying alive in your Wrangler. It's just stupid not to wear it whenever the key is in the ignition. On top of seat belts, every Jeep Wrangler TJ includes a factory roll bar to further ensure occupant safety. The roll bar consists of the hoop section over the front seat and the rear bars, which extend toward the rear wheel wells. The bars above the door are referred to as sport bars and will offer minimal rollover protection, if any.

The best part about the factory roll bar is that it provides an excellent founda-

tion for a complete roll cage. In recent years, a variety of manufacturers have produced some of the finest, easy-to-install roll cage kits. Many of these are bolt-in affairs that draw on support from the factory roll bar and replace the lightweight sport bar components. One of the greatest features of these kits is the price. A custom roll cage usually creeps well above $1,000, whereas a bolt-in cage kit can be obtained for less than $500. Most roll cage kits add new A-pillars that secure to the door pillars and windshield. Some kits also include provisions to extend the door pillar mounts to the floorboards, which is a great means of further increasing occupant protection in the event of a rollover. Weld-in cages are inherently stronger than bolt-in cages and often include more gussets. Your choice should depend on the value of your head. My head is worth over $1,000.

Roll cage kits also have lots of options, such as extra bolt-in bars that can be used in various locations to provide further support. A bar can be installed behind the seats to secure seat belt shoulder harnesses. Grab handles can also be conveniently placed. Dash bars can be added. Weld-in gussets are another option. Poison Spyder Customs offers two roll cage kits for Wranglers, its bolt-in Helldorado system and its weld-in Trail Cage. The weld-in Trail Cage will run you a bit more for installation, but will offer a good deal more strength than the bolt-in style cages.

Some cage kits don't allow use of some factory interior items, such as sound bars, speaker pods, and sun visors. Check with the manufacturer to see what components will be affected, but wouldn't you rather have an intact noodle than overhead speakers?

Carpet Kits and Coatings

I've been thoroughly amazed at the resiliency of the factory carpet. Even after repeated rainstorms, mud, and

Poison Spyder Customs offers two roll cage kits for Wranglers. The weld-in Trail Cage system is shown.

Rock Hard 4x4 Parts has available its Sport Cage, which requires no drilling or welding for installation.

infrequent vacuuming, the carpet still looks good and stays fixed in place. However, this isn't the case with all TJs. Pre-2000 TJs appear to use a carry-over carpet kit from the Wrangler YJ that doesn't fare as well under the elements.

For those in the need of an interior refresher, there are many sources of replacement carpet. Most factory colors are available. Some carpet kits are better than others, and typically, you get what you pay for. Also, some carpets kits are universally cut to easily fit other Jeep models, so pay attention to what you're buying or the install may become more labor intensive than it has to be. The vinyl type carpets seem to hold up better than the plush living-room styles.

Another option is to coat the floor of the tub with a spray-in or brush-on liner. This is a good idea for those in colder, wetter climates, since the liner can inhibit rust. It will also add a bit more insulation from road noise, and can be combined with floor mats or even a carpet kit. Floor liners, which are much easier to clean, are also available.

CBs and GPS

Staying in touch on the trail is a great idea for ensuring trail safety. While hand signals may work if everyone in your group remains within the line of sight, a CB radio is typically the more preferred method. There are a variety of ways to mount a CB in your TJ. One of the easier ways is to install a Tuffy overhead security console, which mounts between the roll bar and the windshield. The console can hold a CB or other piece of electronic equipment, and also features secure compartments for additional small-item storage. Most CBs include a mounting bracket and this can also be utilized in a variety of locations throughout the TJ. One of the more common mounting sites is the forward portion of the center console next to the transfer case shifter. This could present issues for some TJ owners with longer legs, but it seems to suit many.

Using a global positioning system (GPS) is one sure-fire way to not get lost. While Jeepers have been toting handheld GPS units for quite a few years, Mopar Parts and Garmin teamed to create a unit made specifically for the Wrangler. The Trail Guide navigation system mounts to the tray at the top center of the dash and features a display cradle with two speakers for turn-by-turn directions,

The Garmin Trail Guide GPS mounts to the coin tray at the top of the dash bezel. It uses a unique cradle/charging bay with two speakers for turn-by-turn directions and can also be used for storage of the GPS unit.

a charging bay, and a secure storage compartment for when it isn't in use. The GPS unit itself can be removed from the cradle so you can take it with you on foot. It's completely waterproof and offers a full-color screen and uses lithium batteries that provide up to 20 hours of use when it isn't in the charging cradle.

Accessory Switch Control

If you install an accessory, such as a set of lights, you'll need to install a switch to operate this accessory. While it isn't difficult to find a spot for one extra switch on your dash, you can run out of space once you have three or four extra switches. There are a few good places to add switches to the dash. The best spot is below the climate control system next to the ashtray where hard-top models are equipped with factory-placed switches for the rear windshield wiper and rear window defroster. This is where the front and rear locker activation switches are located in the Rubicon. The area is easy to access by removing the center bezel and is near to accessible power sources. I've also experimented with placing

These center switch and/or gauge pods mount over the coin tray on the center dash bezel. This one holds three switches and two gauges.

The sPod windshield switch panel from JC Fab & Design holds seven rocker switches or six switches and one gauge. It installs in factory bolt holes without additional drilling.

The Tuffy locking glove box is made from high-strength 16-gauge steel and includes a high-strength tumbler lock. It replaces the factory plastic glove box and can be keyed to match other Tuffy locking storage pieces.

Bestop offers its Instatrunk as an easy method of creating rear locking storage at the rear of the vehicle. The InstaTrunk isolates the area behind the rear seat so it can only be accessed from the tailgate when it is open. A locked tailgate creates secure storage.

The Bestop Extendatrunk can be installed to factory seat hardware and creates some secure storage when the tailgate is locked. Of course, the rear seat must be removed for use.

switches on the dash panel to the left of the steering wheel. The higher mounted switches fare well but the lower ones take a punch from my knee, every other time I get out of the drivers seat. Both parties suffered, so I've since moved these switches to the center bezel area.

If you have too many switches to fit in the dash, a few switch-center options exist to help centralize your custom-mounted switches. One such option is a center gauge and switch pod that installs over the change tray at the top of the dash. The enclosed panel can be equipped with multiple switches or a few switches and a gauge or two. A variety of sources offer this item, including Tri-County Gear and Kilby Enterprises, among others. For even more accessory switch mounting possibilities, look to the windshield-mounted sPod switch panel, which secures to the windshield frame between the sun visors and can hold up to seven rocker switches or six switches and an air gauge for an onboard air system. The sPod panel is easily mounted and wired thanks to the available wiring harnesses.

Storage and Security

If your Wrangler has ever been broken into, you know that it isn't the most secure vehicle ever made. After all, most TJs don't even have tops on them and some even go doorless. Though lockable factory glove boxes and consoles were optional after 2000, they still don't offer the greatest theft deterrence. Quite a few alternatives exist to replace the factory equipment, including full steel locking glove boxes, locking consoles, and a host of locking storage boxes and compartments. Tuffy Security Products is one of the larger storage purveyors and pretty much has it down pat. Tuffy offers a number of secure storage possibilities, including an overhead console and rear wheel well storage boxes that can be equipped with stereo speakers. The best thing about the Tuffy items is that they all lock securely using heavy-duty tumbler locks and can be keyed alike so you only need one key to access multiple storage compartments. Bestop also offers a few saddlebag options that secure to the roll bar and tailgate, as well as a plastic storage trunk that fits in the rear and secures to the factory seat hardware.

TAKING YOUR TJ OFF THE PAVEMENT

Taking your Wrangler off-road is the ultimate display of pride in ownership. Off-roading is what Jeeps are built for, and it brings out the best in them. However, taking to the trail does require a bit of planning on your part to ensure a successful trip. While a stock Wrangler can easily handle most terrain in stock form, it's important to start small until you're certain of your vehicle's capabilities, as well as your own driving ability. On a number of occasions, I've driven well-equipped loaner Jeeps where I was handed the keys and told to have fun. While I did have fun, it wasn't until I'd taken the time to familiarize myself with the vehicle's trail manners that I could best react to a given driving situation.

Pick Your Terrain

You'll notice that Jeep Wranglers are set up differently, not only to cater to each individual's personal preferences, but also according to how the vehicle is used the most. You also may notice that different regions call for different setups. For example, a lot of guys I know in Kentucky and Tennessee areas roll V-8 engines and 38- to 40-inch mud terrain tires that function well in muddy and wet conditions. Super Swamper tires are

Just as you learned to ride a bike, it's important to start slow when hitting the trail for the first time. Driving over your head or beyond your vehicle's capabilities is a sure-fire way to get stuck, broken, and hurt.

You should seek out the opportunity to drive your Wrangler across multiple terrains. You'll not only gain experience as a driver, but may also discover a fondness for rocks, mud, or sand that you may not have known to exist.

Lots of throttle and picking a good line are the keys to crossing mud holes without getting stuck. If your tires get coated with mud you can expect rock surfaces to feel slicker than usual.

more common in the Southeast for this reason, while desert and rock crawling treads are more prevalent in the Southwest. Most of the TJs you see in California, Nevada, Arizona, and New Mexico, are built to contend with rocks and sand with 35- to 37-inch treads. Those living in snowy areas also adapt their 4x4s for use in such conditions. Studded and/or siped tires are employed to help achieve better traction in snow and ice, and snowplow attachments are also available.

Mud

Driving in mud sucks. Don't get me wrong, I love a good mud drag on television or even in person, but for my own rig, I hate mud. This comes mostly from the fact that I'm very bad at keeping to a car wash schedule of any sort. Even when I wash my Jeep, I find it impossible to remove all remnants of mud after landing in a mud bog. When I sold my '69 CJ-5 back in 1987 it still had mud on top of the frame rails from two years earlier. The buyer noticed it during his pre-purchase inspection. Yet despite my attitude toward boggy mires, I won't ignore the fact that some folks flat-out love hitting mud holes in their TJs.

It requires a good amount of speed to slosh through mud successfully, and depending on the length of the mud hole, you'll also want to maintain a good deal of momentum. This means staying in high gear and not digging in. The faster the wheels spin, the faster the tire tread blocks will self clean and continue grabbing and moving forward. The higher rate of speed also helps the vehicle float across the top of the mud. Successfully attacking an obstacle at speed, however, also requires a good degree of planning. After all, you don't want to blast across unknown territory and end up with a submerged vehicle. Believe it or not, all mud holes aren't just puddles waiting to be splashed through—some are deep enough to swallow a Wrangler whole. Just as you'd carefully examine an obstacle that could result in a rollover, you should do the same when tackling muddy terrain. This is the best defense against vehicle breakage and helps you continue up the trail in one piece.

Your first step should be to size up the mud hole and look for the best route across. Previous successful tracks left by other rigs are sometimes the best option, but don't eliminate the possibility that the previous vehicle across might've been equipped with larger tires than

your rig. Once you pick a line, stick with it. If the front tires want a different line due to a rut beneath the surface, sometimes it's best to let it take you there, but only if you can do so without losing control or momentum. You can help the tires stay on the surface by airing down to create a wider contact patch. Aggressive tread tires with large diameter and width are essential for conquering mud.

Rocks

Just the opposite of mud, rocky terrain calls for slow and steady progress to successfully complete an obstacle. High-RPM attempts are a quick way to break drivetrain parts, but rocks are also partial to damaging steering systems and whatever else gets in their way. Picking the correct line is crucial and can sometimes take a few attempts to accomplish. If an obstacle looks extra difficult, I like to get out and walk the path to get a feel for it, as well as to locate sharp or unstable rocks to avoid. More often than not, I usually end up driving the same route I traveled on foot and imagined in my head. Learning how to read the terrain and knowing how your vehicle reacts to trail conditions is a big part of being successful at rock crawling.

Rock crawling takes a bit of patience to get right but once you're familiar with your vehicle it's a matter of picking the right line and driving consistently.

Some rocky trails seem to never end. Slow and steady gets you through every time.

Airing down for any wheeling situation is a necessity, and it's a particular aid to rock crawling.

The California desert offers ample rock crawling opportunities.

Attacking obstacles at a low speed requires a good amount of low-end torque and plenty of low gearing. The 4.0L engine offers up plenty of torque for the job and the factory 2.72:1 low transfer case ratio is ample for stock and modified vehicles. It may begin to wane in effectiveness with 37-inch and larger tires, but you can compensate for this by installing corresponding axle gears to help maintain the low gear ratio. For those still left wanting, there are many lower-geared transfer case options to explore. Low tire pressure is also necessary for the tires to better conform and adhere to the surface of the rocks. Beadlock wheels also help protect the bead lip and sidewall of the tire from tears.

As if ascending rocky trails wasn't difficult enough, it's a whole new ballgame when things are wet. Previously course-rock surfaces become slick as snot, while once-stable rock footings are washed down the trail. Rain also quickly saturates the dirt beneath the rocks to create mud, which amplifies the difficulty of an obstacle tenfold. Dealing with just rocks or just mud can be trying in itself, but mixed together it can be downright discouraging. It is possible, though; I've seen many prove it so. It essentially becomes a game of "find the traction," and when that tire finally grabs, you just stab the throttle and steer your way through.

Like any obstacle, traversing rocky terrain takes a good bit of planning. In addition to sizing up and sometimes walking a difficult section of a trail, it's also a good idea to continue looking ahead as you make your way up the trail and plan out how you'll hit the obstacle before you get there. After a while you'll know exactly when and where a front tire will contact a rock and pass over it, as well as when and where the rear tire will travel the same path. Just keep it slow and steady and keep your head, and a rocky trail will soon be as easy to conquer as the paved road leading to the trailhead.

Sand

Growing up in Southern California, some of my first experiences in a 4x4 occurred at Oceano Dunes State Vehicular Recreation Area in California. It was always a fun place to camp and the dunes stretched for miles and miles, offering ample off-highway vehicle

There is safety in numbers and that goes for Jeeping, too. Hitting the trail with a group is the best way to ensure that you'll make it home safely.

Though I don't recommend trying it yourself, a rollover can be an awakening experience. I was lucky that I just flopped on a side this time, but I've been on the lid more than once. (Photo courtesy Kevin McNulty)

Once a vehicle has come to stop, it's time to assess the situation and create a plan to right the vehicle. In this case we had enough muscle on hand and a bit of leverage on our side and were able to put the TJ back on the tires without too much trouble. (Photo courtesy Kevin McNulty)

(OHV) recreational opportunities. I remember one of my first times out I got stuck past my frame rails and couldn't understand why my rig wasn't performing as expected. A passerby eventually stopped to see how the dig out was going when he asked how much air pressure I had in the tires. Just off the highway, I was still fully aired and scratched my head at the proposition of dropping the air to 10 psi. I did it anyway, and with just a bit more digging I drove my rig out of the hole successfully. It was a lesson learned, and one I will not forget.

Lowering your tire pressure helps the vehicle float on top of the sand and maintain momentum better so that the vehicle won't dig in as easily. The lower the air pressure the better, but too low and you may slip the tire off the wheel. As with mud, sand requires that you maintain a good bit of speed and momentum. You should use the 4-high range so you can stay in a higher RPM band. Low gears won't cut it because

you'll only dig in and get stuck. Should you lose momentum in the sand or need to get started again after coming to a stop, don't hammer the throttle too hard. Instead, start in first gear and feather the gas pedal until you can get the tires spinning on top of the sand again.

Avoiding Rollover

The first time I rolled a 4x4 I felt like a complete idiot—mainly because I was. I was driving way too fast for the unknown conditions ahead and didn't anticipate a change in terrain. The graded fire road on which I was traveling suddenly dropped into a deep sand wash and made a wide banked left turn. I tried to pull it off, but I hit the brakes in a moment of panic upon dropping off into the wash and the non-power steering wheel took the path of least resistance. My firm grip on the steering wheel quickly slipped away and before I knew it my rig launched into a sand berm that sent it into a spiraling airborne roll. I can still remember a distinct slow motion feeling as I watched a loose wrench float by my face as my untethered toolbox

emptied its contents. After that, it was a quick landing and a short roof-top skid until the sand brought the vehicle to a stop (I did say I was going way too fast, didn't I?).

What did I do wrong? You name it. Inexperience driving the vehicle off-road was my first offense—I was driving over my head. Driving too fast for the conditions and for my vehicle ranks second. But I committed one final error that ultimately led to the rollover: I panicked. Despite my initial errors in judgment, had I kept a clear head and sized up the situation, I could have taken the necessary action and possibly avoided this rollover.

Another thing about my experience that bothered me were the lumps in the back of my head where I was pelted by loose tools. That was a completely avoidable injury. While I did thankfully have the forethought to tie down the heavy spare tire and gas can I had stowed behind the rear seat, the toolbox didn't enter my mind. It was tucked in behind the passenger seat and looked pretty cozy

Unnecessary injury can be avoided during a rollover by having all gear in the vehicle securely stowed or tied down. Be sure to use a spare tire carrier, which can also come in handy for storing other heavy items like gas cans.

There's no replacement for a quality roll cage in a 4x4. It can save your head in the worst of situations and should be on your shopping list above most other items.

for off-road travel. Properly storing all items you carry in your Wrangler is paramount to avoiding injury in a rollover. People are injured by loose objects more often than they are by the other effects of the rollover.

I attribute my first rollover to a moment of idiocy, but the second and third times just happened—driving off-road has its pitfalls. Perhaps I could've done a couple things differently, such as

not listening to the spotter and trusting my own judgment (of course, that would be passing the buck), but for the most part each rollover occurred because sometimes shit happens. Damage was minimal both times and I was able to continue up the trail successfully, so in effect it was pretty much just part of getting from point A to point B. Wheeling isn't for the meek; it's about adventure. Expect body damage. The best way to avoid a rollover—be careful.

If you intend to use your Wrangler off-road then I strongly recommend that you install a roll cage. While the factory roll bar helps protect you from a minor low-speed rollover (even though this type of rollover can be extremely dangerous), you can consider yourself lucky if you emerge uninjured from a more jarring incident involving multiple rolls. A variety of roll cage kits are available from the aftermarket and should be seriously explored if you intend to keep wheeling a fun pastime rather than an ugly reminder of how you could have been better prepared.

Buckle Up

I shouldn't have to remind you to wear a seat belt, but I sometimes find that I have to remind myself from time to time, so I guess it couldn't hurt. Not wearing a seat belt is a dumb move. Plus, it's illegal in most states. I wasn't so fond of the factory seat belts in my TJ because they'd cinch and lock whenever I'd drive off-road. After a while they'd get so snug that I wouldn't be able to lean forward to peer out the side at the terrain. I eventually installed lap belts with optional shoulder harnesses from MasterCraft Race Products and found much greater comfort. I use the lap belt all the time and strap on the shoulder harnesses before stepping into anything too extreme. This is a good solution to maintaining safety if you find yourself not buckling up with the factory belts.

Seat belts should be worn at all times while operating your Wrangler. The stock belts are prone to cinching tight and can be uncomfortable during off-road maneuvers, but they're still a better option than risking injury in a rollover.

Winch Use

If there's anything I've seen too much of on the trail, it's improper winching practices. The worst part is that it isn't that difficult to learn how to correctly and safely operate a winch. The largest infractions include not utilizing proper winch mounting points, not weighting the line during a pull, not using a tree strap, and having too many people standing around during a pull. D-ring shackles should be used to properly secure the winch line to a solid mounting point on the vehicle to be extracted. Many TJ models are equipped with tow hooks from the factory, but even these are questionable mounting points for a winch

A winch is an asset to any 4x4 and can make the difference between getting home or not.

line since they don't offer an enclosed mount and could allow the line to slip free during winching maneuvers. Many aftermarket bumpers incorporate mounting points for D-ring shackles, but you can also install a front receiver hitch and use a removable mount with a shackle attached.

If you're new to wheeling and don't have any experience using a winch, then I recommend taking the time to practice using it before you need it. This can be completed using just one vehicle and a stationary object, but multi-vehicle pulls should also be reviewed. Many 4x4 clubs require such knowledge before participation in events, and many are willing to share their winching expertise with a potential new member to promote responsible use. WARN Industries also offers an excellent winch guide on how to safely operate a winch, including a variety of extraction techniques.

Even a well-equipped TJ will sometimes need winching assistance. This TJ hooked up to avoid a tippy situation. Also, winch line should be weighted during a pull so it (in theory) falls to the ground if it snaps. Winch weights are available from a number of companies and are usually a better option than the jacket off your back (which can actually also serve in a pinch).

You should carry a variety of winch accessories when traveling off-road, including a winch remote control, a snatch block, a tree strap, gloves, a length of chain, and D-ring shackles. A tree strap should be employed when using a tree as an attachment point. The strap is wrapped around the tree and the cable hook is secured to it using a D-ring shackle. The strap is used to protect the tree, but also saves the winch's wire cable from becoming frayed. (Photo courtesy WARN Industries)

You should always attach a winch cable to a stable mounting point, whether it is the vehicle to be pulled or a good-sized tree that won't pull out of the ground or fall over. Don't forget to use a tree strap! (Photo courtesy WARN Industries)

Air Systems

As you experience airing down and airing up tires before and after the trail, you'll quickly find that cheapie 12-volt plug-in compressors just don't cut it. There are, however, a number of available

An electric air compressor can be mounted virtually anywhere in a vehicle and can be plumbed to an onboard air tank. Having air is great for airing tires back up when you're done wheeling for the day.

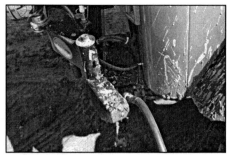

Some aftermarket bumpers are sealed so that they can be used for air storage, but a permanently mounted tank is another good option.

The Kilby On-Board Air system features an engine-driven air compressor that can be used to operate air lockers or simply air up tires after the trail. A remotely mounted air tank is used for air storage. The Kilby kit repositions the alternator and mounts the compressor above it so the pulleys are aligned. A longer drive belt is used to accommodate the compressor.

portable air systems that work quite well—much better than the cheapie units you may be used to. 4WD Products, ARB, and others offer 12-volt plug in and/or battery-clamp connection compressors to quickly air-up tires after a day of wheeling.

Look into an onboard air system if you want to give portable air a new meaning. These come in a variety of shapes and forms, from engine belt-driven compressors to electric units that can be mounted virtually anywhere in the vehicle. Optimum performance requires an air storage tank of some sort, which can also be mounted in a variety of locations. Some aftermarket bumper manufacturers seal their bumpers and install threaded fittings so that they can be used for air storage. I've also seen people seal custom roll cages for air storage.

A remote mounted air tank can be secured beneath the tub floor or to a frame rail. Many sizes are available to accommodate engine-driven and electric air compressors.

For installation on stock vehicles, however, one of the readily available tanks that include mounting hardware is the easiest option. Onboard air systems can also be used for more than just filling tires. I've used a Kilby onboard air system to power air tools while completing trail repairs and even around my garage a few times when the shop compressor crapped out.

Making the Most out of your Stock TJ

It doesn't have to cost loads of dough to go wheeling. After all, you already

shelled out for the rig so what else should you need? The truth is, not that much. A Jeep Wrangler is pretty good to go right out of the box and you shouldn't be wary of stretching its legs in stock form. Still, there are a couple of tips I can offer on how to improve your rig's off-road performance and how to limit the propensity for damage.

Big Tires, No Lift

The first thing most new Wrangler TJ owners want is bigger tires. I'm guilty of it myself. Before even installing a lift, I was already looking for a way to tuck a set of 31s in place of the stock 30s. They did fit 30s under there, so why not 31s? Unfortunately, some tire shops are sticklers about their policy of not installing tires larger than those deemed appropriate by the vehicle manufacturer. "It'll rub the frame rail when you corner," they say. Or, "It'll hit the fender flares when the suspension compresses." "I won't corner so tightly," I reply. "I'll trim the fenders with a Sawzall. Don't worry about it," I say. But that's usually when they start talking about insurance and liability and such and start directing you toward the OE replacement tires that you already know you don't want.

So how do you get bigger tires in there without spending that arm and leg you so desperately want to keep? The cheapest and easiest way to go about it is to buy a set of used Rubicon wheels and

Like any 4x4, a TJ should be built to suit its owner's needs. This TJ received the works so that in could conquer all that Tennessee had to offer. Note the Rockwell axles, 42-inch Swampers, lengthened wheelbase, raked and chopped grille, modified fenders, remote reservoir shocks, and exterior roll cage. This TJ is truly ready for anything.

This Dana 44 axle shaft shows the affects of hard wheeling. The splines are twisted from extreme rotational torque loading.

Even a Ford 9-inch axle can succumb to breakage. This image shows where the pinion gear literally ripped out of the center drop-out, along with half of the case material. The pinion gear, yoke, and driveshaft can also be seen beneath the carnage.

tires and install them. After that, you could invest in a set of wheel spacers that position the wheel further outboard of the vehicle. This creates the appearance of a wheel with greater backspacing and allows fitment of a slightly taller and wider tire. You can also pick up a set of new or used wheels with the appropriate backspacing (up to 3¾-inch works well with stock suspension) to fit up to a 31-inch tire. Here's the thing though: yes, the tire will probably rub the frame rail

during tight cornering, and the turning radius will also increase. They'll also likely mash into the fender flares when you compress the suspension, so you get out the Sawzall. If you hit trails on a regular basis, this will be a larger issue and that can be easily alleviated with a small body lift. This also puts you on a good path toward the next step in prepping your Wrangler for improved off-road use.

Disco the Sway Bar

One of the first steps to increasing a stock Wrangler's trail crawling ability is to disconnect the factory front sway bar. This can be completed rather easily using basic hand tools; doing it every time you hit the trail can get a bit tedious. That's why aftermarket sway bar disconnects have become so popular. You can also disconnect the rear sway bar, and many simply leave it that way. You'll experience a little more body roll during cornering if you leave it disconnected during highway use and you'll certainly feel a much greater "tippy" sensation during off-camber trail maneuvers. When my TJ was still fairly stock, I typically left the rear sway bar connected and simply undid the front. This created a greater degree of available wheel travel up front and allowed me to better place the front tires exactly where I wanted them. The rear end offered plenty of droop, so I left the rear sway bar hooked up—plus, it was pretty much a pain in the ass to hook back up every time.

Remove Vulnerable Equipment

You can decrease your chances of damaging stock equipment on your Wrangler by removing much of it before hitting the trail. The full or half hard doors can be pulled and left at your campsite. Tops can be removed to avoid tears or scratches to the vinyl soft-top windows. Even the windshield frame can be folded down or pulled altogether to keep from cracking the glass or denting the frame. The bumperettes on the ends

Removing hard doors during trail use helps prevent damage and improves visibily. Concentrate behind the wheel and don't take on a trail that's above you and your rig's ability.

Soft tops can become torn on low-hanging trees and rock overhangs. Folding down the windshield and securing it to the hood is another good method of avoiding vehicle damage while on the trail.

of factory bumpers are also easy targets for rocks and other obstacles and can be removed using simple hand tools.

Plan Ahead

If you keep your Wrangler in tiptop condition, it should hopefully make it to the trail and back without issues. This is just about the best way to avoid on-trail repairs. Lack of maintenance is the cause of most on-trail repairs I've completed over the years. Had I taken the time to investigate potential problems and practiced better maintenance habits, I would have spent that time wheeling rather than getting greasy. The worst part is that trailside repairs usually hold up more than just you and your buddies. In some cases, I've seen trail breaks hold up groups of 20 or more after a poorly maintained vehicle clogged a narrow trail. Trail breaks can also end up costing you more money since you typically end up buying parts wherever they're available. You may also have to pay for a tow if you can't fix the problem. I'm not saying that all breaks are preventable, but taking just a few steps before you get to the trail can greatly help the potential for a trouble-free excursion.

Buying Used Parts

One man's junk is another man's treasure, right? That goes for Jeep TJ parts, too. Stock parts aren't all you'll find either. A lot of folks upgrade to taller tires and sell their short adjustable control arms and coil springs to buy long arms and taller coils or coil-over shocks. You might find a set of 31- to 33-inch tires from the same crowd. Sometimes the parts may be a few years old, but in many cases you'll simply need a new set of shocks and you're good to go. A common sight at many 4x4 shops is take-off Rubicon Dana 44s complete with factory lockers, cast aside when the previous owner made the leap to Dana 60s.

These are great bolt-in upgrades for those with Dana 30 and 35c axles. Dana 30s and 35s aren't complete junk, especially if you can find a useable Trac-Lok LSD or pick up a few spare axle shafts. You could also find the complete assembly, along with steering components, needed to upgrade your well-worn 1997 axle to one built in 2004 or later for that "almost" new feel. Tie rod and drag link assemblies are also good picks since you can keep a spare handy in the event of a trail mishap. You can also find a lot of other stock take-off items, such as spare tire carriers with third brake lights, non-bashed bumperettes, fender flares, front and rear seats, full and half doors, soft and hard tops, and other miscellaneous body parts.

Your local wrecking yard should be your first stop and you may find the best deals there as opposed to 4x4 or Jeep-specific yards where you'll often pay a

Steering parts take a tremendous amount of abuse while tackling difficult trails. Many TJ owners carry spare rod ends and even complete tie rod and drag link assemblies as spare parts just in case.

Used Dana 30 axle shafts are a good find and can help you make it home in the event that you break one on the trail.

premium for the convenience of having multiple vehicles to pick from. Catching a mildly totaled TJ amongst a sea of sedans and mini vans can garner most of the above-mentioned items. You can save even more by pulling the parts yourself if the yard permits , so don't be afraid to bring your own tools. Many of the available online 4x4 forums are

other good places to locate used parts cheap. The TJ-specific sites are your best starting point, but even eBay and other auction sites are often overflowing with parts from people who want them out of their garage and are willing to deal.

When buying used parts, pay close attention to what you're getting. Remember, all Wranglers are not the same. The pre-'97 model Wranglers use a bevy of different parts than the TJ, so items such as axles, transfer cases, and others won't be bolt-in swaps. Also, sometimes junk really is junk, so be careful that you don't end up with a boat anchor axle that's no better than the one you've got.

Packing for the Trail

Some people say that if you don't have it with you, then you probably

don't need it. The fact is, wheeling is a dangerous activity at times and if you don't have the right gear, tools, parts, or necessities with you at all times, then you just might be out of luck in the event of serious vehicle failure. What you bring with you is all you have sometimes, so figure out what you can survive on and carry that. If you need me, I'll be the guy keeping warm in a down sleeping bag and bivy sack.

Trail Tools

This is a list of stuff I carry in my TJ whenever the tires touch dirt. I keep the majority of it in a plastic crate, so it's easy to pull in and out of the vehicle without losing everything. Though I prefer carrying a complete set of tools for most excursions, these items alone have saved my ass more than a few times. My advice? Don't leave home without this stuff.

Removing the upper door halves allows greater visibility of the obstacles beneath the vehicle. Don't be afraid to listen to a designated spotter during extra tricky maneuvers.

prepared, while making for a lighter load and slightly better gas mileage.

Wrenches (standard and metric)
Socket set (variety of sizes, don't forget deep and spark plug sockets)
Adjustable wrenches
Pliers (needle-nose, locking grip, channel locks, wire-cutters and crimpers, and snap-ring)
Allen wrenches
Multi-meter and/or test light
Screwdrivers (Phillips and flathead: small, medium, and large)
Hammers (medium mallet, 5-lb sledge, and small and large ball-peens)
Pry bar/breaker bar
Telescoping magnet (for broken axle removal)
Hacksaw
Chisel and punch
Scribe
Sand paper
Wire brush
Hub socket
Locking hub/spindle nut socket
Pickle fork
U-joint tool
Flex-joint tool
½-inch air impact gun
Flaring tool
Soldering gun
Welding rod

Duct tape
Electrical tape
Zip-ties (variety of sizes)
Baling wire
Ratchet strap
WD-40
Multi-tool pocket knife
Tow strap
Fire extinguisher
Flashlight or headlamp
First-aid kit
Drinking water
Ground tarp
Matches or lighter
Warm jacket
Folding shovel
Small socket set
4-in-1 screwdriver
Safety-Seal tire repair kit
Air pressure gauge
Air hose and chuck
Valve core tool and spare valve cores
Jumper cables
Mechanix gloves

Energy bars
Handi wipes or waterless hand cleaner
Lug wrench
Bivouac sack
Toilet paper

Tools

This is pretty much everything needed to get home in one piece. I don't carry all of these items but I wheel with a lot of guys who do. Not to say that I rely on them to be my tool and parts mules, but rather that I do my best to maintain my rig and drive it like it's borrowed to avoid the need for trail repairs. Even so, I have dug into these "shops on wheels" a few times when the need arose and am always grateful that someone in my group is better prepared than I am. If you consistently hit the trail with the same group, consider planning ahead and splitting up some of the items so that each vehicle carries a share. This way all of the rigs will benefit from being well

For those who truly want to be ready for anything, an onboard welder is great. The welder operates off the engine and is capable of producing extremely strong welds.

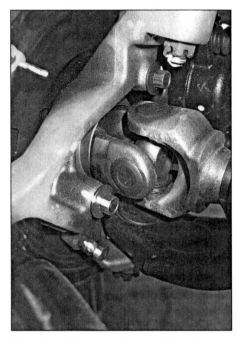

You should always carry at least one extra driveshaft U-joint. Axle shafts can be preassembled with U-joints to make trail repairs take less time.

Welding goggles or shield
Extra set of jumper cables
Torque wrench
Die grinder w/sanding disc and cut-off wheels (for use with OBA systems)
Bench vice (removable clamp-on unit for bumper)
Onboard welder
OBA system, 12V air compressor, or CO_2 tank
Shop rags or paper towels
Ratchet strap
Funnel
Garbage bags
Ziploc bags
Vehicle repair manual
Grease gun
Latex gloves
Spare batteries (as needed)
Hand cleaner
Garden hose repair kit (can be used to fix radiator hoses)
A few pieces of scrap metal

Spare Parts
Drive belt
Radiator and heater hoses
Hose clamps
Fuel line
U-joints (front axle and driveshaft)
U-joint U-bolts or straps
Axle shafts (front/rear)
Driveshafts
Unit bearing hub or locking hub assembly or drive flange
Assorted nuts, bolts, washers, and fasteners
Cotter pins
C-clamps (variety of sizes)
Fuses
Electrical wire and connectors
Brake lines and unions
Tie rod and drag link
Tie rod/drag link ball joints (or Heims for custom steering setups)
Suspension joints (Heim joints, flex-joints, etc.)
Lug nuts
Lug studs
Spare tire

Fluids and Lubrication
Motor oil
Gear oil
Brake fluid
Power-steering fluid
ATF
RTV silicone or gasket maker
Multi-purpose grease
Radiator coolant
Radiator stop-leak
Carburetor cleaner
Gasoline (for longer excursions)
WD-40
Water

Recovery Items
Winch
Extra winch remote control
Winch cable weight
3 or 4 D-ring shackles
Snatch block
Hi-Lift Jack
Snatch straps (multiple lengths)

When trails from afar call my TJ, I'll sometimes tow it to my destination. Though it's no trailer queen, I find this saves a lot of unnecessary wear and tear and also allows me to tackle more extreme trails without abandon. Like they say, go big or go home.

Even some of the most skilled drivers still rely on a spotter to work their way through a tricky obstacle. A spotter's job is to safely direct the driver through a trail and point out potential hazards that could cause vehicle damage. It's important to establish hand signals with your spotter so you'll always know what's going on.

Tree saver winch strap
Come-along (ratcheting cable hand winch)
Chain (10-ft or more)
Leather gloves
Shovel
Axe

Navigation and Communication
Compass
Maps
GPS
CB radio
Cell phone

Survival Gear
Emergency radio
12-hour green light sticks
Emergency strobe

Candles
1 to 3 gallons water
Sleeping bag or bivouac and sleeping pad

The stock bumperettes are shown removed from this stock bumper. Hey, you can break what's not there. Some later-model TJs had bumper end caps instead of the bumperettes.

Tent or emergency shelter
Sunscreen
Bug spray
Ice chest cooler
Warm clothing and rain gear

Everything Else
You can probably leave this stuff home if you're on a short trip but they sure are nice having handy on extended adventures.
Satellite radio receiver
Folding chairs
Umbrella or sun shade
Gasoline generator
Portable toilet
Sun Shower

Acme Accessories For Jeep
www.acmejeepparts.com
800-421-2215

Adobe Off-Road
www.adobeoffroad.com
888-857-5337

Advance Adapters, Inc.
www.advanceadapters.com
800-350-2223

Advanced Air Systems
www.powertank.com
209-366-2163

Advanced Engine Management
(AEM)
www.aempower.com
310-484-2322

Advanced Flow Engineering (AFE)
www.afefilters.com
909-279-4050

Advanced Frame Works
www.advancedframeworks.com
406-538-4996

Adventure Trailers
www.adventuretrailers.com
877-661-8097

Aero Tanks
www.aerotanks.com
800-783-4826

AGR Performance Power Steering
www.agrperformance.com
800-662-3649

Airaid Filter Company
www.airaid.com
800-498-6951

Alcoa Wheel Products
www.alcoawheels.com
800-242-9898

All J Products
www.boulderbars.com
909-352-2556

Allied Racing Wheels
www.alliedrockathons.com
800-52-WHEELS

Alloy USA
www.alloyusa.com
866-352-5569

American Expedition Vehicles
www.aev-conversions.com
406-251-2100

American Racing Wheels
www.americanracing.com
310-761-4033

Aqualu Industries
www.aqualu.com
250-765-6714

ARB 4X4 Accessories
www.arbusa.com
425-264-1391

Art Carr
www.artcarr.com
888-526-5868

Auburn Gear, Inc.
www.auburngear.com
260-925-3200

Auto Meter Products
www.autometer.com
815-895-8141 815-899-0800

Avenger Superchargers
www.avengersuperchargers.com
719-594-4766

Axis Wheels
www.axiswheels.com
562-906-9898

Back Country USA
www.backcountrytrailers.com
661-266-9869

Baer Brake Systems
www.baer.com
602-233-1411

Baja Designs, Inc.
www.bajadesigns.com
760-560-2252

Banks Power
www.bankspower.com
800-601-8072

BDS Suspension Co.
www.bds-suspension.com
517-279-2135

Beard Seats
www.redart.com
714-774-9444

Benchmark Maps
www.benchmarkmaps.com
541-772-6965

Bestop, Inc.
www.bestop.com
303-465-1755

BFGoodrich Tires
www.bfgoodrichtires.com
864-458-4566

Bilstein Shock Absorbers
www.bilstein.com
858-386-5900

Black Diamond Suspension
www.blackdiamondoffroad.com
318-397-3470

B&M Racing
www.bmracing.com
818-882-6422

Body Armor
www.bodyarmor4x4.com
951-808-0750

Borgeson Universal Co., Inc.
www.borgeson.com
860-482-8283

Borla Performance Industries
www.borla.com
805-986-8600

Bridgestone/Firestone
www.bridgestonetire.com
800-807-9555

Bulletproof Manufacturing
www.bulletproofmfg.com
805-967-2005

Bushwacker, Inc.
www.bushwacker.com
503-283-4335

Camburg Engineering, Inc.
www.camburg.com
714-848-8880

Campbell Enterprises
www.campbellent.com
480-782-5337

CA4WD Clubs
www.cal4wheel.com
916-381-8300

CB City
www.cbcity.com
903-526-7838

CB Radio Discount
www.fm2way.com
800-889-2839

Centech, Inc.
www.centechwire.com
610-754-0720

Center Line Wheel Corp.
www.centerlinewheels.com
562-921-9637

Centerforce Clutches & Flywheels
www.centerforce.com
928-771-8422

Central 4 Wheel Drive
www.central4wd.com
800-676-2325

Champion Wheel Co., Inc.
www.championwheel.com
559-275-5183

Classic Tube
www.classictube.com
716-759-1800

Clutch Masters
www.clutchmasters.com
909-877-6800
406-549-0171

Cobra Electronics
www.cobra.com
773-889-3087

Collins Brothers
www.collinsbrosjeep.com
972-442-6189

Competition Cams, Inc.
www.compcams.com
800-999-0853

Cone Industries
www.coneindustries.com
805-239-2663

Cooper Tire
www.coopertire.com
800-854-6288

Corbeau USA LLC
www.corbeau.com
801-255-3737

C.O.R.V.A.
www.corva.org
800-42-CORVA

Cragar & Weld Wheels
www.cragarwheel.com
909-947-1831

Crane Cams
www.cranecams.com
386-252-1151

Crane High Clearance, Inc.
www.highclearance.com
303-917-4851

Cross Enterprises
www.crossenterprises.com
805-499-8169

Crown Automotive
www.crownautomotive.com
781-826-6200

CTM Racing Products
www.ctmracing.com
949-487-0770

Currie Enterprises
www.currieenterprises.com
714-528-6957

Dakota Digital, Inc.
www.dakotadigital.com
605-332-6513
248-576-5741

Dana Corp.
www.dana.com
815-363-9000

Davis Unified Ignition
www.performancedistributors.com
901-396-5782

Daystar Products Intl., Inc.
www.daystarweb.com
623-907-0081

Dedenbear
www.dedenbear.com
925-935-3025

Deist Safety
www.deist.com
818-240-7866

Denny's Driveshafts
www.dennysdriveshaft.com
716-875-6640

Desert Rat Off Road
www.desertrat.com
866-444-5337

Detroit Locker
www.detroitlocker.com
248-776-5758

Dick Cepek Tires
www.mickeythompsontires.com
909-587-0190

Disc Brakes Australia
www.dba.com.au
310-603-8800

Doetsch Suspension Systems
www.doetsch-shocks.com
800-874-6257

Down East Offroad, Inc.
www.downeastoffroad.com
252-246-9440

Drivelines, Inc.
www.drivelinesinc.com
949-951-9673

Drive Train Specialists
www.drivetrainspecialists.com
877-874-7327

Drive Train Warehouse
www.drivetrainwarehouse.com
888-432-7656

Dunlop
www.dunloptire.com
330-796-2121

Durabak
www.durabakbedliner.com
303-690-7190

Durango 4x4 Outfitters
www.durango4x4.com
888-259-8676

Dutchman Motorsports
www.dutchmanms.com
503-257-6604

Dynatrac Products Co., Inc.
www.dynatrac.com
714-596-4461

DynoMax Performance Exhaust
www.dynomax.com
734-384-7807

Edelbrock Corporation
www.edelbrock.com
310-781-2222

Edge Products
www.edgeproducts.com
801-476-3343

Energy Suspension
www.energysuspension.com
949-361-3935

Exide
www.exideworld.com
800-782-7848

Expedition Exchange
www.expeditionexchange.com
310-618-1875

Explorer Pro Comp
www.explorerprocomp.com
619-216-1444

Extreme Outback Products
www.extremeoutback.com
707-447-7711

Fab Fours, Inc.
www.fabfours.com
970-385-1905

Fabtech Motorsports
www.fabtechmotorsports.com
909-597-7800

Firestik Antenna Co.
www.firestik.com
602-273-7151

Flaming River Industries, Inc.
www.flamingriver.com
440-826-4488

Flex-A-Lite Consolidation
www.flex-a-lite.com
253-922-2700

FlowKooler
www.flowkooler.com
805-544-8841

Flowmaster, Inc.
www.flowmastermuffler.com
707-544-4761

4 Wheel Drive Hardware, Inc.
www.4wd.com
800-333-5535
330-482-4924

4WD Products
www.4wdproducts.com
714-556-5661

4 Wheelers Supply, Inc.
www.4wheelers.com
800-639-7195

4 Wheel Parts Wholesalers
www.4wheelparts.com
800-421-1050

FourXDoctor
www.fourxdoctor.com
818-845-2194

Fox Racing Shox
www.foxracingshox.com
619-768-1800

Front Range Off-Road Fabrication
www.frontrangeoffroadfab.com
970-881-2418

Full-Traction Suspension
www.full-traction.com
661-398-9585

Gale Banks Engineering
www.bankspower.com
800-438-7693

Garmin USA
www.garmin.com
913-397-8200

Garvin Industries
www.garvin-industries.com
619-440-7415

Gibson Performance Exhaust
www.gibsonperformance.com
951-372-1220

Goodyear Tire & Rubber Co.
www.goodyear.com
330-796-2121

Go Rhino! Products
www.gorhino.com
714-279-8300

Gorilla Automotive Products
www.gorilla-auto.com
323-585-2852

Go There Engineering
www.gothereengineering.com
334-821-5709

Green Filters
www.greenfilterusa.com
724-430-2050

Hankook Tires
www.hankooktireusa.com
973-633-9000

Hanson Enterprise
www.hansonenterprise.com
831-757-9779

Harbor Freight
www.harborfreight.com
800-423-2567

JeepPart.com
www.jeeppart.com
562-428-3678

Rough Country Suspension
www.roughcountry.com
731-285-9000

Hedman Hedders/Trans-Dapt
www.hedman.com
562-921-0404

Hella, Inc.
www.hella.com
770-631-7517

HESCO, Inc.
www.hescosc.com
205-251-1472

High Angle Driveline
www.highangledriveline.com
530-877-2875
High Impact
www.high-impact.net
888-898-4331

Hi-Lift Jack Co.
www.hi-lift.com
812-384-4441

Holley Performance Products
www.holley.com
270-782-2900

Hooker Headers
www.holley.com
270-782-2900

HOWE Performance
www.howeperformance.com
619-561-7764

Howell Engine Development
www.howell-efi.com
810-765-5100

Husky Liners
www.huskyliners.com
620-221-2268

Hurst Performance
www.mrgasket.com
216-688-8305

Hutchinson Wheels
www.hutchinsoninc.com
609-394-1010

Hypertech Inc.
www.hypertech-inc.com
901-382-1888

Inline Tube
www.inlinetube.com
800-385-9452

Interco Tire Corporation
www.intercotire.com
337-334-3814

Interstate Batteries
www.interstatebatteries.com
866-842-5368

Jack-It Accessories Inc.
www.jackit.com
888-452-2548

Jacobs Electronics
www.jacobselectronics.com
800-627-8800

Jardine Performance &
Doug Thorley Headers
www.jardineproducts.com
909-739-5900

JAZ Products
www.jazproducts.com
805-525-8800

Jet Performance Products
www.jetchip.com
714-848-5515

JBA Performance Exhaust
www.jbaheaders.com
619-229-7797

JB Conversions
www.jbconversions.com
337-625-2379

J.C. Whitney, Inc.
www.jcwhitney.com
800-529-4486

J.E. Reel Driveline
www.reeldriveline.com
909-629-9002

Jeep Box
www.jeepbox.com
877-465-5729

Jeepers Jamboree
www.jeepersjamboree.com
530-333-4771

Jeep Recycling Inc.
www.jeeprecycling.com
888-932-5337

Jeeps by AutoQuest
www.jeepsbyautoquest.com
713-522-6200

JeepSpeed
www.jeepspeed.com
714-538-7434

Jet Performance Products
www.jetchip.com
800-736-4061

JKS Manufacturing, Inc.
www.jksmfg.com
308-762-6949

JP Cooler
www.jpcooler.com
480-234-3500

KarTek Off Road
www.kartek.com
909-737-7223

KC HiLites, Inc.
www.kchilites.com
928-635-2607

Kenne Bell
www.kennbel.net
909-941-6646

Kentrol, Inc.
www.kentrolinc.com
330-549-2235

Kilby Enterprises
www.kilbyenterprises.com
818-565-5945
818-848-2900

King Shock Technology
www.kingshocks.com
714-530-8701

Klune-V
www.klune.com
800-222-3619

K&N Engineering
www.knfilters.com
800-858-3333

Kumho Tires
www.kumhotireusa.com
330-670-2623
909-428-3303

Lightforce
www.lightforce.com
208-476-9814

Line-X
www.goline-x.com
800-831-3232

Lowrance Electronics, Inc.
www.lowrance.com
918-437-6881

Magellan
www.magellangps.com
909-394-5000

Magnaflow Performance
www.magnaflow.com
949-858-5900

Mark Williams Enterprises
www.markwilliams.com
800-525-1963

Marsh Racing Wheels
www.mrt-wheels.com
800-643-3625

Master Power Brakes
www.mpbrakes.com
888-251-2353

Master Pull Recovery Equipment
www.masterpull.com
877-797-0202

Mastercraft Race Products
www.mastercraftseats.com
619-449-9455

Maxxis International
www.maxxis.com
770-962-5932

MEPCO 4X4
www.mepco4x4.com
866-827-4294

MG Industries
www.mean-green.com
724-532-3090

Michelin
www.michelin.com
800-847-3435

Mickey Thompson Tires
www.mickeythompsontires.com
330-928-9092

Mile Marker, Inc.
www.milemarker.com
954-782-0604

Mopar Performance Parts
www.mopar.com
800-846-6727

Moser Engineering
www.moserengineering.com
260-726-6689
219-726-6689

Motive Gear
www.motivegear.com
773-579-3715

Mountain Off-Road Enterprises
(M.O.R.E)
www.mountainoffroad.com
970-625-0500

MSD Ignition
www.msdignition.com
915-857-5200

Mt. Logan Off-Road, LLC
www.mtloganoffroad.com
435-752-4272

Nitto Tire North America, Inc.
www.nittotire.com
714-236-2080

Novak Conversions
www.novak-adapt.com
877-602-1500

Nth Degree Mobility
www.nthdegreemobility.com
775-885-8454

Oasis Mfg.
www.oasismfg.com
949-768-4311

Off Again, Inc. (Jeep)
www.offagain4x4.com
505-325-5761

Off-Camber 4x4
www.offcamber4x4.com
303-791-6195

Off Road Only
www.offroadonly.com
952-226-4317

Off Road Warehouse (ORW)
www.offroadwarehouse.com
800-341-7757

OK Auto, 4WD and Tires
www.ok4wd.com
908-454-6973

Olympic 4x4 Products
www.olympic4x4products.com
323-726-6988

Olympic 4x4 Supply
www.oly4x4.com
800-752-9979

OMF Performance Products
www.omfperformance.com
951-354-8272
909-354-8272

Omix-Ada, Inc.
www.omix-ada.com
770-448-1726

Optima Batteries
www.optimabatteries.com
303-340-7440

ORBA
www.orbanet.org
619-449-0778

O-R Fab (Off-Road Fabrication)
www.orfab.com
602-749-0588

Ox Locker
www.ox-usa.com
877-694-7699

Painless Performance Products
www.painlessperformance.com
817-244-6212

Parnelli Jones Dirt Grip
www.dirtgriptires.com
330-873-9582

PCI Race Radios
www.pciraceradios.com
562-427-8177

Performance Distributors
www.performancedistributors.com
901-396-5782

Perma-Cool
www.perma-cool.com
909-390-1550

PIAA Corporation, USA
www.piaa.com
503-643-7422

Poison Spyder Customs
www.spydercustoms.com
303-777-4820

Poly Performance, Inc.
www.polyperformance.com
805-234-1760

Powermaster
www.powermastermotorsports.com
865-688-5953

PowerTrax/Lock-Right
www.powertrax.com
800-578-1020

Precision Gear
www.precisiongear.com
734-946-0524

Premier Power Welder
www.premierpowerwelder.com
800-541-1817

Premier Racing Products (PRP)
www.prpseats.com
909-506-9969

Procar by SCAT
www.procarbyscat.com
310-370-5501

Pro Comp Suspension
www.explorerprocomp.com
619-216-1444

Pro Comp Tire & Wheel
www.procomptires.com
310-762-6593

Pull-Pal
www.pullpal.com
800-541-1817

Quadratec
www.quadratec.com
800-745-2348

Radflo Suspension Technology
www.radflo.com
714-965-7828

Raingler Ent., LLC
www.raingler.com
303-523-1776

Ramsey Winch
www.ramsey.com
918-438-2760

Rancho Suspension
www.gorancho.com
734-384-7804

Random Technology
www.randomtechnology.com
770-554-4242

Randy's Ring & Pinion
www.ring-pinion.com
888-231-2493

RCD Suspension
www.racecardynamics.com
619-588-4723

Recaro North America, Inc.
www.recaro-nao.com
248-364-3818

Recovery Gear USA
www.recoverygear.com
888-877-6837

Reider Racing Enterprises
www.reiderracing.com
800-356-1330

Rhino Linings
www.rhinolinings.com
800-422-2603

Richmond Gear
www.richmondgear.com
864-843-9231

Road Armor
www.roadarmor.com
425-328-7194

Robby Gordon Offroad
www.robbygordonoffroad.com
714-632-0311

Rock Buggy Supply
www.rockbuggysupply.com
909-926-1142

Rock Hard 4X4 Parts
www.rockhard4x4parts.com
308-750-4690
970-834-0761

Rockcrusher USA
www.rockcrusher-usa.com
330-538-9791

Rock-it Parts
www.rock-it.com
714-639-4933

Rock Krawler Suspension
www.rockkrawler.com
518-270-9822

Rock Krawler Suspension Inc.
www.rockkrawler.com
845-227-2756

Rockstomper
www.rockstomper.com
303-833-1431

Rough Country Suspension
www.roughcountry.com
731-285-9000

Rube Adapters
www.rube-adapter.com
559-299-5736

Rubicon Express
www.rubiconexpress.com
916-858-8575

Russell Performance
www.russellperformance.com
310-781-2222

Rusty's Off-Road
www.rustysoffroad.com
256-442-0607

Safety Seal
www.safetyseal.com
978-531-3044

Sam's Off Road
www.samsoffroad.com
800-446-5503

Scotty's Jeep, Truck & 4x4 (Jeep)
www.scottysjeeptruckand4x4.com
909-829-2913

Shell Valley Companies
www.shellvalley.com
888-246-0900

Sidekick Off-Road
www.sidekickoffroad.com
909-628-7227

Sirius Satellite Radio
www.sirius.com

Skid Row Automotive
www.skidplates.com
800-786-9249

Skyjacker Suspension
www.skyjacker.com
318-388-0816

Smittybilt, Inc.
www.smittybiltinc.com
888-717-6170

SPAL USA
www.spalusa.com
515-239-7000

Spintech Performance Mufflers
www.spintechmufflers.com
888-550-SPIN

SRC Precision Products
www.jeepxtremes.com
908-687-0611

Stainless Steel Brakes Corp.
www.ssbrakes.com
800-448-7722

Stak 4x4
www.stak4x4.com
915-584-2400

Staun Products
www.staunproducts.com
Australia 61-07-5596-0955

Steel Horse Products
www.steelhorseautomotive.com
817-640-2376

Stockton Wheel
www.stocktonwheel.com
800-395-9433

Summit Racing
www.summitracing.com
800-230-3030

Sun Performance Products
www.sunperformance.com
714-708-7730

Sunray Engineering
www.sunrayengineering.com
871-594-9201

Superchips
www.superchips.com
407-585-7000

Superior Axle & Gear
www.superioraxle.com
951-898-2056

Superlift Suspension Systems
www.superlift.com
951-898-2056
800-551-4955

Superwinch, Inc.
www.superwinch.com
860-928-7787

Sway-A-Way, Inc.
www.swayaway.com
818-700-9712

T & J Performance Center
www.tandjperformance.com
714-633-0991

TCI Automotive
www.tciauto.com
662-224-8972

TD Performance Products
www.tdperformance.com
562-921-0404

Tellico 4x4
www.tellico4x4.com
877-465-5729

Tentrax Sport Utility Trailer
www.tentrax.com
541-484-9885

TeraFlex
www.teraflx.com
801-256-9897

Thor Enterprises/Thor
  SoundWedge
www.webcom.com/thor
800-922-5337

Throttle Down Kustoms
www.throttledownkustoms.com
406-374-2285

T-Max Winches
www.t-maxwinches.com
574-266-1444

Tom Wood's Custom Drive Shafts
www.4xshaft.com
804-737-0785

Toyo Tires
www.toyo.com
714-236-2080

Tractech/Detroit Locker
www.tractech.com
800-328-3850

Trail Master Suspension
www.trailmastersuspension.com
888-717-6170

TrailReady
www.trailready.com
425-353-5570

Trail Sport Unlimited
www.trailsport4x4.com
909-825-2818

Tri County Gear
www.tricountygear.com
909-623-3373

TSM
www.tsmmfg.com
303-688-6882

Tuff Country EZ-Ride Suspension
www.tuffcountry.com
801-280-2777

Tuffy Security Products
www.tuffyproducts.com
970-564-1762

Turbo City
www.turbocity.com
www.rock-it.com
714-639-4933

Turn Key Engine Supply
www.turnkeyengine.com
760-941-2741

Tyres International
www.tyres1.com
800-321-7123

UFWDA
www.ufwda.org
928-477-2281

U-Joint Tool Co., Inc.
www.ujointtool.com
909-350-9373

Ultra Wheel Co.
www.ultrawheel.com
714-994-1111

Uniden
www.uniden.com
800-554-3988

Vanco Power Brake Supply
www.vancopbs.com
800-256-6295

Vertically Driven Products
www.vdpusa.com
562 438 5112

Viair Corp.
www.viaircorp.com
949-582-6866

Volant Cool Air Intakes
www.volantperformance.com
909-476-7226

Wagoner Machine Shop, Inc.
www.wagonermachine.com
918-341-1722

Walker Evans Racing
www.walkerevansracing.com
909-784-7223

WARN Industries
www.warn.com
503-722-1200

Warrior, Inc.
www.warriorproducts.com
503-691-8915

Weld Wheel Industries
www.weldracing.com
816-922-6500

West Coast Differentials
www.differentials.com
310-820-4718   800-510-0950

Wet Okole Hawaii
www.wetokole.com
949-548-1543

Wilwood Engineering
www.wilwood.com
805-388-1188

Winch Weight
www.winchweight.com
209-795-1585

Wrangler North West Power
www.wranglernw.com
503-235-4110

Xtreme Crawlers
www.xtremecrawlers.com
918-607-8924

XM Satellite Radio
www.xmradio.com
202-380-4000

Yokohama Tire
www.yokohamatire.com
800-722-9888

Yukon Gear & Axle
www.yukongear.com
800-347-1188

Z&M Conversions (Jeep)
www.zandm.com
408-274-9011

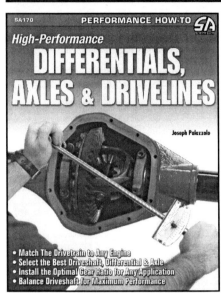

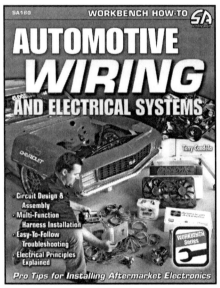

CPSIA information can be obtained at www.ICGtesting.com
Printed in the USA
LVOW090528150613

338753LV00002B/15/P